Programmer's Guide to the AMIBIOS

Includes Descriptions of PCI, APM, and Socket Services BIOS Functions.

American Megatrends, Inc.

Windcrest®/McGraw-Hill

New York San Francisco Washington, D.C. Auckland Bogotá
Caracas Lisbon London Madrid Mexico City Milan
Montreal New Delhi San Juan Singapore
Sydney Tokyo Toronto

Library of Congress Cataloging-in-Publication Data

ISBN 0-07-001562-7 (p)
ISBN 0-07-001561-9 (h)

    2 3 4 5 6 7 8 9 0   FGR/FGR   9 9 8 7 6 5 4

ISBN 0-07-001562-7 (p)
ISBN 0-07-001561-9 (h)

Limitations of Liability
While every precaution has been taken in the preparation of this book, the
author and the publisher assume no responsibility for errors or omissions,
or for the use made of the material contained herein or any decision based
on such use. No warranties are made, express or implied, with regard to
the contents of this work, its merchantability, or fitness for a particular
purpose. In no event shall the publisher or American Megatrends, Inc. be
held liable for any loss, expenses, or damages of any kind whatsoever,
whether direct, special, indirect, incidental, or consequential, arising from
the use or inability to use the contents of this book.

Printed and bound by Fairfield Graphics.

Table of Contents

Table of Contents, Continued

Table of Contents, Continued

Table of Contents, Continued

Table of Contents, Continued

Table of Contents, Continued

Table of Contents, Continued

Preface

Programmer's Guide to the AMIBIOS provides extensive technical details about the operation of the BIOS for ISA and EISA systems, specifically the Hi-Flex AMIBIOS. This book does not specifically discuss the IBM BIOS in IBM PC, XT, AT, or PS/2 computers.

Organization

Chapter	Contents
Chapter 1 Introduction Chapter 2 BIOS Features Chapter 3 AMIBIOS Setup (Before 2/91) Chapter 4 Hi-Flex AMIBIOS Setup	Information useful to the average user of a computer with an AMIBIOS. It is not technically difficult.
Chapter 5 Memory Map Chapter 6 ROM BIOS Data Area Chapter 7 ROM BIOS Data Chapter 8 CMOS RAM Chapter 9 I/O Ports	BIOS data, useful for programmers, software engineers, and those who work with computer architecture.
Chapter 10 POST Chapter 11 Introduction to Interrupts Chapter 12 BIOS Interrupts	The most important part of this book - descriptions of how the BIOS software interrupts work. This information is valuable for engineers and programmers.
Chapter 13 EISA Overview Chapter 14 Keyboard BIOS	Provides advanced technical information about newer BIOS technology, of use to engineers and developers.
Appendix A Error Messages and Beep Codes Appendix B Upgrading the BIOS Appendix C AMIBIOS History Appendix D AMIBIOS ID Strings Appendix E Old AMIBIOS Checkpoint Codes	The appendices contain general reference information for using or upgrading the BIOS in your computer and historical data about AMIBIOS.

Some common acronyms and abbreviations are listed on pages 477 – 480.

Acknowledgments

Many employees of American Megatrends merit special thanks for their contributions in the development of this book. The primary contributors were BIOS engineers Shankar Mandal, Sandip Datta Roy, Sanjeev Kumar, and Debkumar De. They developed BIOS products that consistently achieve performance levels no other BIOS can match. Engineers who also contributed to this book include Bob Gordon, Jeff Kidd, Charles Hanes, Chip Aaron, John Pennington, Lee Davis, Dick Holmberg, Eddy Quicksall, Will Gysin, Terry Lauer, Mohan Nair, Sanjay Sehgal, Nandkumar Phadte, and Vivek Saxena. Special thanks to Sukha Ghosh and Uma S. Mondal. Thanks also to Sam Williams, Manager of Technical Support and the technical support team. This book could not have been produced without those who devoted many nights and weekends to proofreading and copy editing: Julie McDonald, Susan Nease, and Eddy Quicksall. Robert Cheng deserves a special mention for his work on graphics. This book came about in part because of the support and encouragement of Tom Rau, BIOS Sales Manager, and Ray Bridenbaugh, Marketing Director.

But the most important acknowledgment is reserved for Subramonian Shankar, president and founder of American Megatrends, whose leadership, vision, technical knowledge, business acumen, and engineering skills have carried American Megatrends to the forefront in ISA and EISA system development in both BIOS and motherboard technology.

From the Authors

In any writing project that deals with detailed technical complexities, such as this book, errors and omissions occur. If you find an error or have a suggestion for an improvement, please let us know.

Anindya Mukherjee
Paul Narushoff
American Megatrends, Inc.
6145F Northbelt Parkway
Norcross, GA 30071
May, 1993

Notices

Many of the designations used by manufacturers and sellers to distinguish their products are claimed as trademarks. Where those designations appear in this book, and the author and publisher are aware of a trademark claim, the designations have been printed in initial capital letters.

The author acknowledges the following trademarks:

Avocet is a registered trademark of Avocet Systems, Inc.

AMIBIOS, AMIBCP, and AMIDiag are registered trademarks of American Megatrends, Inc.

Cyrix is a registered trademark of Cyrix Corporation.

AMD is a registered trademark of Advanced Micro Devices, Inc.

Intel and Pentium are registered trademarks of Intel Corporation.

Desqview is a registered trademark of Quarterdeck Office Systems Corporation.

C&T is a registered trademark of Chips and Technologies Corporation.

VLSI is a registered trademark of VLSI Corporation.

National Semiconductor is a registered trademark of National Semiconductor Corporation.

MS-DOS, Microsoft Windows, Windows NT, Xenix, and Microsoft are registered trademarks of Microsoft Corporation.

Unix is a registered trademark of American Telephone and Telegraph Company Bell Laboratories.

Weitek is a registered trademark of Weitek Corporation.

IBM, AT, VGA, EGA, XGA, PS/2, MCA, OS/2, and MicroChannel are registered trademarks of International Business Machines Corporation. PC-DOS, XT and CGA are trademarks of International Business Machines Corporation.

Austek is a registered trademark of Austek Corporation.

Novell is a registered trademark of Novell Corporation.

Ethernet is a trademark of Xerox Corporation.

Chapter 1

Introduction

The architecture of the software in ISA (Industry Standard Architecture) and EISA (Extended Industry Standard Architecture) systems is layered. The innermost layer is the computer — the hardware itself. The outer layer is the applications software with which the user interfaces. Systems software lies between applications software and hardware.

Systems software can consist of several elements: the BIOS, the operating system kernel, the operating system shell, and additional device drivers. Operating environments (Microsoft Windows) exist in a layer between the operating system and applications software, as do multitasking supervisors or DOS extenders like Desqview.

The BIOS (Basic Input Output System) is a collection of routines between the hardware and the systems software. The BIOS consists of diagnostic routines, device drivers, interrupt service routines, and other code and data between the hardware and the systems software.

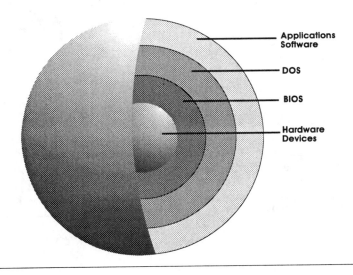

Applications
Software

DOS

BIOS

Hardware
Devices

Introducing the BIOS

The BIOS works in two directions: One part of the BIOS receives and processes requests from programs to perform the standard BIOS I/O services. The other side of the BIOS communicates with the hardware. The mechanism for the requests from programs is called an interrupt, discussed in detail beginning on page 171.

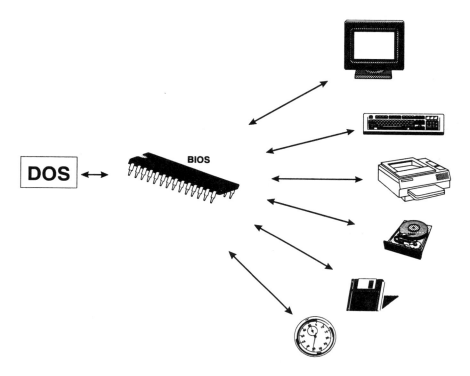

Interrupts are invoked by software programs. In an assembler program, the INT mnemonic is followed by an interrupt number that specifies the type of service and a function number that specifies the exact service to be performed. For example:

```
MOV     AH,00h  ;specifies function 00h get character from keyboard
INT     16h     ;requests INT 16h Keyboard Service
```

BIOS and Hardware

The other side of the BIOS communicates with the hardware (video display, disk drives, keyboard, serial and parallel ports, and so on) in the language used by each device. The computer hardware in an Industry Standard Architecture (ISA or IBM AT-compatible computer) is an inert collection of intricately connected integrated circuits, wires, fiberglass, peripheral I/O devices, and other electronic components.

The hardware side of the BIOS also handles any hardware device-generated interrupts. For example, when a key is pressed on the keyboard, a hardware interrupt (IRQ1) is generated. The BIOS INT 09h interrupt service routine is called to process the keystroke.

A computer can do nothing without software. A computer can't start without software. Starting a computer and keeping it going is easier if some of the software is permanently built into the system. It would be most helpful if the permanent software was the software that deals directly with the hardware — the BIOS.

ROM

Read-Only Memory devices (ROMs) can store software that is permanently built into the system. ROMs store permanently recorded code and data. This information can be modified or erased only by special equipment. ROM devices, although slow compared to RAM (Random Access Memory) devices, are a practical way of storing information that does not change very often and that must be protected from accidental erasure or tampering. In ISA and EISA systems, the BIOS is called the ROM BIOS.

cont'd

ROM Advantages

- ROM-based software is built into the system and does not have to be loaded to memory from the disk drive (as DOS is loaded). Since it is permanent, the ROM BIOS is the foundation on which all other programs (including the operating system) are built.

- ROM-based BIOS software is a standard that all programs for ISA and EISA computers must adhere to, since it is part of the computer architecture.

- As long as the interface between the operating system and the BIOS is standardized, placing the BIOS in ROM allows the hardware to evolve independently from the operating system.

If the BIOS code had been part of the operating system, the operating system would have to be modified every time the hardware changed. Every new peripheral device would require a new operating system release. The BIOS acts as a buffer and permits easier configuration when stored in ROM instead of in the operating system.

Operating System

The last part of the BIOS interface is the operating system, which calls the BIOS directly. The BIOS in ISA and EISA computers supports MS-DOS and PC-DOS. It does not directly support operating environments such as Microsoft Windows, which does not directly call the BIOS. Multitasking operating systems such as Unix do not need BIOS services — they have their own device drivers. IBM OS/2 uses a combination of a standard ISA BIOS, called the CBIOS, and a multitasking BIOS, the ABIOS. Windows NT uses HAL, the Hardware Abstraction Layer, which interfaces between the operating system and the BIOS on ISA and EISA systems.

Parts of the AMIBIOS

The four system ROM elements in a computer with an AMIBIOS are:

POST	Executes at Power-On and System Reset.
BIOS Setup Utility	Executes only when you press <Del> when "Hit <DEL> to run SETUP" is displayed.
Diagnostics and Utility Software	Executes only when you press <Del> when "Hit <DEL> to run SETUP" is displayed.
System BIOS	Always available as interface between hardware and software.

POST

The Power On Self Test (POST), described in detail beginning on page 155, consists of diagnostic and booting code that:

- executes a diagnostic and reliability test of the system, the ROM programs, and system RAM,
- initializes the chips and the standard parts of the computer system and places a record of the system configuration in CMOS RAM and in low system memory,
- sets up the interrupt vector table,
- detects optional equipment in the system, and
- boots the operating system.

cont'd

Parts of the AMIBIOS, Continued

System BIOS

The system BIOS is a part of the code stored in ROM that is actively used the entire time a computer is on. The ROM BIOS provides the fundamental services needed for the proper operation of the system.

The BIOS controls the peripheral devices: the video display, keyboard, disk drives, and serial and parallel ports through device service routines.

Device service routines are the programs that actually perform all the necessary steps when asked to read data from the hard disk drive. They initialize, detect and correct errors, set error codes, and perform all hardware-specific tasks associated with the activity they were asked to perform. Interrupt service routines handle hardware interrupts.

In the broadest sense, the BIOS not only includes the routines that control peripheral devices but also the routines that contain information or perform tasks that are fundamental to all system operations, such as tracking the time, keeping track of hardware device status, and preventing system resource conflicts.

Hard Disk Utility or Diagnostics

You can choose Hard Disk Utility (newer AMIBIOS) or RUN DIAGNOSTICS. The hard disk utilities in the AMIBIOS ROMs include formatting, auto interleave, and media analysis. See page 91 for additional information about the hard disk utilities. These diagnostics have been removed from newer versions of the BIOS to make room for the more complex functions that the BIOS must support. American Megatrends manufactures a standalone diagnostic product — *AMIDiag*, a utility program that tests all system functions and has many other features.

The Diagnostics in the AMIBIOS ROMs include memory, hard disk, floppy disk, video system, keyboard, and serial communications analysis and performance tests. See page 23 for additional information about ROM diagnostics.

Parts of the AMIBIOS, Continued

BIOS Setup Utility

BIOS Setup stores system configuration data in CMOS RAM (permanent, nonvolatile memory). The hard disk drive type, type of floppy drives and monitor, and the day, date, and time can be set by the AMIBIOS Setup utility, specifically through Standard CMOS Setup in the Hi-Flex AMIBIOS. Newer versions of the AMIBIOS have Advanced CMOS Setup and Advanced Chipset Setup to configure more complex system characteristics, such as RAM and ROM wait states, DMA Clock origination, and memory relocation. These additional screens are described starting on page 49.

Types of BIOS

The types of BIOS in ISA and EISA computers include:

- the system BIOS,
- the video BIOS,
- optional adaptor ROM BIOS, and
- the keyboard controller BIOS.

System BIOS

To recapitulate what we have said about the system BIOS, it consists of diagnostic routines, device drivers, interrupt and device service routines, and other code that acts as an interface between the system hardware and the operating system. The system BIOS tests the system components, loads (bootstraps) the operating system, and remains active for requests by the operating system to activate device drivers that service the keyboard, video display, hard drive, floppy drives, real time clock, parallel ports, serial ports, and other components. The system BIOS is a translator. The BIOS takes the instructions from the operating system and translates these commands to the exact instructions that the hardware understands. The BIOS is also the first level of protection and system security. The BIOS maintains data about various system components. The BIOS recognizes when a component is unable to perform and reports it to the operating system.

cont'd

System BIOS Size and Location

The system ROM BIOS code is 64 KB at F0000h – FFFFFh in ISA systems. In EISA systems, it is 128 KB at E0000h – FFFFFh.

Video BIOS

All ISA and EISA systems that use EGA, VGA, or XGA video adapters have video BIOS. The system BIOS has a video service (INT 10h), but it only handles the most basic MDA (Monochrome Display Adapter) and CGA (Color Graphics Adapter) video functions. The video modes defined in other video standards must be translated by a video BIOS, usually installed on the video adapter card. The video BIOS is best discussed in the context of the EGA, VGA, or XGA specifications. They all require a separate BIOS. A comprehensive discussion of the video BIOS is beyond the scope of this book.

Keyboard Controller BIOS

Every ISA and EISA system must also have a keyboard controller BIOS to translate the signals from the keyboard into codes that the BIOS and the system can understand. The keyboard controller BIOS is discussed in detail beginning on page 431.

Adaptor ROM BIOS

Many adapter cards have code in ROM. For example, ESDI hard disk drive controllers have a ROM that assists in translating this interface to code that the computer can understand and vice versa.

Adaptor ROM resides between C8000h and EFFFFh. This area also can be copied to RAM (in a process called shadowing) via AMIBIOS Advanced CMOS Setup to speed operation of devices that have adaptor ROMs, provided that the motherboard or chipset used in the system supports adaptor ROM shadowing.

Chapter 2

AMIBIOS Features

The two types of BIOS features in the BIOS are: standard features, and
BIOS Setup-dependent features.

Standard BIOS Features

AMIBIOS Setup features are accessed by pressing DEL when

`Hit <DEL> if you want to run SETUP` *(or DIAGS in older BIOS)*

ECP and EPP Support

The 08/08/93 and later AMIBIOS support ECP (Extended Capabilities
Port) and EPP (Enhanced Parallel Port) in the INT 17h Parallel Port
Service if the appropriate hardware is present in the computer and the
appropriate I/O support is provided in the BIOS.

Flash EPROM Support

The 08/08/93 and later AMIBIOS provide additional INT 16h
functions to support the American Megatrends Flash Utility.

IDE Block Transfer Mode Support

The 08/08/93 and later AMIBIOS support transfer of multiple sectors
to and from an IDE drive. An AMIBIOS Setup option enables this
feature. An AMIBIOS Setup option specifies the maximum number of
sectors that can be transferred at a time.

PS/2 Keyboard Error Detection

The 08/08/93 core AMIBIOS and any later AMIBIOS displays a
keyboard error if a PS/2 mouse is inserted in a PS/2 keyboard port.

Standard BIOS Features, Continued

IDE Standby Mode Support

The 08/08/93 and later AMIBIOS support IDE Standby mode, which spins down the IDE hard disk drive after a prespecified period of hard disk inactivity expires. IDE Standby mode is not supported by some IDE drives. The timeout period is specified in AMIBIOS Setup.

Green PC Support

The 08/08/93 and later AMIBIOS provide Green PC functions when used in a system with the American Megatrends MegaKey keyboard controller. Green PC features include:

- keyboard clock speed setting,
- selecting hot keys, and
- setting device timeout power down parameters (1 - 255 minutes) for up to five peripheral devices.

AMIBIOS Setup options permit the end user to control the timeout values for each individual power-controlled peripheral device. The Green PC functions cannot be used with the AutoKeyLock feature.

AutoKeyLock

The 08/08/93 and later AMIBIOS support AutoKeyLock. AutoKeyLock can only be used in desktop systems with an AMIBIOS desktop BIOS that also has an American Megatrends MegaKey keyboard controller. An AMIBIOS Setup option sets the AutoKeyLock timeout period. When the AutoKeyLock and Password features are enabled and no system activity occurs for the specified time period, the system locks and the end user must enter the correct password to use the computer. AutoKeyLock cannot be used with the Green PC functions.

Keyboard Speed Switching

You can increase processor speeds at any time by pressing <Ctrl> <Alt> <+>. Processor speed can be decreased by pressing <Ctrl> <Alt> <-> (except in 80486-based systems). An OEM can modify these keychords. The above keychords are the defaults.

Standard BIOS Features, Continued

Enable Cache Memory

Both external and internal (if the CPU is an 80486) cache memory can be enabled by pressing <Ctrl> <Alt> <Shift> <+> or disabled by pressing <Ctrl> <Alt> <Shift> <->. These keychords are the defaults.

Password Deletion

Should you forget the system password and not be able to use the computer, AMIBIOS implements a circumvention in the system hardware design that does not require removal and reinstallation of the CMOS RAM power supply.

Advanced Power Management (APM)

AMIBIOS supports the Intel/Microsoft INT 15h Advanced Power Management BIOS functions.

System Memory Detect

AMIBIOS automatically detects all system memory, the type of processor, and onboard/offboard floppy, IDE, serial, and parallel controllers. AMIBIOS automatically configures onboard controllers to prevent conflicts.

Detects IDE Hard Drive Parameters

If *Autodetect Hard Disk Drive* is selected on the AMIBIOS Setup main menu, AMIBIOS detects and reports all IDE drive parameters.

Local Bus Support

AMIBIOS supports the VESA VL-Bus and Intel PCI local bus standards. AMIBIOS supports all PCI-specific BIOS calls.

Socket Services and Card Services

AMIBIOS supports the INT 1Ah Socket Services and Card Services functions.

Standard BIOS Features, Continued

2.88 MB 3½" Floppy Drive Support

AMIBIOS supports 2.88 MB 3½" floppy drives, configured in
STANDARD CMOS SETUP.

Automatically Detects Processor Type and Speed

AMIBIOS can detect the Intel 386SX, 386DX, 386SL, 486SL, 486SX,
486DX, 486DX2, Pentium, and all other Intel CPUs, IBM Blue
Lightning, 386SLC, and 486SLC2, Cyrix Cx486SLC, Cx486DLC, Cx486S,
Cx486SLC2, Cx486DLC2, Cx486S2, single-clock Cx486DX, double-clock
Cx486DX, and the Texas Instruments Potomac.

AMIBIOS also can detect all other 386- and 486-compatible CPUs and
executes BIOS code accordingly. AMIBIOS also automatically detects
the Cyrix Cx487S math coprocessor when used in conjunction with the
Cyrix 486S or 486S2 CPU in a system.

Automatically Detects Memory Size

AMIBIOS reports system and cache memory on the initial AMIBIOS
screen and the AMIBIOS System Configuration Screen that appears
after POST completes. In systems with more than 1 MB, AMIBIOS
reports 384 KB less RAM than it finds because it accounts for the
address space between 640K and 1024K that is unavailable to DOS.

Peripheral Controller Support

AMIBIOS supports the Intel® 82341, VLSI 82C106 and 82C107, C&T
82C710, 82C711, and 82C721, National Semiconductor PC87310,
PC87311, and PC87312, SMC FCD637C651, FCD637C661, and
FCD637C665 Peripheral Controllers.

Parallel and Serial Port Support

AMIBIOS supports up to four serial ports and four parallel ports. The
fourth parallel port is not supported if PS/2 mouse support is enabled.

Standard BIOS Features, Continued

Memory Test Tick Sound

The 08/08/93 and later AMIBIOS allow you to press ESC or DEL to disable the ticking sound and bypass the memory test

Configures Nonstandard Systems

You can configure systems that are missing a keyboard, monitor, or disk drive through AMIBIOS SETUP. Select *Not Installed* as the setting for the missing device in Standard CMOS Setup. All missing device error messages are suppressed, permitting normal boot.

Supports Hardware-Specific Features

Many ISA systems have paged memory, memory interleaving, EMS, and power management features. The AMIBIOS in your computer may have special BIOS Setup options to configure these features.

Supports Extended BIOS Services

AMIBIOS includes INT 14h Function 04h Extended Initialize and Function 05h Extended Serial Port Control, a PS/2-compatible BIOS feature (see page 233). INT 15h Functions are: C1h and C2h (see page 269) for PS/2-type mouse support, INT 15h Function C3h Fail-Safe Timer Enable, which makes sure a program does not turn off interrupts for too long (see page 278), INT 15H APM functions, and the EISA AMIBIOS supports INT 15h Function D8h, EISA Configuration (see page 279). INT 16h support includes several useful functions that no other BIOS has (see page 316): Function F0h Set CPU Speed, Function F1h Read CPU Speed, Function F4h, Subfunction 00h Read Cache Controller, Subfunction 01h Enable Cache Controller, and Subfunction 02h Disable Cache Controller. INT 1Ah support includes Card Services, Socket Services, and PCI BIOS functions. Both the ISA and EISA AMIBIOS support the use of hardware interrupt IRQ12 for the mouse, described on page 410.

Provides Shadowing

Shadowing copies the BIOS from ROM to RAM to improve system performance. In a system with no shadow option, the ROM BIOS is executed from relatively slow ROM (150 – 250 ns). The BIOS executes much faster when the ROM BIOS is copied to RAM (60 – 100 ns) and the system is instructed to access the BIOS from RAM. In most cases, system BIOS shadowing should never be turned off.

System BIOS ROM Shadowing

The system BIOS resides in the 64 KB address space between F0000h and FFFFFh in ISA systems (and in the 128 KB space between E0000h and FFFFFh in EISA systems). The system BIOS shadow feature is often automatically enabled by the AMIBIOS. If not, it is an option on Standard CMOS Setup or Advanced CMOS Setup screens that should always be enabled to enhance BIOS performance.

High Memory

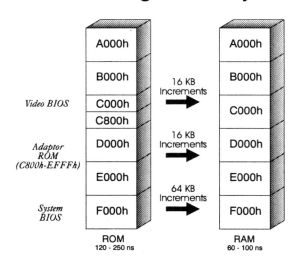

In shadowing, the BIOS code is copied
from slow ROM to faster RAM.

Standard BIOS Features, Continued

Adaptor ROM Shadowing

The area between C8000h and EFFFFh in ISA systems (and C8000h –
DFFFFh in EISA systems) is available for use by other ROM devices.
Often, the hard disk drive controller ROM is stored here. Many
network cards also use this space. AMIBIOS allows this area to be
shadowed from ROM to RAM to speed access to the code in this area.

EGA and VGA RAM Shadowing

Video ROM shadowing can often speed execution in two ways:
running the video BIOS from 16-bit instead of 8-bit memory, and
running the video BIOS from fast RAM instead of relatively slow
ROM. The memory space from C0000h – C7FFFh is reserved for video
ROM. Often, only the EGA BIOS (C0000h – C3FFFh), accessed through
an 8-bit bus, is located in this area. The relatively slow execution of
this device driver from ROM makes the video I/O slow. AMIBIOS
allows you to map this space to system RAM, where it executes about
twice as fast.

Video ROM shadowing copies the video ROM from C0000h – C7FFFh
to RAM. Memory from C0000h – DFFFFh can be accessed on the 16-bit
expansion slot. Any 8-bit I/O memory in that space is automatically
disabled.

Provides Diagnostics

Older AMIBIOS included hardware diagnostic routines. All recent
AMIBIOS include only hard disk drive utilities. See page 19 for more
information about these programs.

Provides Hard Disk Utilities

The Hi-Flex AMIBIOS, available since early 1991, provides several hard
disk utilities, including format, auto interleave, and media analysis. See
page 91 for additional information about these utilities.

AMIBIOS Setup Features

The following AMIBIOS Setup utility features are available only in the Hi-Flex AMIBIOS (available since early 1991) with Advanced CMOS Setup:

Type of Feature	Setup Options
Memory Features	■ **Above 1 MB Memory Test** Executes the POST memory routines on the RAM above 1 MB (if present on the system). If disabled, the BIOS checks only the first 1 MB of RAM. ■ **Memory Test Tick Sound** Turns the ticking sound on or off. ■ **Memory Parity Error Check** Enables or disables parity error checking for all system RAM. ■ **Hard Disk Type 47 RAM Area** Specifies the type 47 data storage area – 0:300h in lower system RAM or in the top 1 KB of memory, starting at address 639K or 511K (depending on the amount of base memory). Type 47 data is stored in shadow RAM if shadowing is enabled. ■ **Fast Gate A20 Option** Fast Gate A20 is a hardware circuit that enables Gate A20 faster. The BIOS controls access to this circuitry. Address Gate A20 in the Intel x86 architecture controls access to memory addresses above 1 MB by enabling or disabling access to processor address line 20. Some programs both enter protected mode and use the CMOS RAM Shutdown byte to return to real mode through the BIOS. For these programs, Gate A20 must be constantly enabled and disabled by the keyboard controller, which is a slow process.

Type of Feature	Setup Options
Cache Memory Control	■ **Internal Cache Memory** appears only on 80486-based systems. It enables or disables access to the 8 KB internal cache in the microprocessor.
	■ **External Cache Memory** appears only on systems that have a caching scheme external to the CPU. This option enables or disables the testing and autosizing of cache memory in POST.
Keyboard and Mouse Control Features	■ **Typematic Rate Programming** Typematic Rate Programming enables or disables the Typematic Rate Delay and Typematic Rate options.
	■ **Typematic Rate Delay (milliseconds) and** ■ **Typematic Rate (Characters per Second)** Typematic Rate Delay and Typematic Rate control the speed at which a keystroke is repeated. The character associated with the keystroke is repeatedly displayed when a key is pressed and held down. After the Typematic Rate Delay, the character repeats at a rate set by the Typematic Rate.
	■ **System Boot Up Num Lock** You can turn off the NUM LOCK function when the system is powered on. You can use both sets of arrow keys on the keyboard when the NUM LOCK function is turned off.
	■ **Mouse Support Option** Enables support for a PS/2-type mouse or pointing device. If this option is disabled, the BIOS does not reserve the top 1 KB of the DOS applications area memory (639K or 511K depending on the amount of base memory) for the extended BIOS Data Area.
Message Display Control Features	■ **Hit <DEL> Message Display** Disabling this option prevents *Hit <DEL> to run Setup* from appearing when the system boots.
	■ **Wait for <F1> if Any Error** Disabling this option eliminates the need for user responses to Press F1 to continue.

Type of Feature	Setup Options
Coprocessor Enable Features	■ **Numeric Processor** Enable BIOS testing for a math coprocessor. ■ **Weitek Processor** Enable BIOS testing for a Weitek math coprocessor.
Boot Up Options	■ **Floppy Drive Seek at Boot** This option performs a Seek on drive A: at system boot. The default is Disabled for a faster boot. ■ **System Boot Up Sequence** The system can boot first from drive A: or drive C:. ■ **System Boot Up Speed** Sets the speed at which the system boots.
Speed Control	■ **Turbo Switch Function** Enables the system turbo (processor speed switching) switch, if this switch is supported in hardware.
Security Features	■ **Password Check Option** The password option prevents unauthorized system boot or AMIBIOS Setup use. ■ **Boot Sector Virus Protection** Newer AMIBIOS products automatically report when any program attempts to format or write to the boot sector on a hard disk drive.

Chapter 3

AMI BIOS Setup (Before 2/91)

Older American Megatrends BIOS Setup utilities had two parts: CMOS Setup and ROM Diagnostics.

CMOS Setup

CMOS Setup permits you to configure system components such as floppy drives, hard disk drives, monitor type, and keyboard. The time and date can also be set.

ROM Diagnostics

ROM Diagnostics performs specialized tests on the hard disk drives, floppy disk drives, keyboard, video adapter card, monitor, and parallel and serial ports. These tests are described in detail below.

Running the Old AMI BIOS Setup

The AMI BIOS Setup utility configures system parameters. BIOS Setup is in ROM and is available when the computer is turned on.

The system parameters (amount of memory, number and type of disk drives, video display types, and so on) are stored in CMOS RAM. A battery provides power to CMOS RAM, which retains the system parameters when computer power is turned off. When the system is turned on, it is configured with the stored system parameters. If the data is CMOS RAM is bad, preconfigured default values are used to configure the system.

Running Setup

The following

```
Hit <DEL> if you want to run SETUP or DIAGS
```

appears during BIOS POST. Press DEL to run Setup or Diagnostics.

Old AMI BIOS Setup Key Use

Keystroke	Action
ESC	Exit Utility and Reboot
→, ←, ↑, ↓	Move the cursor from one option to the next.
PGUP, PGDN	Modify the default value of the options for the highlighted parameter.

Write to CMOS and Exit

The features selected and configured by Setup are stored in CMOS RAM when you leave Setup. A CMOS RAM checksum is calculated and written to CMOS RAM. Control is then passed to the ROM BIOS. Then the following:

```
Write data into CMOS and Exit (Y/N)?
```

appears. Type *N* and press ENTER to return to the Setup Main Menu without saving the new configuration data. Type *Y* and press ENTER to save the system parameters and continue the boot process.

CMOS Setup

The following screen appears when you select CMOS Setup:

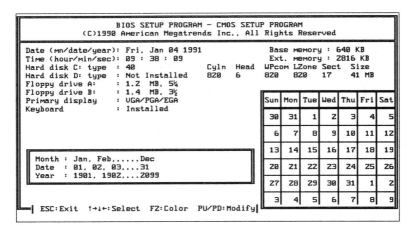

CMOS Setup Options

Daylight Saving Option — Sets Standard Time or Daylight Savings Time. This option is not in AMIBIOS dated 12/12/91 or later.

Date And Day Configuration — Move the cursor to the Date field via the ↑ and ↓ keys. Set the Date and Day by pressing PGUP or PGDN.

Time Configuration — Move the cursor to the Time field with the ↑ and ↓ keys and set the time by pressing PGUP or PGDN.

Hard Disk C: and D: — Move the cursor to these fields via the ↑ and ↓ keys and select a hard disk drive type by pressing PGUP or PGDN. Match the parameters listed in the Hard Disk Drive Type table on page 117 to the parameters provided by the disk drive manufacturer (or listed in the computer owner's manual). Choose:

- Type 47 to configure a drive whose parameters are not listed in the Hard Disk Drive Type table,
- Type 47 to configure an IDE drive,
- Type 1 to configure an ESDI drive, or
- *Not Installed* to configure a SCSI drive.

The hard disk drive parameters are:

Parameter	Description
Type	The drive type number.
Cylinders	The number of cylinders in the disk drive.
Heads	The number of heads in the disk drive.
Write Precompensation	The size of a sector becomes progressively smaller as the track diameter diminishes yet each sector must still hold 512 bytes. Write precompensation circuitry on the hard disk compensates for the physical difference in sector size by boosting the write current for sectors on inner tracks. This is the track number where write precompensation begins.
Landing Zone	The cylinder where the heads park when the system is off.
Sectors	The number of sectors per track. MFM hard drives have 17 sectors per track. ESDI drives have 34 sectors per track. SCSI and IDE drives have even more sectors per track.
Capacity	The formatted capacity of the drive is: Number of heads x Number of cylinders x Number of sectors per track x 512 bytes per sector.

cont'd

CMOS Setup Options, Continued

Floppy Drive A: and Floppy Drive B:

The settings are: *360 KB 5¼ inch, 1.2 MB 5¼ inch, 720 KB 3½ inch, 1.44 MB 3½ inch*, or *Not Installed*. *Not Installed* stops missing drive messages.

Monitor

The settings are: *Monochrome, Color 40x25, VGA/PGA/EGA, Color 80x25*, or *Not Installed*. *Not Installed* stops missing display messages.

Keyboard

The BIOS automatically senses the keyboard type and configures it. *Not Installed* stops missing keyboard messages.

Video BIOS Shadow

The video BIOS code at C0000h – C7FFFh is copied from ROM to RAM and is executed from RAM.

256 KB Memory Relocate

The memory segment from 640 KB to 896 KB is relocated above 1 MB as extended memory. Disable Video BIOS Shadow before enabling this option. The settings are *Enabled* or *Disabled*.

Advanced ROM Diagnostics

Older AMIBIOS include diagnostic utilities for five peripheral devices.

Utility	Purpose	Turn to
Hard Disk	Perform a low-level format of the hard drive, determine the optimum interleave factor, analyze each hard drive to determine usable tracks, test the performance of each hard drive, perform various diagnostic tests.	Page 24
Floppy Disk	Test Disk Formatting, Drive Speed, Read and Write tests, and Disk Change Line test.	Page 28
Keyboard	Scan/ASCII Code Test.	Page 32
Video	Perform sync test, adapter test, attribute test, text and graphics display test, page selection test, and color test.	Page 33
Miscellaneous Tests	Test serial and parallel ports.	Page 34

Each option is explained in this section.

Diagnostics Menu

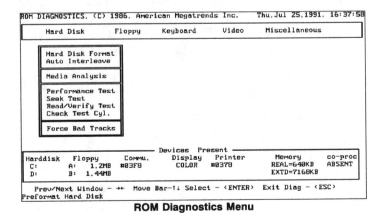

ROM Diagnostics Menu

Hard Disk Diagnostics

Function	Purpose	Turn to
Hard Disk Format	Performs a low level format of the hard drive(s). Read the system or hard disk drive documentation to find out if the hard disk has been preformatted.	Page 24
Auto Interleave	Determines the optimum interleave factor.	Page 25
Media Analysis	Analyzes each hard disk drive track to determine usability. The track is marked bad if unusable.	Page 25
Performance Test	Determines the data transfer rate and track-to-track seek time.	Page 26
Seek Test	Performs a sequential and random head seek to check seek capability.	Page 26
Read/ Verify Test	Performs a sequential and random read and verify operation for a specified cylinder and head range.	Page 27
Check Test Cylinder	Does a write/verify test on the highest cylinder of the hard disk.	Page 27
Force Bad Tracks	Allows you to mark certain tracks as bad.	Page 28

Hard Disk Format

Run the Hard Disk Format routine to integrate a new hard disk to the system or to reformat a used hard disk that has developed bad tracks as a result of aging or poor handling. Select Media Analysis to find bad tracks. The following screen appears when you press ENTER.

```
                    Hard Disk Format
   Disk Drive (C/D)                        ? C
   Disk Drive Type                         ? 47
   Interleave (1—16)                       ?
   Mark Bad Tracks (Y/N)                   ?
   Start cylinder number                   ?
   End cylinder number                     ?
   Start head number                       ?
   End head number                         ?
   Proceed (Y/N)                           ?
```

The first two questions are already completed if a hard disk was selected in CMOS Setup. Type C or D in Disk Drive and press ENTER. The Disk Drive Type is read from CMOS RAM. The interleave factor can be selected manually or determined automatically.

Hard Disk Diagnostics, Continued

The hard disk drive manufacturer usually provides a list of bad tracks. Enter these tracks. They are marked as bad to prevent data from being stored on them. A warning message appears after the starting and ending cylinders and heads are entered. Type Y and press ENTER.

Auto Interleave

Auto Interleave destroys hard disk data. Back up the data on the hard disk before running these programs. Auto Interleave calculates the optimum interleave factor through trial and error by measuring the transfer rates of four interleave values. To determine the best interleave factor, the system formats a portion of the hard disk for each transfer rate. The cylinders, heads, and sectors formatted for each value displayed. This test does not work on an IDE or SCSI hard disk drive. Select Auto Interleave and press ENTER. The following appears:

```
        Auto Interleave Detection
Disk Drive (C/D)              ? C
Disk Drive Type               ? 47
Proceed (Y/N)                 ?
```

After entering the disk drive (C or D) and hard disk drive type, a warning message appears. Type Y and press ENTER to continue.

Media Analysis

Media Analysis lists bad or damaged tracks on the hard disk as a result of aging or poor handling. This test writes to all cylinders and heads on the hard disk to verify any bad tracks. For best results, run the test in its entirety. Media Analysis does not work on an IDE or SCSI hard disk drive. Select Media Analysis from the main Hard Disk Utility Menu and press ENTER.

```
           Media Analysis
Disk Drive (C/D)            ? C
Disk Drive Type            ? 47
Proceed (Y/N)              ?
```

A warning message appears when you type Y. Type Y again and press Enter to perform the hard disk drive analysis.

cont'd

Hard Disk Diagnostics, Continued

Performance Test

Optimize the interleave factor before choosing the Performance Test. The Performance Test determines the data transfer rate and the track-to-track seek time based on transfer size, seek count and data transferred. This information is calculated and displayed. Compare these values to the values in the hard disk drive documentation to determine if they are acceptable. The following screen appears when Performance Test is selected from the Hard Disk Diagnostic menu:

```
┌─────────────────────────────────────────────┐
│           Performance Test                   │
├─────────────────────────────────────────────┤
│ Disk Drive (C/D)              ? C            │
│ Disk Drive Type               ?              │
│ Proceed (Y/N)                 ?              │
└─────────────────────────────────────────────┘
```

Enter the hard disk drive type or press ENTER and the BIOS automatically enters the correct type. If you enter the hard disk drive type, you must know the drive parameters. The table on page 117 lists the standard hard disk drive types.

If none of the listed types match the parameters for the system's hard disk drive, you can use hard disk drive type 47. You must enter the hard disk drive parameters for type 47 in CMOS Setup.

Seek Test

The Seek Test determines the seek capability of the hard disk on the specified cylinder and head range. First, a sequential seek is performed, followed by a random seek. Errors that occur during this test are displayed. The following screen appears:

```
┌─────────────────────────────────────────────┐
│           Hard Disk Seek Test                │
├─────────────────────────────────────────────┤
│ Disk Drive (C/D)              ?              │
│ Disk Drive Type               ?              │
│ Start cylinder number         ?              │
│ End cylinder number           ?              │
│ Start Head number             ?              │
│ End Head number               ?              │
│ Proceed (Y/N)                 ?              │
└─────────────────────────────────────────────┘
```

Press ENTER on each line to permit the BIOS to enter the values for each field.

Hard Disk Diagnostics, Continued

Read/Verify Test

This test performs sequential and random read and verify operations on the specified cylinder and head ranges. The following screen appears when you select Read/Verify:

```
┌─────────────────────────────────────────────┐
│       Hard Disk Read/Verify Test            │
├─────────────────────────────────────────────┤
│ Disk Drive (C/D)              ?             │
│ Disk Drive Type               ?             │
│ Start cylinder number         ?             │
│ End cylinder number           ?             │
│ Start Head number             ?             │
│ End Head number               ?             │
│ Proceed (Y/N)                 ?             │
└─────────────────────────────────────────────┘
```

Press ENTER on each field to permit the BIOS to enter the appropriate values.

Check Test Cylinder

The last cylinder on the hard disk is the test cylinder. This cylinder should be tested if a C: Drive or D: Drive error occurs during POST. A write/verify test is performed on all sectors in the test cylinder. This test should pass in at least one sector. If the test fails in all sectors, the test cylinder is probably faulty. The following screen appears:

```
┌─────────────────────────────────────────────┐
│        Hard Disk Test Cyl. Test             │
├─────────────────────────────────────────────┤
│ Disk Drive (C/D)              ? C           │
│ Disk Drive Type               ?             │
│ Proceed (Y/N)                 ?             │
└─────────────────────────────────────────────┘
```

The BIOS automatically completes both tests if you press ENTER. Type Y in the *Proceed* field. *Write* and *Verify* are highlighted and flash while the test runs.

cont'd

Hard Disk Diagnostics, Continued

Force Bad Tracks

The Force Bad Tracks routine allows you to define a set of tracks as faulty before performing a low level format. This routine accomplishes the same objective as the Hard Disk Format Test. It is a quick way to mark bad tracks before formatting. This routine should be run if you did not enter bad tracks in the Hard Disk Format Test. This routine does not work on IDE or SCSI hard disk drives. The following screen appears when you select Force Bad Tracks from the Hard Disk menu:

```
┌──────────────────────────────────────┐
│            Force Bad Tracks           │
├──────────────────────────────────────┤
│  Disk Drive (C/D)           ? C       │
│  Disk Drive Type            ?         │
│  Interleave (1-16)          ?         │
│  Mark Bad Tracks (Y/N)      ?         │
│  Proceed (Y/N)              ?         │
└──────────────────────────────────────┘
```

Press ENTER at each field to allow the BIOS to enter the correct value. Format is highlighted and flashes while the test is in progress.

Floppy Disk Diagnostics

The five floppy diagnostic tests are:

- Floppy Format Test,
- Drive Speed Test,
- Random Read/Write Test,
- Sequential Read/Write Test, and
- Disk Change Line Test.

Warning

The Disk Format, Random Read/Write, and Sequential Read/Write Tests destroy data on the disk in the tested drive.

Floppy Disk Diagnostics, Continued

Floppy Format Test

This test determines if the floppy disk controller can perform low-level formatting. The floppy format test can only be performed interactively. This test destroys all data on the floppy. Don't use the floppy disk required for this test with any other program. Floppy disks formatted with this option do not have the DOS file structure. Reformat the disk under DOS before using it for any other purpose. The following screen appears when you select Floppy Format:

```
┌──────────────────────────────────────────┐
│              Floppy Format                 │
├──────────────────────────────────────────┤
│ Disk Drive (A/B)              ? A          │
│ Proceed (Y/N)                 ?            │
└──────────────────────────────────────────┘
```

Format is highlighted and flashes.

Drive Speed Test

This test determines the rotation speed of the drive. Consult the floppy drive documentation for acceptable tolerances. The following appears:

```
┌──────────────────────────────────────────┐
│ Insert A Formatted Diskette in Drive       │
│ Press ENTER when ready...                  │
└──────────────────────────────────────────┘
```

The following screen appears after you insert a formatted floppy in the drive and press ENTER:

```
┌──────────────────────────────────────────┐
│ Floppy Disk Drive is 1.44 MB               │
│ Diskette Capacity - 80 trks & 9 secs/trk   │
│ Test in Progress                           │
└──────────────────────────────────────────┘
```

Wait for 2 minutes appears briefly as the test begins. The test records a lower and upper limit. The Current Speed flashes. Press ENTER to return to the Main Menu when the test is done.

cont'd

Floppy Disk Diagnostics, Continued

Random Read/Write Test

This test checks the random seek, read, and write capability of the drive. The disk used in this test must be formatted on the current operating system before running this test.

Warning
This test destroys data on the disk used to perform these tests.

The following message appears when you select Random Read/Write Test from the Floppy Disk menu:

```
                        Random R/W Test
Disk Drive (A/B)              ? A
Proceed (Y/N)                 ?
```

Type *N* to return to the Floppy Drive Menu. Type *Y* to display:

```
Insert A Formatted Diskette in Drive
Press ENTER when ready...
```

After you insert a formatted disk in the drive and press ENTER, the following appears:

```
Floppy Disk Drive is 1.44 MB
Diskette Capacity - 80 trks & 9 secs/trk
Test in Progress
```

Read, Write, and Verify flash in sequence as these operations are performed. The cylinder numbers, head numbers, and sector numbers are read, written, and verified. Press ESC to abort the test. Press ENTER to return to the Main Menu when done.

Sequential Read/Write Test

This routine tests the drive's sequential seek, read, and write capability. The floppy disk used in this test must be formatted on the operating system being used before running the test.

> ### *Warning*
> *This test destroys data on the disk used to perform these tests.*

The following screen appears when you select Sequential Read/Write Test:

```
                    Sequential R/W Test
Disk Drive (A/B)              ? A
Proceed (Y/N)                 ?
```

Type Y. The following screen appears:

```
Insert A Formatted Diskette in Drive A:
Press ENTER when ready...
```

The following appears after you insert a formatted disk in the drive and press ENTER:

```
Floppy Disk Drive is 1.44 MB
Diskette Capacity - 80 trks & 9 secs/trk
Test in Progress
```

Write and Verify flash as these operations are performed. The cylinder numbers, head numbers, and sector numbers are read, written, and verified sequentially by sector number. Press ENTER to return to the Main Menu.

cont'd

Floppy Disk Diagnostics, Continued

Diskette Change Line Test

This test verifies the disk change line feature, which allows the
operating system to recognize that a new disk has been inserted
without accessing the File Allocation Table (FAT). The disk used in
this test must be formatted on the operating system being used. The
following screen appears when you select Disk Change Line Test.

```
                         Disk Change Line Test
  Disk Drive (A/B)              ? A
  Proceed (Y/N)                 ?
```

Type Y. The following screen appears:

```
  Remove Diskette from Drive A:
  Press ENTER when ready...
```

After you insert a formatted disk in the drive and press ENTER, Verify
is highlighted. The cylinder number is 0, the head number 0, and the
sector number 1 are displayed. The following appears:

```
  Reinsert Same Diskette
  Press ENTER when ready...
```

Verify is highlighted when completed. Press ENTER to run the test.
Press ENTER again when the test completes to return to the Main
Menu.

Keyboard Diagnostics

Scan/ASCII Code Test

The Scan/ASCII Code Test determines whether the pressed keys are
the proper Scan and ASCII codes. When you press a key to verify its
code, the key symbol, scan code, and ASCII code of the key are
displayed. Highlight Keyboard in the Main Menu and Scan/ASCII
Code Test. Press ENTER to display a keyboard layout. Scan code and
ASCII Code appear above the keyboard layout. Press the keys on the
keyboard. The scan codes and ASCII codes display in the appropriate
fields for each key as it is pressed. Press CTRL BREAK to exit.

Video Diagnostics

The video tests that can run on a system depend on the type of display adapter card installed. The following table describes the video diagnostic tests:

Diagnostic Test	Description	Can be run on systems with
Adapter Test	Tests the display memory.	Monochrome and color
Attribute Test	Tests the display attributes. Displays a screen with a blinking line, reverse video line, high intensity line, and lines in eight colors.	Monochrome and color
80x25 Display Test	Tests the 80x25 character set of the display adapter, displaying the entire character set in black and white, then in reverse video.	Monochrome and color
40x25 Display Test	Tests the 40x25 character set of the display adapter in black and white, displaying the entire character set in black and white, then in reverse video.	Monochrome and color
320x200 Graphics Test	Displays a black and white 9x13 window and redisplays it in reverse video, a three-color screen, a screen of random colors, a black and white screen, and finally 256 colors.	Color only
640x200 Graphics Test	Displays three black and white boxes, a black screen, a white screen, and a black screen again.	Color only
Page Selection Test	Displays a screen of 0s, 1s, 2s, 3s, and so on, through 7s in black and white, indicating that each video page mode is being used.	Color only
Color Test	Displays eight colors in the foreground, background, and border.	Color only

Performing All Video Tests

To perform all visual tests, Highlight Video in the Main Menu and Run All Tests. Highlight the visual tests below the Sync Test. Press ENTER to begin a test. Follow the onscreen prompts.

Miscellaneous Diagnostics

Printer Adapter Test

This test writes a pattern on the printer. Highlight Miscellaneous in the Main Menu and Printer Adapter Test and press ENTER. The following appears:

```
Checking Printer Port #1
```

Press ENTER to return to the Main Menu.

Printer Adapter Test Error Messages

Printer Out of Paper   Printer Not Selected
Printer Interface I/O Error   Time Out On Printer

All messages except Printer Out of Paper indicate a controller problem.

Serial Communications Adapter Test

The RS-232C jumper settings are displayed and:

```
Are the Pins Connected as Above ? (Y/N)
```

appears. Type Y or N. Checking Serial Port #1 appears. Type Y to begin. This test requires a special RS-232 Turnaround Connector attached to the serial port and jumpered as follows:

- TXD (Pin 2) and RXD (Pin 3) must be shorted,
- RTS (Pin 4) and CTS (Pin 5) must be shorted, and
- DSR (Pin 6) and DTR (Pin 20) must be shorted.

The serial test reads 9600 data transmission rate, odd parity, two stop-bits, and 8-bit data. The test performs a reset function to check for possible errors, a send function, and then a receive function.

Serial Port Diagnostic Test Error Messages

Error - Time out!   Error - Break Detected
Error - Framing error   Error - Parity error   Error - Overrun error

If a timeout error occurs during send and receive, there is a problem in the communication adapter controller.

Chapter 4

Hi-Flex AMIBIOS Setup

This chapter documents the AMIBIOS Setup for an AMIBIOS with a
BIOS Date after January 1991.

Hi-Flex AMIBIOS Setup Options

The Hi-Flex AMIBIOS Setup utility menu options are shown below.
All options do not appear in all AMIBIOS Setup utilities.

- Standard CMOS Setup,
- Advanced CMOS Setup,
- Advanced Chipset Setup,
- Power Management Setup,
- Peripheral Management Setup,
- Auto Configuration with BIOS Setup Defaults,
- Auto Configuration with Power-On Defaults,
- Auto Detect Hard Disk,
- Change Password,
- Hard Disk Utility,
- Write to CMOS and Exit, and
- Do Not Write to CMOS and Exit.

AMIBIOS Setup in your system probably does not display all of these
options.

cont'd

Hi-Flex AMIBIOS Setup Options, Continued

A sample Hi-Flex BIOS Setup Main Menu is shown below. All options may not appear on the BIOS Setup screens in your computer because computer manufacturers can enable or disable individual menu items.

```
AMIBIOS SETUP PROGRAM — BIOS SETUP UTILITIES
(C) Copyright 1993 American Megatrends Inc. All Rights Reserved

                  STANDARD CMOS SETUP
                  ADVANCED CMOS SETUP
                 ADVANCED CHIPSET SETUP
               POWER MANAGEMENT BIOS SETUP
                PERIPHERAL MANAGEMENT SETUP
           AUTO CONFIGURATION WITH BIOS DEFAULTS
          AUTO CONFIGURATION WITH POWER-ON DEFAULTS
                 AUTO DETECT HARD DISK
                   CHANGE PASSWORD
                  HARD DISK UTILITY
                 WRITE TO CMOS AND EXIT
              DO NOT WRITE TO CMOS AND EXIT

STANDARD CMOS SETUP for changing Time, Date, Hard Disk Type, etc.
```

Each option is explained in detail in this section.

Standard CMOS Setup

Standard CMOS Setup configures system components such as floppy drives, hard disk drives, and monitor type. These options are discussed on page 45.

Advanced CMOS Setup

Advanced CMOS Setup configures options such as which drive to boot from, the Typematic Rate and Delay, and error message displays. It is discussed on page 49.

Advanced Chipset Setup

Advanced Chipset Setup configures chipset-specific features and is discussed on page 55.

Power Management BIOS Setup

This option, described on page 81, is used only in notebook, handheld, laptop, and other systems where system power use must be carefully monitored and conserved. It appears in AMIBIOS dated after 12/91.

Peripheral Management Setup

This option, described on page 85, appears only in Hi-Flex AMIBIOS manufactured after 12/91. The screen generated by this part of AMIBIOS Setup allows you to configure advanced system features related to peripheral device control.

Auto Configuration with BIOS Setup Defaults

This option configures a high-performance system. Advanced CMOS Setup, Advanced Chipset Setup, Power Management Setup, and Peripheral Management Setup options have a BIOS Setup default setting that provides optimal performance. Standard CMOS Setup default settings are loaded only if CMOS RAM is corrupt. The defaults disable all peripheral devices. The other AMIBIOS Setup screens have two default values: BIOS Setup and Power-On Default settings.

If CMOS RAM is corrupted, the BIOS Setup defaults are automatically loaded. Type Y and press ENTER. The following appears:

```
Default values loaded. Press any key to continue.
```

Auto Configuration with Power-On Defaults

This option configures a system for safe operation. Advanced CMOS, Advanced CHIPSET, Power Management, and Peripheral Management Setup options have Power-On default settings that provide the safest configuration, but not the best performance. These values are most likely to work when there is a system configuration problem. Choose this option as a diagnostic aid. Type Y and press ENTER. The following appears.

```
Default values loaded. Press any key to continue.
```

cont'd

Auto Detect Hard Disk

This option detects the hard disk parameters for all IDE hard disk drives and some ESDI drives. It displays the parameters that it detects and allows the end user to accept or reject the parameters. If accepted, these parameters are displayed for the hard disk drive in Standard CMOS Setup.

Change Password

Sets the system password (see page 89 for more information about passwords). The system password is not enabled on all systems with an AMIBIOS. The password type is set in Advanced CMOS Setup.

Hard Disk Utility

Executes a hard disk utility.

Write to CMOS and Exit

Stores the features selected and configured in BIOS Setup to CMOS RAM. A checksum is calculated and written to CMOS RAM. The following appears:

```
Write to CMOS and Exit (Y/N)? N
```

Type *N* to return to the Setup main menu. Type *Y* to save the system parameters and continue to boot. The BIOS reboots the system if an option has been selected that changes the memory map.

Do Not Write to CMOS and Exit

This option passes control to the ROM BIOS without writing any changes to CMOS RAM. Type *N* and press ENTER to return to the Main Menu. Type *Y* to continue the boot process without saving any system parameters changed in Setup.

Section 1

Running AMIBIOS Setup

The system parameters (such as amount of memory, disk drives, video displays, and numeric coprocessors) are stored in CMOS RAM. When the computer is turned off, a back-up battery provides power to CMOS RAM, which retains the system parameters. Every time the system is powered on, it is configured with these values, unless CMOS RAM has been corrupted.

The system configuration parameters are set via AMIBIOS Setup. AMIBIOS Setup resides in the ROM BIOS (Read Only Memory Basic Input/Output System) and is available each time the computer is turned on.

Default System Parameters

If CMOS RAM is bad, the system is configured with the default values stored in ROM. There are two sets of BIOS values stored in the ROM file: the BIOS Setup default values and the Power-On default values.

Starting Setup

As POST executes, the following appears:

        Hit <DEL> if you want to run SETUP

Press DEL to run Hi-Flex AMIBIOS Setup.

AMIBIOS Setup Key Use

Keystroke	Action
ESC	Returns to previous screen.
→, ←, ↑, and ↓	Moves the cursor from one option to the next.
PGUP and PGDN CTRL PGUP CTRL PGDN	Modifies the default value of the options for the highlighted parameter. If there are fewer than 10 options, CTRL PGUP and CTRL PGDN operate like PGUP and PGDN. Press CTRL to increment a setting.
F1	Displays Help.
F2	Changes background colors.
F3	Changes foreground colors.
F5	Restores the values resident when the current Setup session began. These values are taken from CMOS RAM if CMOS RAM was uncorrupted at the start of the session. Otherwise, AMIBIOS Setup default values are used.
F6	Loads all features in Advanced CMOS Setup and Advanced Chipset Setup with the BIOS Setup defaults.
F7	Loads all features in Advanced CMOS Setup and Advanced Chipset Setup with the Power-On defaults.
F10	Saves all changes made to Setup and continues the boot process.

Note: The default value for F5, F6, and F7 is always N. To execute these options, change the *N* to *Y* and press ENTER.

AMIBIOS Setup Main Menu

A Hi-Flex AMIBIOS Setup Main Menu is shown below. All options may not appear on the AMIBIOS Setup screens that appears in your computer because you can enable or disable the menu items.

```
        AMIBIOS SETUP PROGRAM - BIOS SETUP UTILITIES
  (C) Copyright 1992 American Megatrends, Inc. All Rights Reserved



                    STANDARD CMOS SETUP
                    ADVANCED CMOS SETUP
                  ADVANCED CHIP SET SETUP
                POWER MANAGEMENT BIOS SETUP
                     PERIPHERAL SETUP
            AUTO CONFIGURATION WITH BIOS DEFAULTS
           AUTO CONFIGURATION WITH POWER-ON DEFAULTS
                     CHANGE PASSWORD
                   AUTO DETECT HARD DISK
                     HARD DISK UTILITY
                   WRITE TO CMOS AND EXIT
                DO NOT WRITE TO CMOS AND EXIT


  Standard CMOS Setup for changing Time, Date, Hard Disk Type, etc.
```

Main Menu Option	Described on
Standard CMOS Setup	page 45
Advanced CMOS Setup	page 49
Advanced Chipset Setup	page 55
Power Management Setup	page 81
Peripheral Management Setup	page 85
Auto Configuration With BIOS Defaults	page 42
Auto Configuration with Power On Defaults	page 42
Change Password	page 89
Auto Detect Hard Disk	page 43
Hard Disk Utility	page 91
Write to CMOS and Exit	page 44
Do Not Write to CMOS and Exit	page 44

BIOS Default Values

AMIBIOS has default settings for many options in the five types of Setup. In Standard CMOS Setup default values are only loaded if CMOS RAM is corrupt. All Standard CMOS Setup default settings are disabled (floppy, hard disk, monitor, keyboard). In all other types of Setup, both BIOS and Power-On defaults are provided for most options.

Auto Configuration With BIOS Defaults

By choosing *Auto Configuration With BIOS Defaults*, you automatically configure the system using the BIOS default values. The BIOS default value are best-case values that should optimize system performance. If CMOS RAM is corrupted, the BIOS defaults are loaded automatically.

To use the BIOS defaults, type Y and press ENTER. The following message appears:

`Default values loaded. Press any key to continue.`

Auto Configuration With Power-On Defaults

By choosing Auto Configuration with Power-On Defaults, you automatically configure the system using the default Power-On values. Power-On default values are worst-case values for system performance, but are the most stable values. Use this option as a diagnostic aid if the system is behaving erratically.

Type *Y* and press ENTER to use the Power-On defaults. The following message appears:

`Default values loaded. Press any key to continue.`

Autodetect Hard Disk

This option detects the hard disk parameters for nonstandard hard disk drives, such as IDE and SCSI drives. It displays the parameters that it detects (see the following screen) and allows the end user to accept or reject the parameters. If accepted, these parameters are displayed in the Hard Disk Drive C: or D: fields in Standard CMOS Setup as Type 47.

```
          AMIBIOS SETUP PROGRAM - HARD DISK AUTO DETECT
      (C) Copyright 1992 American Megatrends, Inc. All Rights Reserved

  HARD DRIVE TYPE      Cyln   Head   WPcom   LZone   Sect   Size

                        960     12     960     960     34    200 MB








     Auto detect hard disk drive parameters.
```

If an IDE drive is found and you accept the parameters, AMIBIOS places the hard disk drive parameters that it finds in the Hard Dive C: or Hard Drive D: field in Standard CMOS Setup and sets Type 47. Press ENTER to accept these values.

Write to CMOS and Exit

The configurations settings are stored in CMOS RAM when this option is selected. A CMOS RAM checksum is calculated and written to CMOS RAM and control is passed to the system BIOS. The following

```
Write to CMOS and Exit (Y/N) ? N
```

appears. Press *N* and ENTER to return to the Main Menu. Press *Y* and ENTER to save the system parameters and continue the boot process. AMIBIOS either reboots the system (if any new settings change the memory map) or continues the boot process.

Do Not Write to CMOS RAM and Exit

This option passes control to the BIOS without writing any changes to CMOS RAM.

Press *N* and ENTER to return to the Main Menu. Press *Y* and ENTER to continue the boot process without saving any system parameters changed in Setup.

Section 2

Standard CMOS Setup

Standard CMOS Setup sets basic system parameters, such as day, date, time, and hard disk type. Use the ↑ and ↓ keys to select Standard CMOS Setup and press ENTER. The following appears:

```
              AMIBIOS SETUP PROGRAM - CMOS SETUP PROGRAM
             (C)1992 American Megatrends Inc., All Rights Reserved

Date (mn/date/year): Fri, Aug 07 1992        Base memory : 640 KB
Time (hour/min/sec): 09 : 38 : 09            Ext. memory : 2816 KB
                                 Cyln  Head  WPcom LZone Sect  Size
Hard disk C: type  : 40          820   6     820   820   17    41 MB
Hard disk D: type  : Not Installed
Floppy drive A:    : 1.2  MB, 5¼
Floppy drive B:    : 1.44 MB, 3½        ┌───┬───┬───┬───┬───┬───┬───┐
Primary Display    : VGA/PGA/EGA        │Sun│Mon│Tue│Wed│Thu│Fri│Sat│
Keyboard           : Installed          ├───┼───┼───┼───┼───┼───┼───┤
                                        │30 │31 │ 1 │ 2 │ 3 │ 4 │ 5 │
                                        ├───┼───┼───┼───┼───┼───┼───┤
                                        │ 6 │ 7 │ 8 │ 9 │10 │11 │12 │
┌─────────────────────────────┐        ├───┼───┼───┼───┼───┼───┼───┤
│Month : Jan, Feb,.....Dec    │        │13 │14 │15 │16 │17 │18 │19 │
│Date  : 01, 02, 03,...31     │        ├───┼───┼───┼───┼───┼───┼───┤
│Year  : 1901, 1902,...2099   │        │20 │21 │22 │23 │24 │25 │26 │
└─────────────────────────────┘        ├───┼───┼───┼───┼───┼───┼───┤
                                        │27 │28 │29 │30 │31 │ 1 │ 2 │
                                        ├───┼───┼───┼───┼───┼───┼───┤
                                        │ 3 │ 4 │ 5 │ 6 │ 7 │ 8 │ 9 │
                                        └───┴───┴───┴───┴───┴───┴───┘
  ESC:Exit  ↑→↓←:Select  F2:Color  PU/PD:Modify
```

Standard CMOS Setup OPTIONS

Date And Day Configuration

Ranges for each value are shown in the lower left corner of the screen. Move the cursor to the Date field via the →, ←, ↑, or ↓ keys and set the Date and Day by pressing PGUP and PGDN.

Time Configuration

This option uses a 24-hour clock format (add 12 for P.M. numbers). Enter 4:30 P.M. as 16:30:00. Move the cursor to the Time field via the →, ←, ↑, or ↓ keys and set the time by pressing PGUP and PGDN to change values.

cont'd

Hard Disk Drive C: and D:

Move the cursor to these fields via the →, ←, ↑, or ↓ keys and press PGUP or PGDN to select a hard disk drive type. *Not Installed* is used for diskless workstations and SCSI hard disk drives. Type 47 can be used for both hard disks C: and D:, and is primarily for IDE drives. The parameters for type 47 for drives C: and D: can be different, permitting user-definable hard disk drives.

Using Auto Detect Hard Disk

If you select the Auto Detect Hard Disk option from the AMIBIOS Main Menu screen, the AMIBIOS automatically finds all IDE hard disk drive parameters. AMIBIOS places the hard disk drive parameters that it finds in the Drive C: or D: field and sets Type 47. Press ENTER to accept these values.

Otherwise, you must enter the hard drive parameters, described in the following table. The hard disk drive type parameters are shown on the following page.

Parameter	Description
Type	The number for a drive with certain identification parameters.
Cylinders	The number of cylinders in the disk drive.
Heads	The number of heads in the disk drive.
Write Precompensation	The size of a sector gets progressively smaller as the track diameter diminishes. Yet each sector must still hold 512 bytes. Write precompensation circuitry on the disk drive compensates for the physical difference in sector size by boosting the write current for sectors on inner tracks. This is the track number where write precompensation begins.
Landing Zone	This number is the cylinder location where the heads normally park when the system is shut down.
Sectors	The number of sectors per track. Hard drives that use MFM have 17 sectors per track. RLL drives have 26 sectors per track. ARLL and ESDI drives have 34 sectors per track. SCSI and IDE drives can have even more sectors per track.
Capacity	The formatted capacity of the drive is the Number of Heads x Number of Cylinders x Number of Sectors per Track x 512 bytes (Bytes per Sector).

Hard Disk Drive Types

Type	Cylinders	Heads	Write Precompensation	Landing Zone	Sectors	Size
1	306	4	128	305	17	10 MB
2	615	4	300	615	17	20 MB
3	615	6	300	615	17	31 MB
4	940	8	512	940	17	62 MB
5	940	6	512	940	17	47 MB
6	615	4	65535	615	17	20 MB
7	462	8	256	511	17	31 MB
8	733	5	65535	733	17	30 MB
9	900	15	65535	901	17	112 MB
10	820	3	65535	820	17	20 MB
11	855	5	65535	855	17	35 MB
12	855	7	65535	855	17	50 MB
13	306	8	128	319	17	20 MB
14	733	7	65535	733	17	43 MB
16	612	4	0	663	17	20 MB
17	977	5	300	977	17	41 MB
18	977	7	65535	977	17	57 MB
19	1024	7	512	1023	17	60 MB
20	733	5	300	732	17	30 MB
21	733	7	300	732	17	43 MB
22	733	5	300	733	17	30 MB
23	306	4	0	336	17	10 MB
24	925	7	0	925	17	54 MB
25	925	9	65535	925	17	69 MB
26	754	7	754	754	17	44 MB
27	754	11	65535	754	17	69 MB
28	699	7	256	699	17	41 MB
29	823	10	65535	823	17	68 MB
30	918	7	918	918	17	53 MB
31	1024	11	65535	1024	17	94 MB
32	1024	15	65535	1024	17	128 MB
33	1024	5	1024	1024	17	43 MB
34	612	2	128	612	17	10 MB
35	1024	9	65535	1024	17	77 MB
36	1024	8	512	1024	17	68 MB
37	615	8	128	615	17	41 MB
38	987	3	987	987	17	25 MB
39	987	7	987	987	17	57 MB
40	820	6	820	820	17	41 MB
41	977	5	977	977	17	41 MB
42	981	5	981	981	17	41 MB
43	830	7	512	830	17	48 MB
44	830	10	65535	830	17	69 MB
45	917	15	65535	918	17	114 MB
46	1224	15	65535	1223	17	152 MB
47	ENTER PARAMETERS PROVIDED BY HARD DRIVE MANUFACTURER					

Floppy Drive A and Floppy Drive B:

Use PGUP or PGDN to select a setting. The settings are: *360 KB 5¼ inch, 1.2 MB 5¼ inch, 720 KB 3½ inch, 1.44 MB 3½ inch, 2.88 MB 3½ inch,* or *Not Installed*, which could be used for diskless workstations. The BIOS does not generate error messages if *Not Installed* is selected.

Primary Display

Use PGUP or PGDN to select a setting. The settings are: *Monochrome, Color 40x25, Color 80x25, VGA/PGA/EGA,* or *Not Installed*, which could be used for network file servers. The BIOS does not generate missing monitor messages if *Not Installed* is selected.

Keyboard

Use PGUP or PGDN to select a setting. The settings are *Installed* or *Not Installed.* Use *Not Installed* in a keyboardless system such as a file server. The BIOS does not generate an error message about a missing keyboard if *Not Installed* is selected.

Section 3

Advanced CMOS Setup

The following screen shows the standard Advanced CMOS Setup options, described in this section:

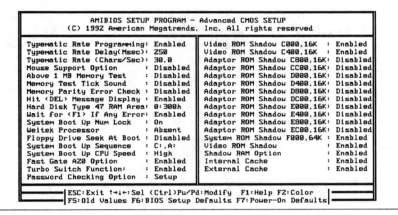

```
                  AMIBIOS SETUP PROGRAM - Advanced CMOS SETUP
              (C) 1992 American Megatrends, Inc. All rights reserved

 Typematic Rate Programming: Enabled    Video ROM Shadow C000,16K  : Enabled
 Typematic Rate Delay(Msec): 250        Video ROM Shadow C400,16K  : Enabled
 Typematic Rate (Chars/Sec): 30.0       Adaptor ROM Shadow C800,16K: Disabled
 Mouse Support Option      : Disabled   Adaptor ROM Shadow CC00,16K: Disabled
 Above 1 MB Memory Test    : Disabled   Adaptor ROM Shadow D000,16K: Disabled
 Memory Test Tick Sound    : Disabled   Adaptor ROM Shadow D400,16K: Disabled
 Memory Parity Error Check : Disabled   Adaptor ROM Shadow D800,16K: Disabled
 Hit <DEL> Message Display : Enabled    Adaptor ROM Shadow DC00,16K: Disabled
 Hard Disk Type 47 RAM Area: 0:300h     Adaptor ROM Shadow E000,16K: Disabled
 Wait for <F1> If Any Error: Enabled    Adaptor ROM Shadow E400,16K: Disabled
 System Boot Up Num Lock   : On         Adaptor ROM Shadow E800,16K: Disabled
 Weitek Processor          : Absent     Adaptor ROM Shadow EC00,16K: Disabled
 Floppy Drive Seek At Boot : Disabled   System ROM Shadow F000,64K : Enabled
 System Boot Up Sequence   : C:,A:      Video ROM Shadow          : Enabled
 System Boot Up CPU Speed  : High       Shadow RAM Option         : Enabled
 Fast Gate A20 Option      : Enabled    Internal Cache            : Enabled
 Turbo Switch Function:    : Enabled    External Cache            : Enabled
 Password Checking Option  : Setup

    ESC:Exit ↑→↓←:Sel (Ctrl)Pu/Pd:Modify  F1:Help F2:Color
    F5:Old Values F6:BIOS Setup Defaults F7:Power-On Defaults
```

Advanced CMOS Setup Options

Typematic Rate Programming, Typematic Rate, and Typematic Rate Delay

Typematic Rate Programming enables or disables the following two options. Typematic Rate Delay (*250, 500, 750, or 1,000 milliseconds*) and Typematic Rate (*6, 8, 10, 12, 14, 16 24, or 30 characters per second*) control the speed at which a keystroke is repeated. A character is displayed when a key is pressed and held down. After a delay set by the Typematic Rate Delay, the character repeats at the Typematic Rate.

cont'd

Advanced CMOS Setup Options, Continued

Mouse Support Option

This option enables or disables PS/2-type mouse support. The settings are *Enabled* or *Disabled*.

Above 1 MB Memory Test

Executes memory routines on the RAM above 1 MB (if present on the system) if enabled. If disabled, the BIOS only tests the first 1 MB of RAM and clears all memory above 1 MB. The settings are *Enabled* or *Disabled*.

Memory Test Tick Sound

This option enables or disables the ticking sound during the memory test. The settings are *Enabled* or *Disabled*.

Memory Parity Error Checking

This option enables or disables parity error checking for all system RAM. The settings are *Enabled* or *Disabled*.

Hit <DEL> Message Display

Disabling this option prevents:

```
Hit <DEL> if you want to run Setup
```

from appearing when the system boots. The settings are *Enabled* or *Disabled*.

Advanced CMOS Setup Options, Continued

Hard Disk Type 47 RAM Area

You can specify a user-definable hard disk type for drive C: and drive D:. The type 47 drive parameters must be entered in Standard CMOS Setup (see page 118). This option specifies the type 47 data storage area – 0:300h in lower system RAM or in the top 1 KB of applications memory, starting at address 639K or 511K (depending on the amount of base memory). Type 47 data is stored in shadow RAM if shadowing is enabled.

Hard Disk Type 47 Data Storage

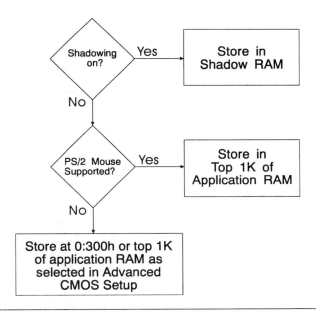

Wait for <F1> If Any Error

Errors displayed by POST are followed by:

```
Press <F1> to continue
```

If this option is disabled, the BIOS does not wait for F1 to be pressed after an error message appears. The settings are *Enabled* or *Disabled*.

cont'd

Advanced CMOS Setup Options, Continued

System Boot Up Num Lock

When enabled, you can turn off the NUM LOCK key when the system is powered on to use both sets of arrow keys on the keyboard. The settings are *Enabled* or *Disabled.*

Numeric Processor Test

This option specifies if a math coprocessor (Intel 80*x*87 or compatible) is installed. The settings are *Enabled* or *Disabled.* If disabled, the BIOS does not check for a math coprocessor.

Weitek Processor

This option specifies that a Weitek math coprocessor is configured. The settings are *Absent* or *Present.*

Floppy Drive Seek At Boot

This option performs a Seek on floppy drive A: at system boot if enabled. The settings are *Enabled* or *Disabled.*

System Boot Up Sequence

Sets the boot drive sequence. The system can be booted from floppy drive A: or hard disk drive C:. The settings are *A:,C:* or *C:, A:.*

System Boot Up CPU Speed

Sets the speed at which the system boots. The settings are *High* or *Low.*

Advanced CMOS Setup Options, Continued

Fast Gate A20 Option

The settings are *Enabled* or *Disabled*. Gate A20 controls access to memory addresses above 1 MB by enabling or disabling access to processor address line 20. To remain XT-compatible and to be able to access conventional memory (from 0 – 1024K), address line A20 must always be low, so Gate A20 must be disabled.

However, some programs both enter protected mode and shut down through the BIOS. For these programs, Gate A20 must be constantly enabled and disabled by the keyboard controller, a slow process.

Fast Gate A20 is a hardware circuit that speeds Gate A20 access, which in turn speeds programs that constantly change from real to protected mode. For example, enabling this option allows network operating systems and Microsoft Windows to execute faster. If the AMIBIOS Setup in your system has this option, it probably should be enabled, since it is likely that Fast Gate A20 circuitry has been incorporated into your computer. This option must be *Disabled* when running DOS 5.00 HIMEM.SYS in some systems.

Turbo Switch Function

This option enables or disables the system turbo (processor speed switching) switch. The settings are *Enabled* or *Disabled*.

Password Checking Option

This option prevents unauthorized system boot or AMIBIOS Setup use by requiring a password. The settings are *Always* or *Setup*. In some older version of AMIBIOS, there is also a *Disabled* setting.

If *Always* is selected, a password prompt appears every time the system is turned on. If *Setup* is chosen, the password prompt appears if BIOS Setup is executed. See page 89 for additional information.

cont'd

Advanced CMOS Setup Options, Continued

Internal Cache Memory and *External Cache Memory* appear in 80486 systems. In 80386 systems, *Cache Memory* may be displayed.

Internal Cache Memory

Appears only on 80486-based systems. Enables or disables the 8 KB microprocessor internal cache. The settings are *Enabled* or *Disabled*.

External Cache Memory

Appears only on systems that have a caching scheme external to the microprocessor. The settings are *Enabled* or *Disabled*.

ROM Shadow

In shadowing, BIOS code is copied from slower ROM to faster RAM. The BIOS is then executed from RAM. In the Hi-Flex AMIBIOS Setup, there are two sets of shadow options:

- Two Advanced CMOS Setup options that can be enabled or disabled: *Shadow Video ROM* (shadows C0000h – C7FFFh) or *RAM Shadow Option* (shadows C8000h – FFFFFh).

- Thirteen shadowing options. All options shadow 16 KB segments except System ROM Shadow (64 KB in ISA systems and 128 KB in EISA systems). If an option is enabled, the code that resides in that segment of ROM is copied to RAM.

There are several other varieties of shadowing options with a 32 KB granularity for some address ranges. The EISA system BIOS is 128 KB long, so the System RAM Shadow option in EISA BIOS Setup is E0000h – FFFFFh, or 128 KB long.

Boot Sector Virus Protection

If enabled, the BIOS displays a message that allows the user to intervene if any program attempts to format the hard disk drive or write to the boot sector. The settings are *Enabled* or *Disabled*.

Section 4

Advanced Chipset Setup

The options that appear in Advanced Chipset Setup vary. There are no standard options. Most of these options are described in this section. The settings for these options are determined by the computer manufacturer, not American Megatrends. Therefore, only generic descriptions are provided.

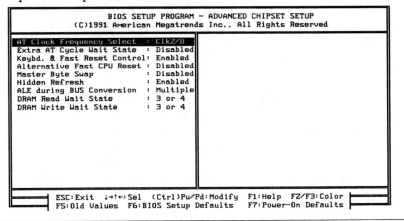

Sample Advanced Chipset Setup Options

8-Bit DMA Active Clock

The settings are *2 CLKs, 3 CLKs,* or *4 CLKs.* This option sets the number of clock cycles that the DMA command is active for during 8-bit DMA cycles.

16-Bit DMA Active Clock

The settings are *2 CLKs, 3 CLKs,* or *4 CLKs.* This option sets the number of clock cycles that the DMA command is active for during 16-bit DMA cycles.

cont'd

8-bit I/O Wait States

This option sets the number of wait states inserted before 8-bit I/O operations. The AT-Compatible value is 4 wait states. The settings are *4 wait states* or *5 wait states*. The settings may be different in 486-based systems.

16-bit I/O Wait States

This option sets the number of wait states inserted before 16-bit I/O operations. The AT-Compatible setting is *0* wait states. The settings are *0* or *1 wait states*.

384 KB Memory Relocation

When this option is enabled, the 384K area between 640K and 1024K is relocated above 1 MB and added to existing extended memory. *This option can be enabled only when the system has a total of either 1 or 2 MB of RAM.* It cannot be used with the EMS option or any shadowing options. If both this option and any shadowing options are enabled, shadowing is enabled and this option is disabled. The settings are *Enabled* or *Disabled*.

16 Bit DMA Wait States

This option sets the number of wait states inserted before 16-bit DMA commands. The settings are *1, 2, 3,* or *4*.

8 Bit DMA Wait States

This option sets the number of wait states inserted before 8-bit DMA commands. The settings are *1 W/S, 2 W/S, 3 W/S,* or *4 W/S*.

Advanced Chipset Setup Options, Continued

82C206 Access Wait State

This option inserts additional wait states into the DMA read/write cycle when high-powered CPUs access the 82C206 DMA Controller. The additional wait states cause the 82C206 to assert a *Not Ready* condition on IOCHRDY (low) when a valid decode from the Top Level Decoder is detected and either XIOR or XIOW is asserted. IOCHRDY remains low for the number of wait states specified in this option. The settings are usually *1 W/S, 2 W/S, 3 W/S,* or *4 W/S.*

Adapter Shadow RAM Cacheable

This option enables caching of the memory segment from C80000h-EFFFFh. The settings are *No* or *Yes.*

Additional AT Cycle Wait State
Extra AT Cycle Wait State
I/O Cycle Delay

When enabled, these options add an additional wait state in the AT cycle. The settings can be *0 ns, 250 ns, 500 ns, 1000 ns, 0 W/S, 1 W/S, Enabled,* or *Disabled.*

ADS Synchronized Internally

When this option is enabled, the ADS signal from the VL-Bus local bus is synchronized with the CPU ADS signal. The settings are *Enabled* or *Disabled.*

Allocation, Non-Cached Area

This option selects whether the noncacheable area applies to the onboard system memory or the AT Bus. The settings are *Sys DRAM* or *AT Bus.*

cont'd

Advanced Chipset Setup Options, Continued

Auto-Configuration

If this option is enabled, the following Advanced Chipset Setup options are automatically configured. The settings are *Enabled* or *Disabled*.

- CAS Width in Read Cycle, Register 0Bh, Bits 3-2,
- ADS Delay, Register 1Ah, Bit 7,
- Register 01h, Bits 7-0,
- Register 04h, Bits 7-4,
- Register 0Bh, Bits 7-4, 1-0,
- Register 12h, Bits 7-4,
- Register 18h, Bits 7-0, and
- Register 1Ah, Bits 6-3, 1-0.

AT Bus Clock Source

This option sets the source for the AT Bus clock. *AUTOSYNC* sets a value based on the CPU clock speed. The settings are *14.3 MHz, SCLK/1, SCLK/1.5, SCLK/2, SCLK/2.5, SCLK/3, SCLK/4, SCLK/5, 16.0 MHz,* or *AUTOSYNC.*

AT Bus 32 Bit Command Delay

This option sets the command delay for 32-bit operations on the AT bus. The settings are *0, 1, 2,* or *3* cycles.

AT Bus 16 Bit Command Delay

This option sets the number of delays inserted before 16-bit operations on the AT bus. The settings are *0, 1, 2,* or *3* cycles.

AT Bus 8 Bit Command Delay

This option sets the number of delays inserted before 16-bit operations on the AT bus. The settings are *0, 1, 2,* or *3* cycles.

Advanced Chipset Setup Options, Continued

AT Bus Address Hold Time

This option provides extra access time for an AT adapter card to improve reliability. The settings are *Enabled* or *Disabled.*

AT Bus I/O Command Delay

This option sets the command delay for I/O operations on the AT bus. The settings are *0 W/S, 1 W/S, 2 W/S,* or *3 W/S.*

AT Bus 32 Bit Wait States

This option sets the number of wait states inserted before 32-bit operations on the AT bus. The settings are *0 W/S, 1 W/S, 2 W/S,* or *3 W/S.*

AT Bus 16 Bit Wait States

This option sets the number of wait states inserted before 16-bit operations on the AT bus. The settings are *0 W/S, 1 W/S, 2 W/S,* or *3 W/S.*

AT Bus 8 Bit Wait States

This option sets the number of wait states inserted before 8-bit operations on the AT bus. The settings are *2 W/S, 3 W/S, 4 W/S,* or *5 W/S.*

AT Clock Frequency Select

This option sets the source for the AT Clock. The settings are usually *CLK2IN/2, CLK2IN/3, CLK2IN/4, CLK2IN/5, CLK2IN/6, CLK2IN/8,* or *CLK2IN/10.*

cont'd

Advanced Chipset Setup Options, Continued

ATCLK Stretch

When enabled, the duty cycle of ATCLK is increased temporarily to avoid a synchronization penalty in order to maximize performance. The settings are *Disabled* or *Enabled*.

AT Cycle Between I/O Cycles
Back to Back I/O
I/O Recovery Time
I/O Recovery Select

Sets the number of wait states, delays, or BCLK cycles added by the hardware when two or more consecutive I/O operations occur. The BIOS Setup and Power-On default (two wait states) usually assures proper operation of most adapter cards. If a slower adapter card is installed, the number of wait states can be increased. If only high speed adapter cards are used, the number of wait states can be decreased (but always set at least 2 wait states). The valid settings are *1 through F*.

BCLK Stretch

Enabling this option improves system performance. BCLK (ISA and EISA Bus Clock) stretching allows the EISA Bus Controller (EBC) to drive the START# signal active without waiting for the next rising edge for BCLK. BCLK is then stretched to allow START# to meet the required pulse width. The settings are *Enabled* or *Disabled*.

Advanced Chipset Setup Options, Continued

BIOS Shadow Segments

The following table lists the effect of each setting:

Setting	Description
Disabled	No System BIOS Shadow
F	64 KB System BIOS Shadow
F+E	128 KB System BIOS Shadow
F+C	64 KB System BIOS Shadow + 64 KB Video Shadow
F+E+D+C	128 KB System BIOS Shadow + 128 KB Video Shadow

Cacheable Region

This option defines an area in memory whose contents are cacheable. The settings are *4 MB through 64 MB* in 4 MB increments, *128 MB*, or *256 MB*.

Cache Burst Read Cycle (Cache Read Cycle) (486 Cache Burst Cycle)

This option sets the secondary cache memory read burst cycle in 486-based systems. The settings are usually *3-1-1-1, 2-1-1-1, 3-2-2-2,* or *2-2-2-2.*

Cache Burst Wait State

This option sets the number of wait states inserted before burst mode cache memory operations. The settings are *0 W/S* or *1 W/S.*

Cache Early Write Enable

This option enables a hardware circuit that writes data/code to cache memory faster. The settings are *Enabled* or *Disabled.*

cont'd

Cache Read Cycle

This option sets the secondary cache memory read burst cycle in 486-based systems. The settings are *2-1-1-1*, *2-2-2-2*, *3-1-1-1*, or *3-2-2-2*.

Cache Read Wait State

This option sets the number of wait states inserted before cache memory read operations. In 486-based systems, the settings are *0 W/S* or *1 W/S*. In 386-based systems, additional wait states may be added.

Cache Write Wait State

This option sets the number of wait states inserted before cache memory write operations. In 486-based systems, the settings are *0 W/S* or *1 W/S*. In 386-based systems, additional wait states may be added.

Cacheable RAM Address Range

This option sets the maximum range for which memory is cacheable. All memory above this address is noncacheable. The settings are *1 MB, 2 MB, 3 MB, 4 MB, 5 MB, 6 MB, 7 MB, 8 MB, 9 MB, 10 MB, 11 MB, 12 MB, 13 MB, 14 MB, 15 MB,* or *16 MB*.

CAS Precharge

This option sets the length of the CAS precharge cycle. The settings are usually *1 CLK* or *2 CLKs*.

CAS Delay

The CAS delay is the length of time that the CAS signal is delayed before the CAS signal becomes active. The settings are *0 CLK* or *0.5 CLK*.

Advanced Chipset Setup Options, Continued

CAS Read Delay

The CAS read delay is the length of time that the CAS signal is delayed before memory read activities. The settings are *0 CLK* or *1 CLK*.

CAS Pulse Width

This option sets the CAS pulse width. The CAS pulse width is the length of time during which the CAS pulse should be active. The settings are *3 CLK2* or *2 CLK2*.

Command Delay, 8-Bit Cycle

This option adds an extra command delay for 8- and 16-bit I/O and 8-bit memory cycles. The settings are *No* or *Yes*.

Command Delay, 16-Bit Cycle

This option adds an extra command delay for 16-bit memory cycles. The settings are *No* or *Yes*.

Concurrent Refresh

This option enables concurrent refresh, a method of refreshing system memory without holding the CPU. Memory refresh can be either *AT classic* or *concurrent*, which shortens the delay built into the AT-compatible refresh cycle. The settings are *Enabled* or *Disabled*.

Coprocessor Wait States

This option sets the number of wait states inserted before coprocessor operations. The settings are usually *0 W/S* or *1 W/S*.

cont'd

Coupled Refresh Mode

When enabled, this option couples the refresh mode for onboard and offboard memory. The settings are *Enabled* or *Disabled*. The defaults are *Enabled*.

CPU Address Pipeline Mode

When enabled, this option enables the use of the CPU address pipelining feature. The settings are *Enabled* or *Disabled*.

CPU Time-Slice Priority

CPU Time-Slice Priority is the number of BCLKs the Integrated System Peripheral waits between a HOLD request input (from DMA, a bus master, or other device) and a HOLD request to the CPU.

A higher number allows the CPU to continue running a little longer before it is placed in HOLD. The settings are *0 through 1F*.

CRD Generation

This option permits the use of slower SRAMs by generating the CRD0- and CRD1- signals earlier. The settings are *T2/4, CLK2/4-4, CLK2/2-2,* or *CLK2/2*.

Cycle Early Start

Enabling this option allows the cycle to begin ½ cycle earlier to provide extra access time. The settings are *Enabled* or *Disabled*.

Decoupled Refresh

When this option is enabled, hardware circuitry that makes the system DRAM memory refresh function asynchronous with the CPU cycle is enabled. The settings are Enabled or Disabled.

Advanced Chipset Setup Options, Continued

DMA CAS Timing Delay

When enabled, CAS is delayed by 1 T-state. If disabled, CAS is not delayed. The settings are *Enabled* or *Disabled*.

DMA Clock

This option sets the source for the DMA clock. The settings are *SCLK/2* or *SCLK*.

DMAMEMR Assertion Delay

If disabled, the assertion of the DMAMEMR signal is not delayed. If enabled, the assertion of this signal is delayed.

DMA Fast Sample

The BIOS automatically disables this option if the 80486 CPU clock speed is 20 MHz or less. The BIOS automatically enables this option if the system speed is 25 MHz or greater. The settings are *Enabled* or *Disabled*.

DRAM RAS Precharge T-Cycles

2.5 T or 3.5 T cycles may be assured for DRAM RAS precharge time. The settings are *2.5 T* or *3.5 T*.

DRAM State Machine select

This option selects whether the cache controller is to be included in the state machine cycle. The settings are *Cache* or *No Cache*.

cont'd

Drive Current

This option sets the amount of current needed to drive the memory line. The settings are *150 pF, 300 pF, 450 pF,* or *600 pF* of memory line capacitance.

Early READY Enable

When enabled, the READY signal is generated early. The settings are *Enabled* or *Disabled.*

EISA BCLK

This option sets the source for the EISA bus clock. The settings are usually *CLK2, CLK2/2, CLK2/2.56, CLK2/3, CLK2/4, CLK2/5,* or *CLK2/6.*

EMS & Relocation Wait State

This option inserts additional wait states in the EMS and relocation memory cycles. The settings are *EMS+Rel, EMS Only, Rel Only,* or *None.*

EMS+Rel adds an additional wait state to both the EMS and the relocation memory cycles, a total of two wait states for each cycle. *EMS Only* adds an additional wait state to the EMS memory cycle (a total of two wait states) and none to the relocation memory cycle. *Rel Only* adds an additional wait state to the relocation memory cycle (a total of two wait states) and none to the EMS memory cycle. *None* adds no additional wait states to either cycle.

EMS Base Address Pages 0-3

This option sets the base addresses for EMS pages. The settings are usually the values in the first column below.

Setting	Page 0	Page 1	Page 2	Page 3
C0-CC000	C0000	C4000	C8000	CC000
C4-D000	C4000	C8000	CC000	D0000
C8-D400	C8000	CC000	D0000	D4000
CC-D800	CC000	D0000	D4000	D8000
D0-DC00	D0000	D4000	D8000	DC000
D4-E000	D4000	D8000	DC000	E0000
D8-E400	D8000	DC000	E0000	E4000
DC-E800	DC000	E0000	E4000	E8000
E0-EC00	E0000	E4000	E8000	EC000

EMS Page Registers

This option sets the base address for the EMS page registers.

Setting	Page Register
EMS 0	0208h, 0209h, and 020Ah
EMS 1	0218h, 0219h, and 021Ah

EMS Page Reg I/O Address (hex)

This option sets the base address for the EMS page register I/O ports. The settings are *208/209, 218/219, 258/259, 268/269, 2A8/2A9, 2B8/2B9,* or *2E8/2E9.*

EMS Page Register Map

This option sets the map for the EMS page register. The settings are *Map 0* or *Map 1. Map 0* maps the page registers to C*xxxx*h, D*xxxx*h, or E*xxxx*h. *Map 1* maps the page registers to A*xxxx*h, B*xxxx*h, or F*xxxx*h.

cont'd

Extended DMA Memory Read

The settings are *Disabled* (delay the -MEMR signal one clock cycle after the -IOW signal) or *Enabled* (start -MEMR at the same time as -IOW).

Extended I/O Decode

When enabled, more than 10 address lines (A9-A0) are used for I/O addressing. The settings are *Enabled* or *Disabled*.

Ext. Parity Error Input

When enabled, bit 8 of the cache tag is used to generate parity and normal operations are disabled. The settings are *Enabled* or *Disabled*.

Fast BUS CLK Divider

This option sets the BUSCLK divider to establish the Fast BUSCLK speed. The settings are /2, /4, /6, or /8. If BUSOSC is not connected, TCLK/2 is divided, but the settings change, as shown below.

Setting if BUSOSC	If TCLK/2
/2	/4
/4	/6
/6	/8
/8	/12

Fast Decode Enable

When enabled, this option speeds DRAM access in systems running at 20 or 25 MHz. The settings are *Enabled* or *Disabled*.

Advanced Chipset Setup Options, Continued

Fast Keyboard Reset

The settings are *Slow* (the BIOS waits for a HALT instruction after a keyboard reset command) or *Fast* (it does not wait).

Fast I/O Speed Option

When using offboard memory and peripherals, this option can be disabled to slow the system clock to 8 MHz. The settings are *Enabled* or *Disabled*.

Fast Reset Control

When enabled, a HLT instruction is required before CPURST can be generated. The settings are *Enabled* or *Disabled*.

First Serial Port Address

This option enables serial port 1 on the motherboard, if installed. The settings are any valid I/O port address, usually *3F8h, 3E8h, 2F8h,* or *2E8h.*

GA20 Line After System Boot

Gate A20 on the keyboard controller controls switching between real and protected mode. Some operating environments and operating systems such as OS/2, Microsoft Windows, and Novell NetWare change address modes frequently. If the Gate A20 hardware has timing problems, software may not run properly. Enable this option when using the above operating systems.

Hidden Refresh

Hidden refresh is a special hardware circuit that allows memory refresh to occur without holding the CPU. The settings are *Enabled* or *Disabled.* If enabled, the Hidden Refresh feature must be supported by the type of system memory used in the system.

cont'd

Interleave Type

This option defines the boundary that memory interleave operates on for Memory Bank B. Select *0* to set interleave on a word boundary. Choose *1* to set interleave on a block boundary. The settings are *0* or *1*.

Internal/External Cache

This option enables both the internal cache of the 80486 processor and the cache memory on the motherboard. The settings are:

Setting	Description
Disabled	the 80486 internal cache and the system cache memory are both disabled.
Internal	Only the internal cache on the 80486 is disabled.
Both	All cache is enabled.

Internal MUX Clock Source

Selecting AUTOSYNC causes the BIOS to set the Internal MUX Clock Source option based on the CPU clock speed. The settings are *14.3 MHz, SCLK/1, SCLK/2, SCLK/3, SCLK/4, SCLK/5, 16.0 MHz,* or *AUTOSYNC.*

IOR/IOW Wait States

This option sets the number of wait states inserted before I/O read and write commands. The settings are *1 W/S, 2 W/S, 3 W/S,* or *4 W/S.*

Keyboard Frequency Select
KBCLK Select

These options set the source for the keyboard clock. The settings are usually *7.0MHz* or *BUSCLK.*

Keyboard Reset Control

If this option is enabled, the HALT instruction must be executed before the SYSC generates CPURST from the keyboard reset. The settings are *Enabled* or *Disabled*. If the system does not reset in any situation or configuration, you may have to disable this option.

Local Bus Ready

The settings are *SYNC* (the system is using a synchronous Local Bus Ready signal) or *ASYNC* (the system is using an asynchronous Local Bus Ready signal.

Local Memory Access, Block-1

This option specifies if the Block-1 memory area is accessed by local memory or the AT Bus. The settings are *Yes* (access to the memory area defined in Block-1 is directed to local DRAM) or *No* (access to the memory area defined in Block-1 is directed to nonlocal memory).

Late -RAS Mode

This option controls the generation of RAS signals during DRAM cycles. Late -RAS Mode permits the use of slower Tag RAM. The Settings are *Enabled* or *Disabled*.

Local Memory Access, Block 1

This option specifies if memory accesses to the Block 1 memory area are to a local memory or to the AT bus. Block 1 is defined in *Non-Cacheable Block-1 Size* and *Non-Cacheable Block-1 Base*. The settings are *Yes (local Memory)* or *No (AT Bus)*.

cont'd

Local READY Delay

When enabled, a delay is inserted to generate the RDY# signal output. If disabled, RDY# output is not generated. The settings are *Enabled* or *Disabled.*

Local Ready Synchronized

When this option is enabled, the READY signal from the VL-Bus local bus is synchronized with the CPU READY signal. The settings are *Enabled* or *Disabled.*

Low CPU Clock Speed

This option sets the source of the Low CPU clock speed (there are two speeds in an AMIBIOS: Low and High). The settings are usually *CXIN, CXIN/2, CXIN/4,* or *CXIN/8.*

Memory addr. delay from RAS

This option sets the length of time that RAS is delayed after the memory address has been found. The settings are *0 CLK* or *0.5 CLK.*

Memory Read Wait State

This option sets the number of wait states inserted before system memory read operations. In 486-based systems, the settings are usually *0 W/S, 1 W/S,* or *2 W/S.* Additional wait states are often added in 386-based systems.

Memory Write Wait State

This option sets the number of wait states inserted before system memory write operations. In 486-based systems, the settings are usually *0 W/S, 1 W/S, 2 W/S,* or *3 W/S.* Additional wait states are often added in 386-based systems.

Middle BIOS (Below 16 MB)

Enable this option to execute some older applications. When enabled, the System BIOS appears at the 128 KB BIOS boundary (E000h). Residing at the E000 – EFFFh memory segment permits the BIOS to address up to 16 MB of main memory. Systems with more than 16 MB of main memory will not be able to access memory above 16 MB if this option is enabled. The settings are *Enabled* or *Disabled*.

Multiple ALE Enable

If this option is enabled, the SYNC signal activates multiple ALE signals instead of single ALEs during the bus conversion cycle. The settings are *Enabled* or *Disabled*.

Non-Cacheable Block*x* Base

This option sets the start (or base address) of a region of memory in which cache is disabled. Generally, the setting of this option must change in increments equal to the corresponding Non-Cacheable Block*x* Size setting. The settings are *0 KB, 64 KB, 128 KB, 512 KB, 1 MB,* or *2 MB*.

Non-Cacheable Block*x* Size

This option sets the size of a region of memory in which cache is disabled. The settings are *0 KB – 1024 KB*.

Non-Cacheable Boundary > 1M

The memory above this boundary is not cached by the external cache controller. The boundary must be specified in 16 KB (400h) increments. The settings are *any memory address on a 16 KB boundary between 4000h and FFC000h*.

cont'd

Advanced Chipset Setup Options, Continued

Non-Cacheable Bound. Start

The memory from this start address to the Non-Cacheable Boundary End is not cached by the external cache controller. The settings are *any memory address on a 16 KB boundary between 4000h and FFC000h.*

Non-Cacheable Bound. End

The memory from the Non-Cacheable Boundary Start to this address is not cached by the external cache controller. The settings are *any memory address on a 16 KB boundary between 4000h and FFC000h.*

NMI Power Failure Warning

This option enables the warning signal when NMI power fails. The settings are *Enabled* or *Disabled.*

On Board Floppy Controller

Enable this option to use the onboard floppy controller. The settings are *Enabled* or *Disabled.*

On Board IDE Controller

Enable this option to use the onboard IDE hard disk drive controller. The settings are *Enabled* or *Disabled.*

Page Mode

Page mode permits 0 wait state operation on system memory, resulting in faster system RAM performance. DRAM chips must support page mode in order to use this option. The settings are *Enabled* or *Disabled.*

Parallel Port Address

This option enables the parallel port on the motherboard, if installed. The settings are *any valid I/O port address.*

POST Write

If the motherboard has four 245 transceivers between the D and MD bus (often used with external cache memory), the BIOS enables the POST Write buffer option in chipset register 04h bit 7. The number of wait states for the POST write buffer are set automatically if *Auto-configuration* is enabled or the BIOS uses the Power-On default value. *If POST write buffers are not implemented on the motherboard, this option cannot be used. This option should be used only by OEMs. It should not be made available to end users.* The settings are *Enabled* or *Disabled*.

Programming Option

The settings are *Auto* or *Manual*. When set to *Auto*, the BIOS automatically detects all adapter cards installed in the system and configures the onboard ports accordingly. If *Manual* is selected, the settings selected by the end user in AMIBIOS Setup are used.

RAS* Timeout Counter

If the system is not utilizing page mode/interleave memory methods, the RAS* timeout counter can be disabled. The settings are *Enabled* or *Disabled*.

RAS Precharge Time

This option sets the RAS precharge time. The RAS Precharge Time is the amount of time required for the RAS signal to stabilize when memory access shifts from one page to another. The settings are *6 CLK2* or *4 CLK2*.

cont'd

RAS to CAS Delay

RAS to CAS Delay is the delay between CAS (column address strobe) signal and the RAS (row address strobe) signal after the RAS signal has stabilized. The settings are *3 SYSCLK, 2 SYSCLK,* or *1 SYSCLK.*

RC Emulation

When enabled, this option enables the Reset Computer feature, which emulates the keyboard reset. The settings are *Enabled* or *Disabled.*

Relocated 256 KB Cacheable

If the memory between 640 KB and 1 MB (relocatable 384 KB) is remapped to extended memory (above 1 MB), it can also be cached. The settings are *Yes* or *No.*

Remap Memory

1. If enabled, the 256K memory segment from A0000h – BFFFFh and D0000h – EFFFFh are remapped to the top of conventional or extended memory. This option is automatically disabled if more than 12 MB of DRAM is installed on the motherboard. The settings are *Enabled* or *Disabled.*

2. If enabled, the BIOS remaps the 384 KB of memory from A0000h – FFFFFh to the top of conventional or extended memory. If the CPU clock is greater than 33 MHz, this option is automatically disabled. Any RAM used as shadow RAM is not remapped. Because of the 128K granularity of this option, shadowing may limit the amount of memory that is remapped. The settings are *Enabled* or *Disabled.*

Advanced Chipset Setup Options, Continued

Second Serial Port Address

This option enables serial port 2 (if installed) on the motherboard and sets the serial port base address. The settings are *any valid I/O port address*.

Single ALE Enable

If enabled, SYSC activates Single ALEs instead of multiple ALEs during the bus conversion cycle. The settings are *Yes* or *No*.

Slow BUS CLK Divider

This option sets the BUSOSC divider to establish the Slow BUSCLK speed. The settings are */2, /4, /6,* or */8*. If BUSOSC is not connected, TCLK/2 is divided, but the settings change, as shown below:

Setting if BUSOSC	Setting if TCLK/2
/2	/4
/4	/6
/6	/8
/8	/12

Slow Refresh

Slow Refresh is four times slower (about once every 63 μseconds) than the normal refresh rate (about once every 15.8 μseconds). Slowing the memory refresh allows the CPU to execute more instructions instead of having to refresh memory every 15.8 μseconds. The settings are *Enabled* or *Disabled*.

cont'd

Advanced Chipset Setup Options, Continued

Slow Memory Refresh Divider

This option sets the source for the slow memory refresh circuit.

Setting	Value
CLKIN	15.8 μs (Standard)
CLKIN/2	30 μs
CLKIN/4	60 μs
CLKIN/8	120 μs

Staggered Refresh

This option staggers memory refresh between memory banks to decrease memory access time. The settings are *Enabled* or *Disabled*. If enabled, the Staggered Refresh feature must be supported in the type of memory used in the system.

System Shadow RAM Cacheable

This option enables caching of the memory segment from F0000h-FFFFFh. The settings are *No* or *Yes*.

Advanced Chipset Setup Options, Continued

Turbo Memory Settings

Disabled sets the following memory timings and wait state-related options to the Power-On Defaults (the slowest settings):

- Hidden Refresh,
- Staggered Refresh,
- CAS Active Time (Reads),
- CAS Active Time (Writes),
- CAS Delays (Reads),
- CAS Delays (Writes),
- CAS Burst Delay,
- CAS Precharge,
- CAS Hold on RAS,
- RAS Precharge,
- RAS Active (Reads),
- RAS Active (Writes), and
- RAS Delay.

If *Manual* is selected, the BIOS uses the Power-On Default settings selected by the OEM in AMIBCP to permanently set all Advanced Chipset Setup options. If *Auto* is selected, the BIOS determines the CPU clock frequency and programs the timing settings to optimal values. These values will be different, depending on whether the CPU clock frequency is 25, 33, or 40 MHz. The settings are *Disabled, Auto,* or *Manual.*

Video BIOS Area Cacheable

If enabled, the video BIOS shadow RAM area can be cached, which speeds video performance. However, you must be certain that no program will write to the video BIOS area when this option is enabled (*Yes* is chosen). This option may be enabled only when Video BIOS Shadow is enabled in Advanced CMOS Setup. The settings are *Yes* or *No.*

cont'd

Advanced Chipset Setup Options, Continued

Video Shadow RAM Cacheable

This option enables caching of the memory segment from C0000h – C7FFFh. However, you must be certain that no program will write to the video BIOS area when this option is enabled (*Yes* is chosen). The settings are *Yes* or *No*.

Section 5

Power Management Setup

The Power Management AMIBIOS Setup screen includes options that control power management and power conservation features. A sample power management BIOS Setup screen is shown below:

```
┌─────────────────────────────────────────────────────────────────────┐
│         BIOS SETUP PROGRAM — POWER MANAGEMENT SETUP                  │
│         (C) 1993 American Megatrends Inc. All rights reserved        │
├──────────────────────────────────────────┬──────────────────────────┤
│ LCD Power Down Timeout      : 1 min.      │                          │
│ Hard Disk Idle Timeout      : 1 min.      │                          │
│ Sleep Mode Timeout          : Disabled    │                          │
│ Suspend Timeout             : 1 min.      │                          │
│ Manual Suspend Mode         : Disabled    │                          │
│ Hot Key Power Down          : Disabled    │                          │
│ Software Power Down Mode    : Disabled    │                          │
│ Low Battery Power Warning   : Disabled    │                          │
│                                           │                          │
│                                           │                          │
│                                           │                          │
├──────────────────────────────────────────┴──────────────────────────┤
│ ESC:Exit ↑→↓←:Sel (Ctrl)Pu/Pd:Modify  F1:Help F2:Color │            │
│ F5:Old Values F6:BIOS Setup Defaults F7:Power-On Defaults│           │
└─────────────────────────────────────────────────────────────────────┘
```

Power Management Setup Options

LCD Power Down Timeout

The LCD and back light are turned off at the end of the selected timeout period if the system does not find any external activities (such as keyboard activity). Shadowing cannot be disabled if a setting other than *Disabled* is chosen. The settings are *Disabled, 1 min., 2 min., 3 min., 4 min., 5 min., 6 min., 7 min., 8 min., 9 min., 10 min., 11 min., 12 min., 13 min., 14 min., 15 min., 16 min., 17 min., 18 min., 19 min., 20 min.,* or *Reserved*.

Hard Disk Idle Timeout

The hard disk is set to power save mode at the end of the selected timeout period if not accessed. Shadowing cannot be disabled if a setting other than *Disabled* is chosen. The settings are *Disabled, 1 min., 2 min., 3 min., 4 min., 5 min., 6 min., 7 min., 8 min., 9 min., 10 min., 11 min., 12 min., 13 min., 14 min., 15 min., 16 min., 17 min., 18 min., 19 min., 20 min.,* or *Reserved*.

cont'd

Sleep Mode Timeout

Sleep Mode is entered at the end of the selected timeout period if no external activities (such as keyboard activity) occur. Shadowing cannot be disabled if a setting other than *Disabled* is chosen. The settings are *Disabled, 1 min., 2 min., 3 min., 4 min., 5 min., 6 min., 7 min., 8 min., 9 min., 10 min.,* or *Reserved.*

Suspend Timeout

The system is suspended at the end of the selected timeout period if no external activities (such as keyboard activity) occurs. Shadowing cannot be disabled if a setting other than *Disabled* is chosen. The settings are *Disabled, one minute increments from 1 min. through 30 min.,* or *Reserved.*

Manual Suspend Timeout

The system is suspended via an external switch. Shadowing cannot be disabled if a setting other than *Disabled* is chosen. The settings are *Disabled* or *Enabled.*

Hot Key Power Down

The system state is changed when CTRL ALT ENTER is pressed if enabled. Shadowing cannot be disabled if the setting is not *Disabled.* The settings are *Disabled, Sleep,* or *Suspend. Sleep* puts the system in Sleep Mode when the hot key is pressed. *Suspend* puts the system in Suspend Mode when the hot key is pressed.

Low Battery Power Warning

The system issues warnings if low power conditions occur. Shadowing cannot be disabled if a setting other than *Disabled* is chosen. The settings are *Beep* (the system beeps 4 times every minute), *Sleep* (the system beeps 4 times every minute, then enters Sleep Mode), or *Suspend* (the system beeps 4 times every minute and the initiates a Suspend state).

Power Management Setup Options, Continued

Relax Mode Timeout

The BIOS enters Relax Mode from Full On Mode after the timeout period set in this option. Relax mode saves power even during user keyboard activity. The settings are *Disabled, ¼ sec, ½ sec, 1 sec,* or *2 sec.*

Nap Mode Timeout

The BIOS enters Nap Mode from Relax Mode after the timeout period set in this option. Nap Mode provides considerable power savings because it turns off the LCD backlight and waits for any external user activity. The settings are *Disabled* or *1 minute intervals from 1 – 15 minutes.*

Trance Mode Timeout

Trance mode provides DRAM refresh power only and the CPU runs at its lowest clock setting. Static CPUs actually stop. The settings are *Disabled* or *1 minute intervals from 1 – 20 minutes.*

Manual Trance Mode

The OPTi 82C461 chipset allows the user to switch the system to Trance Mode via an external switch. This option enables the external switch. The settings are *Enabled* or *Disabled.*

Software Power Down

Any application software can initiate any power down state by issuing a Software Power Management Interrupt (SPMI) — INT 77h in the AMIBIOS. The settings are *Disabled, Relax, Nap,* or *Trance.* If Trance is set, the external switch must be used to resume normal operation and the Manual Trance Mode option setting (see above) must be *Enabled.*

cont'd

Power Management Setup Options, Continued

CPU Type

Specifies the type of CPU. If a *Dynamic* CPU, the CPU runs at the lowest clock rate in Trance Mode. If a *Static* CPU, the CPU shuts down during Trance Mode.

Keyboard Sentinel

The BIOS keeps a keyboard activity timeout counter. If the value in the counter is reached before any keyboard activity, the system enters Trance Mode. If enabled, any keyboard access restarts the counter. The settings are *Enabled* or *Disabled*.

LCD Sentinel

The BIOS keeps an LCD timeout counter. If the value in the counter is reached before any LCD activity takes place, the system enters Trance Mode. If enabled, any LCD activity restarts the LCD timeout counter. The settings are *Enabled* or *Disabled*.

Hard Disk Drive Sentinel

The BIOS keeps a hard disk drive timeout counter. If the value in the counter is reached before any hard disk drive activity, the system enters Trance Mode. If enabled, any hard drive activity restarts the counter. The settings are *Enabled* or *Disabled*.

Serial/Parallel Port Sentinel

The BIOS keeps a serial/parallel port timeout counter. If the value in this counter is reached before any port activity takes place, the system enters Trance Mode. If enabled, any port activity restarts the timeout counter. The settings are *Enabled* or *Disabled*.

Auto Manager

Sets optimum default values for all Power Management Setup options for maximum battery life. All user settings will be overridden. The settings are *Enabled* or *Disabled*.

Section 6

Peripheral Management Setup

The Peripheral Management Setup screen includes options that must be configured appropriately for proper operation of a system that uses an external peripheral controller, such as a Chips and Technologies 82C710, 82C711, or 82C712, VLSI 82C106 or 82C107, Intel 82341, or National Semiconductor 87C310 or 87C311.

This BIOS Setup screen appears only in AMIBIOS dated 12/91 or later. This screen is configured by the OEM via AMIBCP. A sample Peripheral Management Setup screen is shown below. The options for this screen are described in the following pages. Peripheral Management Setup on your system may be entirely different than the following:

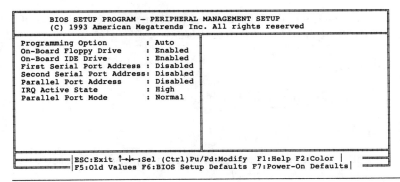

Peripheral Management Setup Options

On Board Floppy Drive

This option enables the use of the floppy drive controller on the motherboard, if installed. The settings are *Enabled* or *Disabled*.

cont'd

Peripheral Management Setup Options, Continued

On Board IDE Drive

This option enables the use of the IDE controller on the motherboard, if installed. The settings are *Enabled* or *Disabled*.

First Serial Port Address

This option enables the use of serial port 1 on the motherboard, if installed. The settings are *Enabled* or *Disabled*.

Second Serial Port Address

This option enables the use of serial port 2 on the motherboard, if installed. The settings are *Enabled* or *Disabled*.

Parallel Port Address

This option enables the use of the parallel port on the motherboard, if installed. The settings are *Enabled* or *Disabled*.

IRQ Active State

This option selects IRQ active low or high.

Parallel Port Mode

Extended parallel mode allows the parallel port to send and receive. The settings are *Extended* or *Normal*.

Peripheral Management Setup Options, Continued

Programming Option

The settings are *Auto* or *Manual*. When set to *Auto*, the BIOS automatically detects all adapter cards installed in the system and configures the onboard I/O (serial ports, parallel ports, floppy controllers, and IDE controller) automatically. All other Peripheral Management Setup option settings are ignored. Any serial port, parallel port, floppy controller, or IDE controller on an adapter card in an expansion slot is configured before onboard I/O. If *Auto* is selected, the BIOS also attempts to avoid IRQ conflicts.

If the offboard serial ports are configured to specific starting I/O ports via jumper settings, the BIOS will configure the onboard serial ports to avoid conflicts. For example, if the default serial port starting I/O ports (serial port1 - 3F8h, serial port2 - 2F8h, serial port3 - 3E8h, serial port4 - 2E8h) are used, the following serial port configurations are possible:

If there are...	the ports are configured as...	and the two onboard serial ports are configured as...
two offboard serial ports	3E8h and 2F8h	3E8h and 2E8h
two offboard serial ports	3F8h and 3E8h	3F8h and Disabled
one offboard serial port	2F8h	3F8h and Disabled
one offboard serial	3F8h	2F8h and Disabled

If *Manual* is selected, the settings chosen by the end user in Peripheral Management Setup apply.

AMIBIOS reports any I/O conflicts after displaying the BIOS Configuration Summary Screen, but only if *Manual* is chosen.

cont'd

Peripheral Management Setup Options, Continued

Serial Ports 1 & 2 Addresses

This option enables serial port 1 and 2 on the motherboard (if installed).

Settings
Dis, Dis
3F8, 2F8
Dis, 2F8
3F8, Dis
2F8, 3F8
Dis, 3F8
2F8, Dis

The Power-On default must not be changed.

Mouse Port Address

The settings are *Enabled* or *Disabled*. If enabled, the keychord CTRL PGUP increments the mouse port address by 40h and CTRL PGDN decrements the mouse port address by 40h.

Mouse IRQ Active State

The settings are *High* or *Low.*

Floppy IRQ Active State

The settings are *High* or *Low.*

Parallel IRQ Active State

The settings are *High* or *Low.*

Serial IRQ Active State

The settings are *High* or *Low.*

Section 7

AMIBIOS Password Support

The Hi-Flex AMIBIOS Setup has an optional password feature. The system can be configured so you must enter a password every time the system boots, or when an attempt is made to enter Setup. The Password Check Setup option is described on page 53.

Changing a Password

Enable *Password Checking* to change the password. The password (1 – 6 characters) is stored in CMOS RAM. To change a password:

Step	Action
1	Select the Change Password option from the main Setup screen and press ENTER.
2	Enter a password or press ENTER to select the password function. The typed characters do not display. The default password can be changed by the OEM via AMIBCP. AMIBIOS manufactured after 12/91 do not have a default password. The default for older AMIBIOS is *AMI*.
3	After the current password has been correctly typed, you are prompted to retype it.
4	If the password confirmation is incorrect, an error message appears. Retype the correct password.
5	If the new password confirmation is entered without error, press ESC to return to the Main Setup menu.

cont'd

Password Support, Continued

Password Storage

The password is stored in CMOS RAM after Setup completes. The next time the system boots, you must enter the password.

Password Option Control Prompt

When and if the password prompt appears depends on the options chosen in Advanced CMOS Setup.

Setup Password Option	Action
Always	The prompt appears each time the system is powered on.
Setup	The prompt does not appear when the system is powered on, but appears each time Setup is run.

Remember the Password

You must enter the new password when the password prompt appears and then press ENTER. You can use the default password if CMOS RAM is corrupted.

You should keep a record of the new password every time the password is changed. If you forget the password and password protection is enabled, the only way to boot the system is to disable CMOS RAM by removing the battery for at least 20 minutes, replacing it, rebooting, and reconfiguring the system.

If the motherboard in your system has a CMOS Drain jumper, you may be able to quickly drain CMOS power by temporarily changing a jumper setting.

Section 8

Hard Disk Utility

AMIBIOS includes three hard disk utilities:

Utility	Purpose	Turn to
Hard Disk Format	Performs a low-level format of the hard drive(s). Read the system or hard disk drive documentation to find out if the hard disk has been preformatted.	Page 93
Auto Interleave	Determines the optimum interleave factor and then performs a low-level format of the hard disk drive.	Page 95
Media Analysis	Analyzes each hard disk drive track to determine whether it is usable. The track is labeled bad if unusable.	Page 96

The hard disk utility error messages are described on page 97.

These routines work on drives that use the MFM, RLL, ARLL, or ESDI data recording techniques. *They do not work on IDE or SCSI Disk Drives.*

Warning
AMIBIOS Hard Disk Utilities destroy all hard disk data. Back up the data on the hard disk before running this utility.

When to Use AMIBIOS Hard Disk Utilities

When	Conditions	Run...
Installing a new hard disk.	The hard disk drive manufacturer provides a list of bad tracks, the system documentation includes the optimum interleave factor, and the drive is preformatted.	None
Installing a new hard disk.	You do not have a list of bad tracks.	Media Analysis
Installing a new hard disk.	You do not know the optimum interleave factor.	Auto Interleave
Installing a new hard disk.	The drive is not formatted.	Hard Disk Format
Installing a used hard disk drive.	N/A	All Hard Disk Utilities

When Hard Disk Diagnostics is selected, the following screen appears:

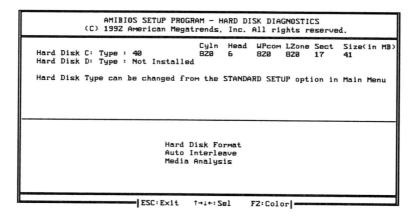

```
                AMIBIOS SETUP PROGRAM - HARD DISK DIAGNOSTICS
                (C) 1992 American Megatrends, Inc. All rights reserved.

                                      Cyln  Head  WPcom LZone Sect  Size(in MB)
    Hard Disk C: Type : 40            820   6     820   820   17    41
    Hard Disk D: Type : Not Installed

    Hard Disk Type can be changed from the STANDARD SETUP option in Main Menu




                        Hard Disk Format
                        Auto Interleave
                        Media Analysis




        ━━━━━━━━━━━━┥ESC:Exit   ↑→↓←:Sel    F2:Color┝━━━━━━━━━━━━
```

Select an option and press ENTER.

Hard Disk Format Utility

> **Warning**
> The Hard Disk Format utility destroys all hard
> disk data. Back up the data on the hard disk
> before running this utility.

This routine does not work on IDE or SCSI drives. Use Hard Disk
Format to integrate a new hard disk to the system, or to reformat a
used hard disk that has developed bad tracks as a result of aging or
poor handling. Select Media Analysis to find bad tracks. The following
screen appears when Hard Disk Format is selected.

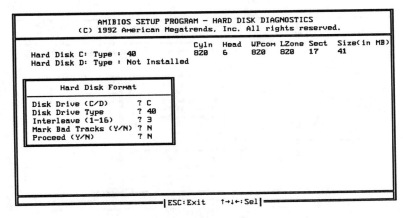

Hard Disk Format Screen

cont'd

Answer the questions on the screen. The first two questions are already completed if only one hard disk drive was selected in Standard CMOS Setup and the cursor is on *Interleave*. The Disk Drive Type is read from CMOS RAM. The interleave factor can be selected manually or determined by the Auto Interleave routine.

The hard disk drive manufacturer usually provides a list of bad tracks. Enter these tracks. They are then labeled as bad to prevent data from being stored on them. The following screen is displayed after entering Y in Mark Bad Tracks, pressing ENTER, and selecting add, delete, revise, or clear from the Bad Track Edit Menu:

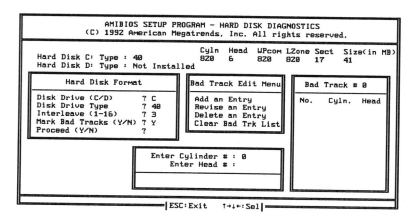

Type *Y* and press ENTER. A warning screen appears. Press any key to continue.

> ***Warning***
> Data on the hard drive will be irrevocably lost.

Auto Interleave Utility

> **Warning**
> The Auto Interleave utility destroys hard disk
> data. Back up the data on the hard disk before
> running this utility.

The Auto Interleave utility calculates the optimum interleave factor
through trial and error by measuring the transfer rate for four different
interleave values. To determine the best interleave factor, the system
formats a portion of the hard disk for each transfer rate calculated. The
cylinders, heads, and sectors formatted for each value appears. The
Auto Interleave routine does not work on IDE or SCSI drives.

Select Auto Interleave on the main Hard Disk Utility Screen and press
ENTER. The following appears:

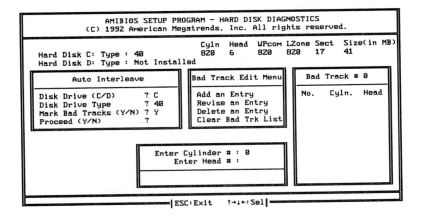

The cursor is on Mark Bad Tracks. The default is *N*. To mark
additional bad tracks, type *Y* and press ENTER. After selecting options
from the Bad Tracks Edit Menu, press ESC. Type *Y* and press ENTER to
proceed with the Auto Interleave process. A warning screen appears.
Press ENTER to return to the main Hard Disk Utility screen. To
proceed, type *Y* and press ENTER.

Media Analysis Utility

The Media Analysis utility performs a series of tests to locate bad or damaged tracks on the hard disk as a result of aging or poor handling. This utility locates all bad tracks and lists them in the Bad Track List Box. Since this test writes to all cylinders and heads on the hard disk to verify any bad tracks, the test requires several minutes to complete. For best results, run this test in its entirety. Media Analysis does not work on IDE or SCSI drives.

Select Media Analysis from the main Hard Disk Utility Menu and press ENTER. The following screen appears:

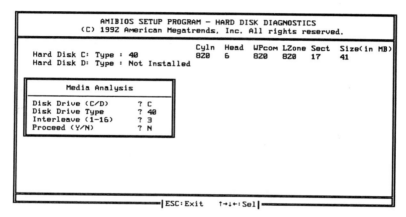

Media Analysis Screen

The cursor is on Proceed. The warning screen appears. Press ENTER to stop. The main Hard Disk Utility screen appears. Type Y and press ENTER to perform the hard disk drive analysis.

Hard Disk Utility Error Messages

Initialization Errors

Message	Explanation
No Hard Disk Installed	There is no hard disk drive in the system but Hard Disk Utility was selected.
FATAL ERROR Bad Hard Disk	No response from the hard disk, or the hard disk is not repairable. Check all cable and power connections to the hard disk.
Hard Disk Controller Failure	Error response from the reset command sent to the hard disk controller. The controller may not be seated properly in the BUS slot.
C: (D:) Hard Disk Failure	The hard disk drive (C: or D:) is not responding to commands. Check power and cable connections to the hard disk.

cont'd

Operation Errors

Message	Explanation
Address Mark Not Found	The address mark (initial address) on the hard disk could not be found.
Attachment Failed to Respond	No response has been received from the hard disk drive.
Bad ECC on Disk Read	When the hard disk drive utility writes to the disk, it also calculates an ECC (Error Correction Code) value for the data being written. This ECC value is written to the drive and then read back. The value read back is different from the one calculated.
Bad Sector Flag Detected	An operation was performed on a sector that has been flagged as bad.
Controller Has Failed	A diagnostic command issued to the controller failed.
Drive Not Ready	An operation on the hard disk drive has timed out. The hard disk drive utility has waited beyond a preset specified time limit.
Drive Parameter Activity Failed	A reset command was sent to the controller followed by drive parameters. Using these parameters, the controller did not get a response from the hard disk. Make sure the drive type is correct.
ECC Corrected Data Error	The ECC value (explained above) read from the disk is not the same value which was written to the disk. The data is not correct. An attempt was made to correct the data, but the ECC value is not corrected.
Requested Sector Not Found	The requested sector could not be found.
Reset Failed	The reset command did not properly reset the hard disk.
Seek Operation Failed	A seek command failed. A seek operation is the act of finding a particular sector on the hard disk.
Undefined Error - Command Aborted	An unidentifiable error condition occurred.
Write Fault on Selected Drive	A write fault occurred during the write operation on the hard disk drive.

Chapter 5

System Memory

The following graphic depicts the layout of conventional memory in ISA and EISA systems:

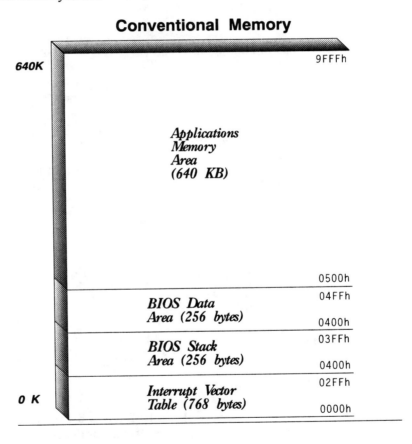

Conventional Memory

Upper memory is allocated as follows in ISA and EISA systems:

Upper Memory Blocks

High Memory Area (64 KB)	An extra 64K accessed via an EMS driver. Controlled by either DOS, Windows, a Network, or Desqview.	

1024K

ISA System BIOS (64 KB)	FFFFFh
	F0000h
EISA System BIOS, Network, or Adaptor ROMs (64 KB)	EFFFFh
	E0000h
Adaptor ROM (64 KB)	DFFFFh
	D0000h
Adaptor ROM (32 KB)	C8FFFh
	C8000h
EGA and VGA Video BIOS (32 KB)	C7FFFh
	C0000h

32 KB Video Buffer BFFFFh **for CGA, EGA color, and VGA color.** B8000h		BFFFFh
32 KB Video Buffer B7FFFh **for MDA, CGA monochrome, and VGA monochrome.** B0000h	**EGA and VGA Video Buffer (128 KB)**	
Video Memory AFFFFh **(64 KB)**		

640K

A0000h		A0000h

Extended and Expanded Memory

Extended Memory is the memory above 1 MB. This memory can be used only by programs that operate in protected mode, such as Microsoft Windows. Extended memory is memory that is made available to DOS programs through an Expanded Memory Manager (EMM) that uses a UMB to bank-switch data.

Chapter 6

BIOS Data Area

The BIOS Data Area is created by the BIOS at location 000400h in RAM when the computer is turned on. It is 256 bytes in length (000400 – 0004FFh), and contains information about the system environment. This information can be accessed (it can even be changed) by any program, not just the system BIOS.

Much of the operation of ISA and EISA computers is controlled by the data in the BIOS Data Area, which is loaded by BIOS POST during the boot process.

The following table lists the contents of all BIOS data area locations. All addresses are offsets from 000400h.

Offset	BIOS Service	Description
00h	INT 14h	Serial Port (COM) 1 — least significant byte.
01h	INT 14h	Serial Port (COM) 1 — most significant byte.
02h	INT 14h	Serial Port (COM) 2 — least significant byte.
03h	INT 14h	Serial Port (COM) 2 — most significant byte.
04h	INT 14h	Serial Port (COM) 3 — least significant byte.
05h	INT 14h	Serial Port (COM) 3 — most significant byte.
06h	INT 14h	Serial Port (COM) 4 — least significant byte.
07h	INT 14h	Serial Port (COM) 4 — most significant byte.
08h	INT 17h	Parallel Port (LPT) 1 — least significant byte.
09h	INT 17h	Parallel Port (LPT) 1 — most significant byte.
0Ah	INT 17h	Parallel Port (LPT) 2 — least significant byte.
0Bh	INT 17h	Parallel Port (LPT) 2 — most significant byte.
0Ch	INT 17h	Parallel Port (LPT) 3 — least significant byte.
0Dh	INT 17h	Parallel Port (LPT) 3 — most significant byte.
0Eh	POST	Extended BIOS Data Area Segment address — least significant byte.

BIOS Data Area, Continued

Offset	BIOS Service	Description
0Fh	POST	Extended BIOS Data Area Segment address — most significant byte.

10h – 11h	INT 11h	Equipment List
		Bits 15–14 Number of parallel adapters
		         00b None installed
		         01b One installed
		         10b Two installed
		         11b Three installed
		Bits 13–12 Reserved
		Bits 11–9 Number of serial adapters installed
		         000b None installed
		         001b One installed
		         010b Two installed
		         011b Three installed
		         100b Four installed
		Bit 8 Reserved
		Bits 7–6 Number of floppy disk drives.
		         00b One drive
		         01b Two drives
		Bits 5–4 Initial video mode
		         00b EGA or PGA
		         01b 40 x 25 color
		         10b 80 x 25 color
		         11b 80x25 Monochrome
		Bit 3 Reserved
		Bit 2 PS/2-type pointing device present if set.
		Bit 1 Math coprocessor present if set.
		Bit 0 Floppy disk drive A: present if set.

12h	POST	Interrupt Flag used in POST.
13h	INT 12h	Memory size in KB — least significant byte.
14h	INT 12h	Memory size in KB — most significant byte.
15h – 16h		Reserved
17h	INT 16h	Keyboard Status Byte Bit 7 System in Insert Mode if set. Bit 6 CAPS LOCK key on if set. Bit 5 NUM LOCK key on if set. Bit 4 SCROLL LOCK key on if set. Bit 3 Right ALT key pressed if set. Bit 2 Right CTRL key pressed if set. Bit 1 Left SHIFT key pressed if set. Bit 0 Right SHIFT key pressed if set.

BIOS Data Area, Continued

Offset	BIOS Service	Description
18h	INT 16h	Extended Keyboard Status Byte Bit 7 INS key pressed if set. Bit 6 CAPS LOCK key pressed if set. Bit 5 NUM LOCK key pressed if set. Bit 4 SCROLL LOCK key pressed if set. Bit 3 CTRL NUM LOCK state active Bit 2 SYSREQ key pressed if set. Bit 1 Left ALT key pressed if set. Bit 0 Left CTRL key pressed if set.
19h		Reserved
1Ah – 1Bh	INT 16h	Pointer to the address of the next character in the keyboard buffer.
1Ch – 1Dh	INT 16h	Pointer to the address of the last character in the keyboard buffer.
1Eh – 3Dh	INT 16h	Keyboard buffer (32 bytes). If the address in 1Ah is the same as the address in 1Ch, the buffer is empty. If the address in 1Ch is two bytes from the address in 1Ah, the buffer is full.
3Eh	INT 13h	Floppy Disk Drive Calibration Status Bits 7–4 Reserved. Should be 00h. Bits 3–2 Reserved Bit 1 Floppy Drive B: needs recalibration if 0. Bit 0 Floppy Drive A: needs recalibration if 0.

3Fh	INT 13h	Floppy Disk Drive Motor Status
		Bit 7 0 Current operation is Write or Format.
		            1 Current operation is Read or Verify.
		Bit 6 Reserved
		Bits 5–4 Drive select
		            00b Drive A: select
		            01b Drive B: select
		Bits 3–2 Reserved
		Bit 1 Drive A: motor is on if set.
		Bit 0 Drive B: motor is on if set.

40h	INT 13h	Floppy Disk Drive Motor Timeout This value is decremented by one 18.2 times per second (via the INT 08h timer interrupt). The drive motor is powered off when the value reaches zero. The value refers to the last disk drive accessed.

Offset	BIOS Service	Description
41h	INT 13h	Floppy Disk Drive Status. These values are valid for the last floppy disk drive accessed. Bit 7 Drive not ready if set. Bit 6 Seek error detected if set. Bit 5 Floppy disk controller failed if set. Bits 4–0 Error Codes 00h No error occurred. 01h Illegal function requested. 02h Address mark not found. 03h Write protect error. 04h Sector not found. 06h Drive door was opened. 08h DMA overrun error. 09h DMA boundary error. 0Ch Unknown media type. 10h CRC failed on floppy read. 20h Controller failure. 40h Seek failed. 80h Timeout.
42h – 48h	INT 13h	Floppy disk controller status bytes and command bytes for the hard disk controller.
49h	INT 10h	Current Video Display Mode setting.
4Ah – 4Bh	INT 10h	Number of text columns per line of current video mode.
4Ch – 4Dh	INT 10h	Current page size, in bytes.
4Eh – 4Fh	INT 10h	Offset address of current display page. The offset is relative to the start of video RAM. Video RAM starts at B800h in CGA. Video RAM starts at B000h in MDA.
50h – 5Fh	INT 10h	Current cursor position for each video page. Up to eight display pages are possible. Two bytes per page are used to store the current cursor position for each page. The most significant byte specifies the row (line) value and the least significant byte specifies the column value of the cursor. Change the cursor position using INT 10h functions. *Do not change the values in this location.*
60h	INT 10h	Starting line of the cursor.
61h	INT 10h	Ending line of the cursor.
62h	INT 10h	Current video display page number.
63h – 64h	INT 10h	I/O Port address of the video display adapter. This is the CRT Controller address register. It is 3B4h if a monochrome adapter is used and 3D4h if color is used.

Offset	BIOS Service	Description
65h	INT 10h	Value of video display adapter mode register. The mode register is at I/O port 3B8h if a monochrome adapter is used, 3D8h if a CGA adapter is used, or 3D9h if EGA or VGA is used.
66h	INT 10h	Current palette color.
67h – 6Bh		Adaptor ROM address.
6Ch – 6Fh	INT 1Ah	Counter used by INT 1Ah Real Time Clock Service. This counter is incremented by one every time the INT 08h timer interrupt occurs (18.2 times per second). This counter is reset to 0 every 24 hours.
70h	INT 1Ah	Timer 24-hour flag. This flag is set to 0 when the timer is between 0 and 24 hours. When the time crosses 24 hours, the flag is set to one. The flag must be manually reset.
71h	INT 16h	Break Key pressed flag Bit 7 Set if either CTRL BREAK or CTRL C is pressed.
72h – 73h	POST	Soft reset flag. If this word contains a 1234h, the memory test is skipped on reboot by POST.
74h – 77h	INT 13h	Status of last hard disk drive operation. 00h No error. 01h Invalid function request. 02h Address mark not found. 04h Sector not found. 05h Reset failed. 07h Drive parameter activity failed. 08h DMA overrun on operation. 09h Data boundary error. 0Ah Bad sector flag selected. 0Bh Bad track detected. 0Dh Invalid number of sectors on format. 0Eh Control data address mark detected. 0Fh DMA arbitration level out of range. 10h Uncorrectable ECC or CRC error. 11h ECC corrected data error. 20h General controller failure. 40h Seek operation failed. 80h Timeout. AAh Drive not ready. BBh Undefined error occurred. CCh Write fault on selected drive. E0h Status error, or error register is 0. FFh Sense operation failed.

Offset	BIOS Service	Description
75h	13h	Number of hard disk drives
76h – 77h	13h	Hard disk drive work area
78h	INT 17h	Parallel port 1 timeout counter
79h	INT 17h	Parallel port 2 timeout counter
7Ah	INT 17h	Parallel port 3 timeout counter
7Bh		Reserved
7Ch	INT 14h	Serial port 1 timeout counter
7Dh	INT 14h	Serial port 2 timeout counter
7Eh	INT 14h	Serial port 3 timeout counter
7Fh	INT 14h	Serial port 4 timeout counter
80h – 81h	INT 16h	Starting address of the keyboard buffer (usually 01Eh).
82h – 83h	INT 16h	Ending address of the keyboard buffer (usually 03Eh).
84h	INT 10h	Number of displayed character rows minus one.
85h – 86h	INT 10h	Height of character matrix.
87h	INT 10h	Bit 7 Equal to bit 7 of the video mode number passed to INT 10h by the programmer. Bits 6–4 Video RAM 000b 64K 001b 128K 010b 192K 011b 256K 100b 512K 110b 1024K Bit 3 0 Video subsystem active. 1 Video subsystem not active. Bit 2 Reserved Bit 1 0 Color monitor 1 Monochrome monitor Bit 0 0 Alphanumeric cursor emulation disabled. 1 Alphanumeric cursor emulation enabled.
88h	INT 13h	Data transmission speed of the hard disk drive.

BIOS Data Area, Continued

Offset	BIOS Service	Description
89h	INT 10h	VGA Video Flags Bits 7,4 Mode 00 350-line mode 01 400-line mode 10 200-line mode Bit 6 0 Display switch disabled. 1 Display switch enabled. Bit 5 Reserved Bit 3 1 Default palette loading enabled. 0 Default palette loading disabled. Bit 2 0 Color monitor 1 Monochrome monitor Bit 1 0 Gray scale summing disabled. 1 Gray scale summing enabled. Bit 0 0 VGA inactive. 1 VGA active.
8Ah – 8Bh		Reserved
8Ch – 95h	INT 13h	Hard disk and floppy disk drive variables.
96h	INT 16h	Extended Keyboard Status Bit 7 Read ID in progress if set. Bit 6 Last code was first ID if set. Bit 5 Forced Num Lock if set. Bit 4 101 and 102-key keyboard used if set. Bit 3 Right ALT key active if set. Bit 2 Right CTRL key active if set. Bit 1 Last code was E0h if set. Bit 0 Last code was E1h if set.
97h	INT 16h	Extended Keyboard Status Bit 7 Keyboard error occurred if set. Bit 6 LED is being updated if set. Bit 5 Resend code received if set. Bit 4 Acknowledge code received if set. Bit 3 Reserved Bit 2 Caps Lock LED is on if set. Bit 1 Num Lock LED is on if set. Bit 0 Scroll Lock LED is on if set.
98h – 99h		Segment part of user wait flag address.
9Ah – 9Bh		Offset part of user wait flag address.
9Ch – 9Fh		Wait count
A0h	INT 1Ah	Wait active flag Bit 7 Wait time has elapsed if set. Bits 6–1 Reserved Bit 0 INT 15h AH = 86h occurred if set.

BIOS Data Area, Continued

Offset	BIOS Service	Description
A1h – A7h		Reserved
A8h – ABh	INT 10h	INT 10h pointer to EGA and VGA parameter control block.
ACh – EFh		Reserved
F0h – FFh		Intra-Applications Communication Area. Stores data that can be used by different applications programs.

Chapter 7

ROM BIOS Data

The system BIOS stores parameters for peripheral devices that help it to initialize the system. This information is stored in arrays and tables in the BIOS. A complete map of the locations of these tables and of all device service routines is included in the ROM BIOS and is listed in this chapter.

In This Chapter

The following topics are discussed in this chapter:

- ROM Compatibility Table,
- Floppy Disk Drive Parameter Table,
- Hard Disk Drive Parameter Table,
- Hard Disk Drive Types,
- Hard Disk Drive Data Transfer Rates,
- Video Parameter Table,
- System Configuration Data Table, and
- Data Transmission Rate Initialization Table.

z

ROM Compatibility Table

Both the ISA and EISA system BIOS assure compatibility with older PC and XT standards by maintaining a list of vectors to the IBM-compatible interrupt routine and data table vectors.

Vector	to
FE05Bh	POST entry point
FE2C3h	NMI Handler entry point
FE3FEh	INT 13h Hard Disk Drive Service entry point
FE401h	Hard Disk Drive Parameter Table
FE6F2h	INT 19h Bootstrap Loader entry point
FE6F5h	Configuration Data Table
FE729h	Data Transmission Rate Generator Table
FE739h	INT 14h Serial Communications Service entry point
FE82Eh	INT 16h Keyboard Service entry point
FE987h	INT 09h Keyboard Service entry point
FEC59h	INT 13h Floppy Disk Service entry point
FEF57h	INT 0Eh Floppy Disk Hardware Interrupt Service Routine entry point
FEFC7h	Floppy Disk Controller Parameter Table
FEFD2h	INT 17h Parallel Printer Service entry point
FF045h	INT 10h Video Service Functions 00h through 0Fh entry point
FF065h	INT 10h Video Service entry point
FF0A4h	MDA and CGA Video Parameter Table (INT 1Dh)
FF841h	INT 12h Memory Size Service entry point
FF84Dh	INT 11h Equipment List Service entry point
FF859h	INT 15h Systems Services entry point
FFA6Eh	Low-order 128 characters of the 320 x 200 and 640 x 200 graphics fonts
FFE6Eh	INT 1Ah Real Time Clock Service entry point
FFEA5h	INT 08h System Timer Interrupt Service Routine entry point
FFEF3h	Initial Interrupt Vector offsets loaded by POST
FFF53h	IRET Instruction for Dummy Interrupt Handler
FFF54h	INT 05h Print Screen Service entry point
FFFF0h	Power-On entry point
FFFF5h	ROM Date (in ASCII). Eight characters in mm/dd/yy format.
FFFFEh	System Model ID (always FCh)

Floppy Drive Parameters

The floppy diskette parameter table is pointed to by the INT 1Eh vector. The table is eleven bytes long.

Offset	Description
00h	**Bits 7–4** Head Unload Time in milliseconds. The amount of time needed to allow the drive head to settle after it is lifted from the drive surface. 0h — 32 ms 1h — 64 ms 2h — 96 ms 3h — 120 ms — The default for 2.88 MB drives. 4h — 160 ms 5h — 192 ms 6h — 240 ms — The default for 1.2 MB 5¼ inch floppy drives and 1.44 MB 3½ inch drives. 7h — 256 ms 8h — 288 ms 9h — 320 ms Ah — 352 ms Bh — 384 ms Ch — 399 ms — The default for 360 KB floppies in a 1.2 MB 5¼ inch floppy drive. Dh — 448 ms Eh — 480 ms — The default for 360 KB 5¼ inch and 720 KB 3½ inch floppy drives. 0Fh — 512 ms **Bits 3–0** Step Rate in milliseconds. The amount of time needed for a drive head to move from one track to another. 00h — 2 ms — The default for 1.2 MB and 2.88 MB floppy drives is 3.0 ms. 01h — 4 ms — The default for 360 KB floppy in 1.2 MB drive is 4.8 ms. 02h — 6 ms — The default for 360 KB, 720 KB, and 1.44 MB floppy drives. 03h — 8 ms 04h — 10 ms 05h — 12 ms 06h — 14 ms 07h — 16 ms 08h — 18 ms 09h — 20 ms 0Ah — 22 ms 0Bh — 24 ms 0Ch — 26 ms 0Dh — 28 ms 0Eh — 30 ms 0Fh — 32 ms

Floppy Drive Parameters, Continued

Offset	Description
01h	Head Load Time. The amount of time in milliseconds needed to allow the drive head to settle after it is lowered onto the drive surface. The value ranges from 00h – 7Fh in increments of 4 milliseconds. See the following table on page 114 for the default values. Bits 7–0 00h 4 ms 01h 8 ms 02h 12 ms 03h 16 ms 04h 20 ms 05h 24 ms 06h 28 ms 07h 32 ms 08h 36 ms 09h 40 ms ... ... 7Fh 512 ms Bit 0 Non-DMA Mode Flag (always 0 to indicate that DMA is used).
02h	Motor Wait Timer. The amount of time that a floppy drive can be inactive before the drive motor is shut off. This value ranges from 0 to 255 in increments of 1. The timer ticks approximately 18.2 per second. The Motor Wait Time value can be calculated as follows: TIME = Selected timer tick value divided by 18.2 Bits 7–0 00h 0 timer ticks 01h 1 timer tick 02h 2 timer ticks ... ... 37h 37 timer ticks (Default for all floppy drives – approximately 2.03 seconds) ... ... FFh 255 timer ticks
03h	Number of Bytes per Sector Bits 7–0 00h 128 bytes per sector 01h 256 bytes per sector 02h 512 " " " (Default for all floppy drives). 03h 1024 bytes per sector
04h	Number of Sectors Per Track Bits 7–0 08h 8 sectors per track (320 KB 5¼" drives) 09h 9 sectors per track (360 KB 5¼" drives) 15h 15 sectors per track (1.2 MB 5¼" drives) 12h 18 sectors per track (720K and 1.44 MB 3½" drives) 24h 36 sectors per track (2.88 MB 3½ drives)

Floppy Drive Parameters, Continued

Offset	Description
05h	Gap Length. The length of the gap between sectors. Bits 7–0 00h 0 01h 1 ... ... 1Bh 27 The default for 1.2 MB, 1.44 MB, and 2.88 MB drives. ... ... 2Ah 42 The default for 360 KB and 720 KB floppy drives. ... ... FFh 255
06h	Data Length — always set to FFh.
07h	Gap Length For Format. This value is used for the same purpose as the gap length, but it is used in formatting only. Bits 7–0 00h 0 01h 1 ... ... 50h 80 The default for 360 KB, 720 KB, and 2.88 MB floppy drives. 51h 84 The default for 1.2 MB floppy drives. ... ... 57h 108 The default for 1.44 MB floppy drives. ... ... FFh 255
08h	Fill Byte for Formatting — always set to F6h
09h	Head Settle Time. The amount of time in milliseconds that must elapse to allow the heads to settle after a Seek operation. Bits 7–0 00h 0 ms 01h 1 ms 02h 2 ms ... ... 0Fh 15 ms The default for all floppy drives. ... ... FFh 255 ms
0Ah	Motor Start Time. The amount of time it takes the drive motor to reach optimal speed. The values are in eighths of a second. Bits 7–0 00h 0 01h 1 ⅛th of a second 02h 2 ¼ second ... ... 08h 8 one second (the default for all floppy drives). ... ... FFh 255 31⅞ of a second

Summary of Default Settings for Floppy Drives

The following table summarizes the default settings for all floppy disk parameter table values in AMIBCP. All floppy drives summarized below have two read/write heads.

Parameter	360 KB Floppy in 360KB Drive	360 KB Floppy in 1.2 MB Drive	1.2 MB Floppy in 1.2 MB Drive	720 KB 3½"	1.44 MB 3½"	2.88 MB 3½
Step Rate (ms)	6.0	4.8	3.0	6.0	6.0	3.0
Head Unload Time (ms)	480	399	240	480	240	120
Head Load Time (ms)	4.0	3.3	2.0	4.0	2.0	1.0
Motor Wait Time (in timer ticks)	37	37	37	37	37	37
Gap Length	42	42	27	42	27	27
Gap Length for Format	80	80	84	80	108	80
Head Settle Time (ms)	15	15	15	15	15	15
Motor Start Time (in ⅛ths of a second)	8	8	8	8	8	8
Number of Bytes per Sector	512	512	512	512	512	512
Cluster Size	1024	1024	512	1024	512	512
Tracks	40	40	80	80	80	80
Sectors per Track	9	9	15	9	18	36

Hard Disk Parameter Table

The hard disk drive parameter table (drive type table) is located at F000:E401h. The vector table entries for INT 41h contains the entry points for the hard disk drive types selected via BIOS Setup for hard disk drive C:. INT 46h contains the vector for hard disk drive D:. Each drive type entry consists of 16 bytes, in the following format:

Offset	Description
00h – 01h	Number of Cylinders. Byte 01h is the most significant byte.
02h	Number of heads.
03h – 04h	Reserved
05h – 06h	Starting write precompensation cylinder. Byte 06h is the most significant byte. The size of a sector becomes progressively smaller as the track diameter diminishes when writing to inner tracks. Yet each sector must still hold 512 bytes. Write precompensation circuitry on the hard disk compensates for the physical difference in sector size by boosting the write current for sectors on inner tracks. This parameter is the track number where the write precompensation circuitry begins operating.
07h	Reserved

08h	Control Byte
	Bits 7–6 Enable or Disable Retries
	          00h Enable retries.
	          All other values disable retries.
	Bit 5 Set if defect map is located at last cylinder plus one.
	Bit 4 Reserved. Always set to 0.
	Bit 3 Set if more than 8 heads.
	Bits 2–0 Reserved. Always set to 0.

09h – 0Bh	Reserved
0Ch – 0Dh	Landing Zone. This number is the cylinder location where the heads normally park when the system is shut down.
0Eh	Number of Sectors per Track. Hard disk drives that use MFM have 17 sectors per track. RLL drives have 26 sectors per track. RLL and ESDI drives have 34 sectors per track. SCSI and IDE drives may have even more sectors per track.
0Fh	Reserved

Hard Disk Drive Types

The system BIOS uses a standard hard disk drive type table that has 45 entries for drive types 0 – 14 and 16 – 46. See page 117 for a complete list of the hard disk drive parameters. These drive types can be used to configure DOS drives C: and D:.

User-Definable Drives

AMIBIOS also supports a user-definable drive (Type 47), used for hard disk drives not defined in the standard drive table. *Not Installed* is used for diskless workstations and SCSI hard drives. Either drive C: or D: or both can use Type 47. Type 47 must be used for IDE drives. You must enter the driver parameters via Standard CMOS Setup when specifying Type 47.

Location of Hard Drive Parameters

The hard disk drive parameters are stored in CMOS RAM registers 1Bh – 23h (drive C:) and 24h – 2Ch (drive D:). The format is shown on page 115. The BIOS rewrites these parameters at system boot to a different location to permit quicker access.

Hard Disk Drive Type Selection

The BIOS first makes sure that shadow RAM is enabled. If so, the BIOS copies these parameters to the locations in the drive table specified by the INT 41h (Drive C:) and INT 46h (Drive D:) vectors.

If shadow RAM is disabled or the system does not support shadow RAM, the parameters are copied to either of two secondary locations:

- the BIOS Stack Area (000300h – 000301h), or

- the upper 1 KB of DOS memory (09FFFEh – 09FFFFh).

The OEM selects the secondary location that is to be used through AMIBCP, or can allow the end user to choose the secondary location via AMIBIOS Setup.

Hard Disk Drive Types, Continued

Type	Cylinders	Heads	Write Precompensation	Landing Zone	Sectors	Capacity
1	306	4	128	305	17	10 MB
2	615	4	300	615	17	20 MB
3	615	6	300	615	17	31 MB
4	940	8	512	940	17	62 MB
5	940	6	512	940	17	47 MB
6	615	4	65535	615	17	20 MB
7	462	8	256	511	17	31 MB
8	733	5	65535	733	17	30 MB
9 *	900	15	65535	901	17	112 MB
10	820	3	65535	820	17	20 MB
11	855	5	65535	855	17	35 MB
12	855	7	65535	855	17	50 MB
13	306	8	128	319	17	20 MB
14	733	7	65535	733	17	43 MB
16	612	4	0	663	17	20 MB
17	977	5	300	977	17	41 MB
18	977	7	65535	977	17	57 MB
19	1024	7	512	1023	17	60 MB
20	733	5	300	732	17	30 MB
21	733	7	300	732	17	43 MB
22	733	5	300	733	17	30 MB
23	306	4	0	336	17	10 MB
24	925	7	0	925	17	54 MB
25 *	925	9	65535	925	17	69 MB
26	754	7	754	754	17	44 MB
27 *	754	11	65535	754	17	69 MB
28	699	7	256	699	17	41 MB
29 *	823	10	65535	823	17	68 MB
30	918	7	918	918	17	53 MB
31	1024	11	65535	1024	17	94 MB
32 *	1024	15	65535	1024	17	128 MB
33	1024	5	1024	1024	17	43 MB
34	612	2	128	612	17	10 MB
35 *	1024	9	65535	1024	17	77 MB
36	1024	8	512	1024	17	68 MB
37	615	8	128	615	17	41 MB
38	987	3	987	987	17	25 MB
39	987	7	987	987	17	57 MB
40	820	6	820	820	17	41 MB
41	977	5	977	977	17	41 MB
42	981	5	981	981	17	41 MB
43	830	7	512	830	17	48 MB
44 *	830	10	65535	830	17	69 MB
45 *	917	15	65535	918	17	114 MB
46 *	1224	15	65535	1223	17	152 MB
47	ENTER HARD DRIVE PARAMETERS SUPPLIED BY MANUFACTURER					

* Control Byte is 80h

cont'd

Hard Disk Drive Types, Continued

Control Byte Parameter

The Control Byte (see page 115) is almost always 00h. The only exceptions are types 9, 25, 27, 29, 32, 35, 44, 45, and 46, where it is 80h.

You must enter the drive parameters when using Type 47. The table on the previous page includes the default hard drive table in the AMIBIOS. The OEM can customize this table via AMIBCP. The table for BIOS Setup in your computer may be different.

Hard Disk Drive Data Transfer Rates

Drive Interface Type	Data Transfer Rate (Mbs)	Data Transfer Rate (MBs)
ST506, ST412, MFM	5 Mbs	0.625 MBs
RLL	7.5 Mbs	0.9375 MBs
IDE	7.5 Mbs	0.9375 MBs
ESDI	10 Mbs	1.25 MBs
SCSI-2	80 – 320 Mbs	10 – 40 MBs

Hard Disk Drive Capacity

The capacity of a hard disk drive can be determined using the following formula:

(Number of heads) X (Number of cylinders) X (Number of sectors per track) X (512 - Number of bytes per sector)

Video Parameter Table

This table always contains one or more entries for each available video mode, including video modes specified in the MDA, CGA, EGA, PGA, XGA, or VGA standards. If VGA is used in the system, this table contains at least 29 entries in the following format:

Offset	Description
00h	Number of displayed character columns (the same value as in 40:49h).
01h	Number of displayed character rows - 1 (the same value as in 40:84h).
02h	Height of character matrix (the same value as in 40:85h).
03h	Size of video buffer in bytes (the same value as in 40:4Ch).
05h	The value for Sequencer Registers 1 through 4.
09h	The value for the Miscellaneous Output Register.
0Ah	Values for CRTC Registers 00h through 18h.
23h	The values for Attribute Control Registers 00h through 13h.
37h	The values for Graphics Controller Registers 0 through 8.

System Configuration Data

The System Configuration Table is at F000:E6F5h. It can be moved to system memory by invoking INT 15h Function C0h.

Offset	Description
00h	Number of bytes in this table. It must be at least eight bytes.
02h	Model Byte (always FCh).
03h	Submodel Byte (always 01h).
04h	BIOS Revision Level. Should be zeros if the first release of the BIOS.
05h	Feature Information Byte 1 Bit 7 If set, the hard disk drive BIOS is using DMA Channel 3. Bit 6 If set, a second interrupt controller chip is present in the system. Bit 5 If set, a Real Time Clock is present. Bit 4 If set, a Keyboard Intercept (INT 15h Function 4Fh) has been called by the keyboard interrupt service (INT 09h). Bits 3–0 Reserved, should be zeros.
06h	Reserved, should be zeros.
07h	Reserved, should be zeros.
08h	Reserved, should be zeros.
09h	Reserved, should be zeros.

Data Transmission Rate Initialization Table

The data transmission rate initialization table is located at F000:E729h in the ROM BIOS.

Data Transmission Rate	Divisor
110	0417h
150	0300h
300	0180h
600	00C0h
1200	0060h
2400	0030h
4800	0018h
9600	000Ch
19200	0006h

Data Transmission Rate Divisors

The input frequency to the device is 1.8432 MHz. The values in the table are calculated as follows:

```
1,843,200/16 = 115,200/data transmission rate = Divisor
```

For example, a data transmission rate of 2400 has a divisor of 115,200/2,400, which equals 30h.

Chapter 8

CMOS RAM Map

Systems that adhere to ISA standards (AT-compatible systems) have at least 64 bytes of CMOS RAM to store system initialization and configuration parameters.

How CMOS RAM is Configured

Most of these parameters are set by the system manufacturer and the user via the AMIBIOS Setup utility. AMIBIOS Setup resides in the BIOS ROM and can be accessed when the system is booting.

Accessing CMOS RAM Directly

You can access CMOS RAM via an assembly language program. To read CMOS RAM, use the following Intel x86 assembler instructions:

```
OUT     70h,Register Number
IN      71h
```

To write to CMOS RAM, use the following instructions:

```
OUT     70h,Register Number
OUT     71h,New_Value
```

If the most significant bit of the *Register Number* is set when reading or writing CMOS RAM, the Nonmaskable Interrupt (NMI) is disabled during the operation.

How CMOS RAM is Organized

CMOS RAM is divided into several parts:

Location	Length	Description
00h – 0Fh	16 bytes	Real Time Clock data.
10h – 2Fh	32 bytes	ISA configuration data.
30h – 3Fh	16 bytes	BIOS-specific configuration data.
40h – 7Fh	64 bytes	Extended CMOS RAM. Available in many systems. Many chipsets incorporate this additional CMOS RAM to store advanced configuration information.

EISA CMOS RAM

EISA Extended CMOS RAM stores EISA-specific information and is configured by the EISA Configuration Utility (ECU). See page 419 for additional information about EISA.

EISA Extended CMOS RAM consists of between 4,096 and 8,192 bytes of CMOS memory and is accessed via INT 15h Function D8h.

EISA Extended CMOS RAM can also be accessed via a series of I/O ports. An I/O port map that describes the EISA CMOS RAM I/O ports is shown on pages 133 through 150.

CMOS RAM Map

A map of CMOS RAM as configured by the AMIBIOS is shown in the following table.

This section assumes that a Motorola MC146818 or compatible Real Time Clock is used. For some registers, only the definitions used during initialization are shown.

Offset	Description
00h	Real Time Clock — Seconds field Contains the seconds value of the current time.
01h	Real Time Clock — Seconds Alarm Contains the seconds value for the RTC alarm.
02h	Real Time Clock — Minutes field Contains the minutes value of the current time.
03h	Real Time Clock — Minutes Alarm Contains the minutes value for the RTC alarm.
04h	Real Time Clock — Hours Contains the hours value of the current time.
05h	Real Time Clock — Hours Alarm Contains the hour value for the RTC alarm.
06h	Real Time Clock — Day of Week Contains the current day of the week.
07h	Real Time Clock — Date Contains the day field (0 – 31) of the current date.
08h	Real Time Clock — Month Contains the month field of the current date.
09h	Real Time Clock — Year Contains the year field of the current date.
0Ah	Status Register A Bit 7 Update in progress if set. 0 Can read date or time. 1 Can't read date or time, update in progress. Bits 6–4 Divider that identifies the time-based frequency to use. The BIOS initializes this field to 010b, a 32.768 KHz time base. Bits 3–0 Rate selection bits that define output frequency and periodic interrupt rate. The BIOS initializes these bits to 0110b, which sets a 1.024 KHz square wave clock pulse and a 976.562 second interrupt rate.

Offset	Description
0Bh	Status Register B
	Bit 7 Halt Cycle to Set Clock
	0 Update counter once per second.
	1 Halt the counter to set the clock.
	Bit 6 Periodic Interrupt
	0 Disable
	1 Enable
	Bit 5 Alarm Interrupt
	0 Disable
	1 Enable
	Bit 4 Update-Ended Interrupt
	0 Disable
	1 Enable
	Bit 3 Square Wave
	0 Disable square wave.
	1 Use the square wave rate set in Status Register A.
	Bit 2 Date and Time Mode
	0 Use BCD format.
	1 Use binary format.
	Bit 1 24 or 12 Hour Mode
	0 Set 12 hour mode.
	1 Set 24 hour mode.
	Bit 0 Daylight Savings Time
	0 Disable
	1 Enable
0Ch	Status Register C
	Bit 7 IRQ Flag (read-only)
	Bit 6 Periodic Interrupt Flag (read-only)
	Bit 5 Alarm Interrupt Flag (read-only)
	Bit 4 Update Interrupt Flag (read only)
	Bits 3–0 Reserved (should be set to 0).
0Dh	Status Register D
	Bit 7 Valid CMOS RAM
	0 CMOS battery low, CMOS RAM invalid.
	1 CMOS RAM battery good, CMOS RAM valid.
	Bits 6–0 Reserved (should be set to 0).

Offset	Description
0Eh	**Diagnostic Status**
	Bit 7 RTC Chip Power
	0 Power valid.
	1 Power invalid.
	Bit 6 CMOS RAM Checksum error
	0 CMOS RAM checksum valid.
	1 CMOS RAM checksum invalid.
	Bit 5 CMOS RAM Configuration Mismatch
	0 CMOS RAM configuration matches the newly determined configuration.
	1 CMOS RAM configuration does not match newly determined configuration.
	Bit 4 CMOS RAM Memory Size Mismatch
	0 CMOS RAM memory size matches newly determined memory size.
	1 CMOS RAM memory size does not match determined memory size.
	Bit 3 Hard disk drive C: initialization
	0 Initialization passed, attempting to boot.
	1 Failed initialization. No boot attempt.
	Bit 2 Time status indicator
	0 Time is valid.
	1 Time is not valid.
	Bits 1–0 Reserved. Should be 0.
0Fh	**Shutdown Status.** The contents of the CPU registers are saved to memory and the CPU is reset when switched from protected to real mode. If a program requests a shutdown (using a DWORD JMP instruction), the address of the program is stored in 40:67h (segment) and 40:69h (offset). Just before reset, a shutdown code is written to 0Fh so that after reset, the BIOS knows the reason for the shutdown.

Code	Explanation
00h	Normal POST execution.
01h	Chipset initialization for real mode reentry.
02h–03h	Used internally by the BIOS.
04h	Jump to bootstrap code.
05h	User-defined shutdown. Issue an EOI, flush the keyboard buffer, and jump to the doubleword pointer at 40:67h. The interrupt controller and math coprocessor are initialized.
06h	Jump to the doubleword pointer at 40:67h with no EOI.
07h	Return to INT 15h Function 87h.
08h	Return to POST memory test.
09h	INT 15h Function 87h Block Move shutdown request.
0Ah	User-defined shutdown requested. The interrupt controller and math coprocessor are not initialized. The BIOS returns via a jump to the DWORD pointer at 40:67h with no EOI.

CMOS RAM Map, Continued

Offset	Description

10h	Floppy Drive Type
	Bits 7–4 Drive A: Type
	      0h No drive
	      1h 360 KB 5¼" drive
	      2h 1.2 MB 5¼" drive
	      3h 720 KB 3½" drive
	      4h 1.44 MB 3½" drive
	      5h 2.88 MB 3½" drive
	      6h – Fh Undefined
	Bits 3–0 Drive B: Type
	      0h No drive
	      1h 360 KB 5¼" drive
	      2h 1.2 MB 5¼" drive
	      3h 720 KB 3½" drive
	      4h 1.44 MB 3½" drive
	      5h 2.88 MB 3½" drive
	      6h – Fh Undefined

11h	Bit 7 Mouse Support Option
	      0 Disable
	      1 Enable
	Bit 6 Above 1 MB Memory Test
	      0 Disable
	      1 Enable
	Bit 5 Memory Test Tick Sound
	      0 Disable
	      1 Enable
	Bit 4 Memory Parity Error Check
	      0 Disable
	      1 Enable
	Bit 3 Hit <DEL> Message Display
	      0 Disable
	      1 Enable
	Bit 2 Hard Disk Type 47 RAM Area
	      0 Store at 0:300h
	      1 Store in Upper 1K of DOS area
	Bit 1 Wait for <F1> if Any Error
	      0 Disable
	      1 Enable
	Bit 0 System Boot Up Num Lock
	      0 Off
	      1 On

Offset	Description
12h	Hard Disk Data Bits 7–4 Hard Disk Drive C: Type 0000b No drive installed 0001b Hard Drive Type 1 0010b Hard Drive Type 2 ... ... 1110b Drive Type 14 1111b Hard Disk Type 16 – 46 (actual hard disk drive type is at CMOS RAM location 19h) Bits 3–0 Hard Disk Drive D: Type 0000b No drive installed 0001b Hard Drive Type 1 0010b Hard Drive Type 2 ... ... 1110b Drive Type 14 1111b Hard Disk Type 16 – 46 (actual hard disk drive type is at CMOS RAM location 1Ah)
13h	Keyboard Typematic Data Bit 7 Enable Typematic 0 Disabled 1 Enabled Bits 6–5 Typematic Rate Delay in milliseconds 00 250 ms 01 500 ms 10 750 ms 11 1000 ms Bits 4–2 Typematic Rate in characters per second 000 6 cps 100 15 cps 001 8 cps 101 20 cps 010 10 cps 110 24 cps 011 12 cps 111 30 cps

Offset	Description
14h	Equipment Byte Bits 7–6 Number of Floppy Drives 00b No Drive 01b One Drive 10b Two drives Bits 5–4 Monitor Type 00b Not CGA or MDA 01b 40x25 CGA 10b 80x25 CGA 11b MDA (Monochrome) Bit 3 Display Enabled 0 Not installed 1 Installed Bit 2 Keyboard Enabled 0 Not installed 1 Installed Bit 1 Math coprocessor Installed 0 Absent 1 Present Bit 0 Floppy Drive Installed. Always set to 1.
15h	Base Memory (in 1K increments), least significant byte.
16h	Base Memory (in 1 K increments), most significant byte.
17h	Extended Memory (in 1K increments), least significant byte.
18h	Extended Memory (in 1 K increments), most significant byte.
19h	Hard Disk C: Drive Type if Bits 7–4 of 12h are 1111b. 00h–0Fh Reserved 10h–2Eh Hard Drive Type 16 – 46
1Ah	Hard Disk D: Drive Type if Bits 7–4 of 12h are 1111b. 00h–0Fh Reserved 10h–2Eh Hard Drive Type 16 – 46
1Bh	User-Defined Drive C: Number of Cylinders, least significant byte.
1Ch	User-Defined Drive C: Number of Cylinders, most significant byte.
1Dh	User-Defined Drive C: Number of Heads.
1Eh	User-Defined Drive C: Write Precompensation Cylinder, least significant byte.
1Fh	User-Defined Drive C: Write Precompensation Cylinder, most significant byte.
20h	User-Defined Drive C: Control Byte (80h if the number of heads is equal or greater than eight).
21h	User-Defined Drive C: Landing Zone, least significant byte.
22h	User-Defined Drive C: Landing Zone, most significant byte.
23h	User-Defined Drive C: Number of Sectors

CMOS RAM Map, Continued

Offset	Description	
24h	User-Defined Drive D:	Number of Cylinders, least significant byte.
25h	User-Defined Drive D:	Number of Cylinders, most significant byte.
26h	User-Defined Drive D:	Number of Heads
27h	User-Defined Drive D:	Write Precompensation Cylinder, least significant byte.
28h	User-Defined Drive D:	Write Precompensation Cylinder, most significant byte.
29h	User-Defined Drive D:	Control Byte (80h if the number of heads is equal or greater than 8).
2Ah	User-Defined Drive D:	Landing Zone, least significant byte
2Bh	User-Defined Drive D:	Landing Zone, most significant byte.
2Ch	User-Defined Drive D:	Number of Sectors

2Dh	Bit 7 Weitek Processor
	    0 Absent
	    1 Present
	Bit 6 Floppy Drive Seek At Boot
	    0 Disable
	    1 Enable
	Bit 5 System Boot Up Sequence
	    0 C:, A:
	    1 A:, C:
	Bit 4 System Boot Up CPU Speed
	    0 High
	    1 Low
	Bit 3 External Cache Memory. Set to 0 if no external cache in the system.
	    0 Disable
	    1 Enable
	Bit 2 Internal Cache Memory. Set to 0 if no internal cache memory in the system.
	    0 Disable
	    1 Enable
	Bit 1 Fast Gate A20 Option. Set to 0 if system does not have Fast Gate A20.
	    0 Disable
	    1 Enable
	Bit 0 Turbo Switch Function
	    0 Disable
	    1 Enable	

2Eh	Standard CMOS checksum, most significant byte.	
2Fh	Standard CMOS checksum, least significant byte.	
30h	Extended memory found by BIOS, least significant byte.	

Offset	Description
31h	Extended memory found by BIOS, most significant byte.
32h	Century byte. The BCD value for the century of the current date.
33h	Information Flag Bit 7 BIOS Length 0 64 KB 1 128 KB Bits 6–1 Reserved. Should be 0. Used as scratchpad for chipset-specific functions during POST. Bit 0 POST Cache test 0 Cache bad 1 Cache good
34h	Bit 7 Boot sector virus protection (only used if BIOS Date is 06/06/92 or later). 0 Enabled 1 Disabled Bit 6 Password 0 Always 1 Password checking only when entering AMIBIOS Setup. Bits 7-6 Password in older AMIBIOS 00 Disabled 01 Always 11 Setup Bit 5 Adaptor ROM Shadow C800,16K 0 Disabled 1 Enabled Bit 4 Adaptor ROM Shadow CC00,16K 0 Disabled 1 Enabled Bit 3 Adaptor ROM Shadow D000,16K 0 Disabled 1 Enabled Bit 2 Adaptor ROM Shadow D400,16K 0 Disabled 1 Enabled Bit 1 Adaptor ROM Shadow D800,16K 0 Disabled 1 Enabled Bit 0 Adaptor ROM Shadow DC00,16K 0 Disabled 1 Enabled

CMOS RAM Map, Continued

Offset	Description
35h	**Bit 7** Adaptor ROM Shadow E000,16K 0 Disabled 1 Enabled **Bit 6** Adaptor ROM Shadow E400,16K 0 Disabled 1 Enabled **Bit 5** Adaptor ROM Shadow E800,16K 0 Disabled 1 Enabled **Bit 4** Adaptor ROM Shadow EC00,16K 0 Disabled 1 Enabled **Bit 3** System ROM Shadow F000,64K 0 Disabled 1 Enabled **Bit 2** Video ROM Shadow C000,16K 0 Disabled 1 Enabled **Bit 1** Video ROM Shadow C400,16K 0 Disabled 1 Enabled **Bit 0** Numeric Processor Test 0 Disabled 1 Enabled
36h	Chipset-specific information.
37h	Password Seed and Color Option **Bits 7–4** Password Seed used in the password encryption algorithm. *Do not modify this value.* **Bits 3–0** AMIBIOS Setup screen color 07h White (light gray) on black. 70h Black on white (light gray). 17h White (light gray) on blue. 20h Black on green. 30h Black on turquoise. 47h White (light gray) on red. 57h White (light gray) on magenta. 60h Black on brown (dark yellow). 70h Black on white (light gray). Monochrome Table (see page 132).
38h – 3Dh	The AMIBIOS Password (unpublished proprietary encryption format).
3Eh	MSB of Extended CMOS Checksum (includes 34h – 3Dh).
3Fh	LSB of Extended CMOS Checksum (includes 34h – 3Dh).

AMIBIOS Setup Color Tables

Monochrome

Color Number	Third Window	First Window	Second Window	Main Window
0	07h	70h	70h	07h
1	70h	70h	70h	70h
2	07h	07h	07h	07h
3	70h	07h	07h	70h
4	70h	70h	07h	07h
5	07h	70h	70h	70h
6	07h	07h	07h	70h
7	70h	07h	07h	07h
8	70h	70h	70h	07h
9	07h	70h	07h	07h
A	07h	07h	70h	70h
B	70h	07h	70h	07h
C	07h	70h	07h	70h
D	07h	07h	70h	07h
E	70h	07h	70h	70h
F	70h	70h	07h	70h

AMIBIOS Setup Color Table

Color Number	Third Window	First Window	Second Window	Main Window
0	57h	60h	17h	20h
1	20h	47h	30h	57h
2	70h	30h	57h	60h
3	60h	17h	20h	70h
4	57h	30h	47h	20h
5	20h	17h	60h	57h
6	17h	60h	57h	30h
7	30h	47h	20h	17h
8	70h	20h	17h	60h
9	60h	57h	30h	70h
A	70h	70h	70h	70h
B	07h	07h	07h	07h
C	70h	07h	70h	07h
D	07h	70h	07h	70h
E	17h	20h	47h	30h
F	30h	57h	60h	17h

Chapter 9

I/O Port Addresses

The microprocessor communicates with and controls many parts of the system via the I/O ports. The I/O ports are like doorways through which information passes as it travels from an I/O device (such as a keyboard or serial port) to the microprocessor and vice versa.

The ISA architecture includes a 64 KB I/O memory area used to access external devices. Intel 80386 and 80486 architecture allows for 8-, 16-, or 32-bit I/O ports. The I/O ports from 0000h – 00FFh address devices on the motherboard. I/O port addresses 0100h – 02FFh are used by devices attached to the system via expansion slots. I/O port addresses 01F0h – 01F8h are reserved for a hard disk controller.

Accessing I/O Ports

Components that Use the I/O Ports

Most of the support chips (or equivalents) in an ISA system (Intel 8259 Programmable Interrupt Controller, Intel 8254 Programmable Interval Timer, Intel 8237 Programmable DMA Controller) use the I/O port to communicate with other parts of the system.

How Ports Are Identified

Each port is identified by a 16-bit port number from 0 – 65,535 (0000h – FFFFh).

cont'd

Ports Accessed by Hex Port Number

The microprocessor sends data or control information to a specific I/O port by specifying the port number. The I/O port responds by passing data or status information through the port to the microprocessor.

Just as it does when accessing memory, the microprocessor uses the data and address buses as paths for communication with the I/O ports.

To access a port, the microprocessor first sends a signal on the control bus. This signal notifies all I/O devices that the information on the bus is an I/O port address. Then it sends the I/O port address. The device that is assigned to that specific I/O port responds.

The I/O port number addresses a memory location that is part of the I/O device, but is not part of system memory. Special assembler I/O instructions are used to signal a port access and send information to and from I/O devices.

Programmer Access

A programmer can use the Intel assembly language instructions IN and OUT to write to and read from I/O port addresses. For example:

```
MOV    DX,03CCh      ;read video register address
IN     AL,DX         ;read byte from I/O port
OR     AL,10h        ;set bit 4 for RAMDAC control
MOV    DX,03C2h      ;write register address
OUT    DX,AL         ;write value to I/O port
```

ISA and EISA I/O Port Assignments

All ISA and EISA computers use the standard I/O port assignments. The standard I/O port addresses are listed in the following tables. Some systems also use customized I/O port assignments.

Hardware I/O Port Addresses

Addresses from 0000h–00FFh are used by motherboard components.

I/O Port	Read/ Write	Description
		0000h – 001Fh are used by the 8237 DMA Controller 1
0000h	R/W	DMA channel 0 address byte 0 (low byte), followed by byte 1.
0001h	R/W	DMA channel 0 word count byte 0 (low byte), followed by byte 1.
0002h	R/W	DMA channel 1 address byte 0 (low byte), followed by byte 1.
0003h	R/W	DMA channel 1 word count byte 0 (low byte), followed by byte 1.
0004h	R/W	DMA channel 2 address byte 0 (low byte), followed by byte 1.
0005h	R/W	DMA channel 2 word count byte 0 (low byte), followed by byte 1.
0006h	R/W	DMA channel 3 address byte 0 (low byte), followed by byte 1.
0007h	R/W	DMA channel 3 word count byte 0 (low byte), followed by byte 1.
0008h	R	DMA channels 0–3 status register Bit 7 1 Channel 3 request Bit 6 1 Channel 2 request Bit 5 1 Channel 1 request Bit 4 1 Channel 0 request Bit 3 1 Terminal count on channel 3 Bit 2 1 Terminal count on channel 2 Bit 1 1 Terminal count on channel 1 Bit 0 1 Terminal count on channel 0

0008h	W	DMA channels 0–3 command register
		Bit 7 0 DACK sense active low
		          1 DACK sense active high
		Bit 6 0 DREQ sense active low
		          1 DREQ sense active high
		Bit 5 0 Late write selection
		          1 Extended write selection
		Bit 4 0 Fixed priority
		          1 Rotating priority
		Bit 3 0 Normal timing
		          1 Compressed timing
		Bit 2 0 Enable controller
		          1 Disable controller
		Bit 1 0 Disable memory-to-memory transfer
		          1 Enable memory-to-memory transfer
		Bit 0 Reserved

0009h	W	DMA write request register

I/O Port	Read/ Write	Description

000Ah	R/W	DMA channel 0–3 mask register
		Bits 7–3 Reserved
		Bit 2 0 Clear mask bit
		       1 Set mask bit
		Bits 1–0 Channel select
		       00 Channel 0
		       01 Channel 1
		       10 Channel 2
		       11 Channel 3

000Bh	W	DMA channel 0–3 mode register
		Bits 7–6 Mode select
		       00 Demand mode
		       01 Single mode
		       10 Block mode
		       11 Cascade mode
		Bit 5 0 Address increment select
		       1 Address decrement select
		Bit 4 0 Disable autoinitialization
		       1 Enable autoinitialization
		Bits 3–2 Select type of operation
		       00 Verify operation
		       01 Write to memory
		       10 Read from memory
		       11 Reserved
		Bits 1–0 Channel select
		       00 Channel 0
		       01 Channel 1
		       10 Channel 2
		       11 Channel 3

000Ch	W	DMA clear byte pointer flip/flop
000Dh	R	DMA read temporary register
000Eh	W	DMA clear mask register
000Fh	W	DMA write mask register
I/O ports 0020h – 0021h are used by the programmable interrupt controller.		

0020h	W	If bit 4 is set, this is the programmable interrupt controller Initialization Command Word 1 (ICW1).
		Bits 7–5 000 Only used in 8080 or 8085 mode
		Bit 4 1 Using ICW1
		Bit 3 0 Edge-triggered mode
		       1 Level-triggered mode
		Bit 2 0 Successive interrupt vectors separated by eight bytes
		       1 Successive interrupt vectors separated by four bytes
		Bit 1 0 Cascade mode
		       1 Single mode. ICW3 is not necessary
		Bit 0 0 ICW4 is not necessary
		       1 ICW4 is necessary

EISA and ISA I/O Ports, Continued

I/O Port	Read/ Write	Description

0021h	W	This port can represent ICW2, ICW3, and ICW4 in sequence after ICW1 is written to I/O port 0020h.
		
		If ICW2
		Bits 7–3 Address lines A0 – A3 of the base vector address for the interrupt controller.
		Bits 2–0 Reserved (should be zeroes)
		
		If ICW3 for the slave controller (00A1h)
		Bits 7–3 Reserved
		Bits 2–0 Slave ID
		
		If ICW4
		Bits 7–5 Reserved (should be zeroes)
		Bit 4 0 No special fully nested mode
		      1 Special fully nested mode
		Bits 3–2 Mode
		      00 Nonbuffered mode
		      01 Nonbuffered mode
		      10 Buffered mode/slave
		      11 Buffered mode/master
		Bit 1 0 Normal EOI
		      1 Auto EOI
		Bit 0 0 8085 mode
		      1 8086 and 8088 mode

0021h	R/W	Programmable interrupt controller master interrupt mask register — Operation Command Word 3 (OCW1) Bit 7 0 Enable parallel printer interrupt Bit 6 0 Enable floppy disk drive interrupt Bit 5 0 Enable hard disk drive interrupt Bit 4 0 Enable serial port 1 interrupt Bit 3 0 Enable serial port 2 interrupt Bit 2 0 Enable video interrupt Bit 1 0 Enable keyboard/mouse/RTC interrupt Bit 0 0 Enable timer interrupt

0020h	W	If Bits 4 and 3 are 0, Programmable interrupt controller OCW2.
		Bits 7–5 000 Rotate in automatic EOI mode (clear)
		      001 Nonspecific EOI
		      010 No op
		      011 Specific EOI
		      100 Rotate in automatic EOI mode (set)
		      101 Rotate on nonspecific EOI command
		      110 Set priority command
		      111 Rotate on specific EOI command
		Bits 4–3 Reserved (should be zeroes)
		Bits 2–0 The interrupt request to which the command applies

EISA and ISA I/O Ports, Continued

I/O Port	Read/Write	Description

0020h	R	Programmable interrupt controller Interrupt request and In-Service registers programmed by OCW3
		
		Interrupt request register
		Bits 7 – 0 0 No active request for the corresponding interrupt line
		          1 Active request for the corresponding interrupt line
		
		Interrupt in-service register
		Bits 7 – 0 0 The corresponding interrupt line is not being serviced now
		          1 The corresponding interrupt line is being serviced now

0020h	W	If Bit 4 is 0 and Bit 3 is 1, Programmable interrupt controller OCW3
		Bit 7 Reserved (should be zero)
		Bits 6 – 5 00 No op
		          01 No op
		          10 Reset special mask
		          11 Set special mask
		Bit 4 Reserved (should be zero)
		Bit 3 Reserved (One)
		Bit 2 0 No poll command
		          1 Poll command
		Bits 1 – 0 00 No op
		          01 No op
		          10 Read interrupt request register on next read of port 0020h
		          11 Read interrupt in-service register on next read of port 0020h

I/O ports 0040 – 005Fh can be used by the Programmable Interrupt Timer.		
0040h	R/W	Programmable interrupt timer R/W counter 0, keyboard controller channel 0
0041h	R/W	Programmable interrupt time channel 1
0042h	R/W	Programmable interrupt timer miscellaneous register channel 2

0043h	W	Programmable interrupt timer mode port. Control word register for counters 0 and 2
		Bits 7 – 6 00 Counter 0 select
		          01 Counter 1 select
		          10 Counter 2 select
		Bits 5 – 4 00 Counter latch command
		          01 R/W counter bits 7 – 0 only
		          10 R/W counter bits 15 – 8 only
		          11 R/W counter bits 7 – 0 first, then bits 15 – 8.
		Bits 3 – 1 Select mode
		          000 Mode 0 programmable one-shot
		          x10 Mode 1 rate generator
		          x11 Mode 3 square wave generator
		          100 Mode 4 software-triggered strobe
		          101 Mode 5 hardware-triggered strobe
		Bit 0 0 Binary counter is 16 bits
		          1 Binary code decimal (BCD) counter

0044h	W	Programmable interrupt controller miscellaneous register (EISA)y

I/O Port	Read/Write	Description

0047h	W	Programmable interrupt timer Control word register four counter 0 (EISA)
		Bits 7 – 6 00 Counter 0
		          All other values reserved
		Bits 5 – 4 00 Counter latch command select counter 0
		          01 R/W counter bits 7 – 0 only
		          All other values reserved

0048h	R/W	Programmable interrupt Timer

0060h	R	Keyboard controller data port or keyboard input buffer. If Keyboard input buffer (can also be 64h):
		Bit 7 0 Keyboard inhibited
		Bit 6 0 Primary display is VGA
		            1 Primary display is MDA.
		Bit 5 0 System BIOS performs diagnostics on the motherboard in an infinite loop.
		            1 Any other diagnostic function
		Bit 4 Motherboard RAM
		            0 256 KB
		            1 512 KB or greater
		Bits 3 – 1 Reserved
		Bit 0 0 The motherboard passed the diagnostics tests when diagnostic mode was enabled. The LED blinks in manufacturing diagnostic mode.

0060h	W	Keyboard output port (can also be port 64h)
		Bit 7 0 Keyboard data is being transferred
		Bit 6 0 The keyboard clock signal is being used in data transfer
		Bit 5 0 PC-type mouse being used
		            1 PS/2-type mouse being used
		Bit 4 0 Output buffer full, IRQ1 generated
		            1 Output buffer not full
		Bits 3 – 2 Reserved
		Bit 1 0 The system processor address 20 line is inhibited on the system bus.
		            1 Address line 20 is not inhibited
		Bit 0 0 Reset system processor
		            1 This bit should always be kept at 1.

0061h	R	Port B control register (EISA systems) Bit 7 1 Parity check Bit 6 1 Channel check Bit 5 1 Timer 2 output Bit 4 1 Toggles with each refresh request Bit 3 1 Channel check enable Bit 2 1 Parity check enable Bit 1 1 Speaker data enable Bit 0 1 Timer 2 gate to speaker enable
0061h	W	Port B Control register (EISA systems) Bits 7 – 4 Reserved Bit 3 1 Channel check enable Bit 2 1 Parity check enable Bit 1 1 Speaker data enable Bit 0 1 Timer 2 gate to speaker enable

I/O Port	Read/ Write	Description

0064h	R	Keyboard controller read status
		Bit 7 0 No parity error
		          1 Parity error on last byte of transmission from keyboard
		Bit 6 0 No timeout
		          1 Received a timeout on last transmission
		Bit 5 0 No timeout
		          1 Transmission from keyboard controller to keyboard timed
		          out
		Bit 4 0 Keyboard inhibited
		          1 Keyboard not inhibited
		Bit 3 0 Data. System writes to input buffer via I/O port 60h
		          1 Command. System writes to input buffer via I/O port 64h
		Bit 2 System Flag status. Set to 0 after a power on reset. The
		          keyboard controller sets this bit according to the command
		          from the system.
		Bit 1 0 Input buffer (60h or 64h) is empty
		          1 Input buffer full
		Bit 0 0 Output buffer has no data
		          1 Output buffer full

0070h	R	Real Time Clock (CMOS RAM) register and NMI mask Bit 7 1 NMI disabled Bits 6 – 0 0 CMOS RAM index
0071h	R/W	CMOS RAM data register port
0080h	R	Manufacturing test port (POST checkpoints can be accessed via this port).
0080h	R/W	Temporary storage for additional DMA page register
0081h	R/W	DMA channel 2 address byte 2
0082h	R/W	DMA channel 2 address byte 3
0083h	R/W	DMA channel 1 address byte 2
0084h	R/W	Additional DMA page register
0085h	R/W	Additional DMA page register
0086h	R/W	Additional DMA page register
0087h	R/W	DMA channel 0 address byte 2
0088h	R/W	Additional DMA page register
0089h	R/W	DMA channel 6 address byte 2
008Ah	R/W	DMA channel 7 address byte 2
008Bh	R/W	DMA channel 5 address byte 2
008Ch	R/W	Additional DMA page register
008Dh	R/W	Additional DMA page register
008Eh	R/W	Additional DMA page register
008Fh	R/W	DMA refresh page register
00A0h – 00A1h are used for the slave programmable interrupt controller. Except for the differences noted below, the bit definitions are the same as those for addresses 0020h – 0021h.		
00A0h	R/W	Programmable interrupt controller 2

I/O Port	Read/ Write	Description
00A1h	R/W	Programmable interrupt controller 2 mask (OCW1) Bit 7 0 Reserved Bit 6 0 Enable hard disk drive interrupt Bit 5 0 Enable coprocessor exception interrupt Bit 4 0 Enable mouse interrupt Bits 3 – 2 Reserved (should be zeroes) Bit 1 0 Enable redirect cascade Bit 0 0 Enable real time clock interrupt
00C0h	R/W	DMA channel 4 memory address bytes 1 and 0 (low)
00C2h	R/W	DMA channel 4 transfer count bytes 1 and 0 (low)
00C4h	R/W	DMA channel 5 memory address bytes 1 and 0 (low)
00C6h	R/W	DMA channel 5 transfer count bytes 1 and 0 (low byte)
00C8h	R/W	DMA channel 6 memory address bytes 1 and 0 (low byte)
00CAh	R/W	DMA channel 6 transfer count bytes 1 and 0 (low byte)
00CCh	R/W	DMA channel 7 memory address bytes 1 and 0 (low byte)
00CEh	R/W	DMA channel 7 transfer count bytes 1 and 0 (low byte)
00D0h	R	DMA channels 4 – 7 status register Bit 7 1 Channel 7 request Bit 6 1 Channel 6 request Bit 5 1 Channel 5 request Bit 4 1 Channel 4 request Bit 3 1 Terminal count on channel 7 Bit 2 1 Terminal count on channel 6 Bit 1 1 Terminal count on channel 5 Bit 0 1 Terminal count on channel 4

00D0h	W	DMA channel 4 – 7 command register
		Bit 7 0 DACK sense active low
		          1 DACK sense active high
		Bit 6 0 DREQ sense active high
		          1 DREQ sense active low
		Bit 5 0 Late write selection
		          1 Extended write selection
		Bit 4 0 Fixed priority
		          1 Rotating priority
		Bit 3 0 Normal timing
		          1 Compressed timing
		Bit 2 0 Enable controller
		          1 Disable controller
		Bit 1 0 Disable memory-to-memory transfer
		          1 Enable memory-to-memory transfer
		Bit 0 Reserved

00D2h	W	DMA channel 4 – 7 write request register

I/O Port	Read/Write	Description

00D4h	W	DMA channel 4 – 7 write single mask register bit
		Bits 7 – 3 Reserved (should be zeroes)
		Bit 2 0 Clear mask bit
		            1 Set mask bit
		Bits 1 – 0 00 Channel 4 select
		            01 Channel 5 select
		            10 Channel 6 select
		            11 Channel 7 select

00D6h	W	DMA channels 4–7 mode register
		Bits 7 – 6 00 Demand mode
		            01 Single mode
		            10 Block mode
		            11 Cascade mode
		Bit 5 0 Address increment select
		            1 Address decrement select
		Bit 4 0 Disable Autoinitialization
		            1 Enable autoinitialization
		Bits 3 – 2 00 Verify operation
		            01 Write to memory
		            10 Read from memory
		            11 Reserved
		Bits 1 – 0 00 Channel 4 select
		            01 Channel 5 select
		            10 Channel 6 select
		            11 Channel 7 select

00D8h	W	DMA channel 4 – 7 clear byte pointer flip/flop
00DAh	R	DMA channel 4 – 7 read temporary register
00DAh	W	DMA channel 4 – 7 master clear
00DCh	W	DMA channel 4 – 7 clear mask register
00DEh	W	DMA channel 4 – 7 write mask register
00F0h		Math coprocessor clear busy latch
00F1h		Math coprocessor reset
00F28–00FFh	R/W	Math coprocessor
I/O ports 0170h – 0177h are used as a secondary hard disk area. See the definition of I/O ports 01F0 – 01F7h for the bit definitions.		
0170h	R/W	Hard disk 1 data register
0171h	R	Hard disk 1 error register
0171h	W	Hard disk 1 write precompensation register
0172h	R/W	Hard disk 1 sector count
0173h	R/W	Hard disk 1 sector number
0174h	R/W	Hard disk 1 number of cylinders, low byte
0175h	R/W	Hard disk 1 number of cylinders, high byte
0176h	R/W	Hard disk 1 drive/head register
0177h	R	Hard disk 1 status register
0177h	W	Hard disk 1 command register

EISA and ISA I/O Ports, Continued

I/O Port	Read/ Write	Description
01F0h	R/W	Hard disk 0 data register base port

01F1h	R	Hard disk 0 error register
		Diagnostic mode
		Bits 7 – 3 Reserved
		Bits 2 – 0 Diagnostic mode errors
		    001 No errors
		    010 Controller error
		    011 Sector buffer error
		    100 ECC device error
		    101 Control processor error
		Operation mode
		Bit 7 0 Block is not bad
		    1 Bad block detected
		Bit 6 0 No error
		    1 Uncorrectable ECC error
		Bit 5 Reserved
		Bit 4 0 ID not found
		    1 ID found
		Bit 3 Reserved
		Bit 2 0 Command aborted
		    1 Command completed
		Bit 1 0 Track 000 found
		    1 Track 000 not found
		Bit 0 0 DAM found (CP-3002 is always 0)
		    1 DAM not found

01F1h	W	Hard disk 0 write precompensation register
01F2h	R/W	Hard disk 0 sector count
01F3h	R/W	Hard disk 0 sector number
01F4h	R/W	Hard disk 0 number of cylinders, low byte
01F5h	R/W	Hard disk 0 number of cylinders, high byte

01F6h	R/W	Hard disk 0 drive/head register
		Bit 7 1
		Bit 6 0
		Bit 5 1
		Bit 4 Drive select
		    0 first hard disk drive
		    1 Second hard disk drive
		Bits 3 – 0 Head select bits

01F7h	R	Hard disk 0 status register Bit 7 1 Controller is executing a command Bit 6 1 Drive is ready Bit 5 1 Write fault Bit 4 1 Seek complete Bit 3 1 Sector buffer requires servicing Bit 2 1 Disk data read corrected Bit 1 An index. Set to 1 at each disk revolution Bit 0 1 Previous command ended with an error
01F7h	R	Hard disk drive 0 command register

EISA and ISA I/O Ports, Continued

I/O Port	Read/ Write	Description
0200 – 020Fh	R/W	Game controller ports
0201h	R/W	Game port I/O data
020C – 020Dh		Reserved for special use by AMIBIOS.
021Fh		Reserved for special use by AMIBIOS.
0278 – 027Fh		Parallel port 2. See the descriptions of I/O ports 0378h – 037Ah for the parallel port bit definitions.
02E8h – 02EFh		Serial port 4. See the descriptions of I/O ports 03F8h – 03FFh for the serial port bit definitions.
02F8 – 02FFh		Serial port 2. See the descriptions of I/O ports 03F8h – 03FFh for the serial port bit definitions.
0300 – 031Fh		Prototype card
0364 – 0367h		Reserved for special use by AMIBIOS.
036C – 036Fh		Reserved for special use by AMIBIOS.
I/O ports 0372h – 0377h are used for the secondary floppy disk controller. See the definitions of I/O ports 03F2h – 03F7h for the bit definitions.		
0372h	W	Floppy disk controller 2 digital output register
0374h	R	Floppy disk controller 2 status register
0375h	R/W	Floppy disk controller 2 data register
0376h	R/W	Floppy disk controller 2 control register
0377h	R	Floppy disk controller 2 digital input register
0377h	W	Select register for floppy disk data transfer rate
0378h	R/W	Parallel port 1 data port
0379h	R/W	Parallel port 1 status port Bit 7 0 Busy Bit 6 0 Acknowledge Bit 5 1 Out of paper Bit 4 1 Printer is selected Bit 3 0 Error Bit 2 0 IRQ occurred Bits 1 – 0 Reserved
037Ah	R/W	Parallel port 1 control port Bits 7 – 5 Reserved Bit 4 1 Enable IRQ Bit 3 1 Select printer Bit 2 0 Initialize printer Bit 1 1 Automatic line feed Bit 0 1 Strobe

EISA and ISA I/O Ports, Continued

I/O Port	Read/ Write	Description
037Bh	R/W	Hercules configuration switch registers Bits 7 – 2 Not used Bit 1 0 Disable upper 32 KB of graphics mode buffer 1 Enable upper 32 KB of graphics mode buffer at B800:0000h Bit 0 0 Disable graphics mode
03B0– 03B3h	R/W	Video registers. See the Video I/O Port tables on page 153 for more information about video I/O ports.
03B4h	R/W	MDA CRTC index register
03B5h	R/W	MDA CRTC data registers
03B8h	R/W	MDA mode control register
03BCh – 03BFh		Parallel port 3. See the descriptions of I/O ports 0378h – 037Ah for the parallel port bit definitions.
03C0 – 03CFh		EGA and VGA video subsystem
03C2h	R	CGA input status register
03C3h	R/W	Video subsystem enable
03C4h	R/W	CGA sequencer index register
03C5h	R/W	Other CGA sequencer registers
03CAh	R	CGA feature control register
03D4h	W	Video CRTC index register
03D5h	W	Other CRTC registers
03D8h	R/W	CGA mode control register
03D9h	R/W	CGA palette register
03E8 – 03EFh		Serial port 3. See the descriptions of I/O ports 03F8h – 03FFh for the serial port bit definitions.
03F2h	W	Floppy disk controller digital output register Bits 7 – 6 Reserved. Should be zero. Bit 5 1 Enable motor on floppy drive 1 Bit 4 1 Enable motor on floppy drive 0 Bit 3 1 Enable DMA for floppy drives Bit 2 0 Controller reset Bit 1 Reserved. Should be zero. Bit 0 0 Select floppy drive 0 1 Select floppy drive 1
03F4h	R	Floppy disk controller status register Bit 7 1 data register is ready Bit 6 0 Transfer from system to controller 1 Transfer from controller to system Bit 5 1 Non-DMA mode Bit 4 1 Floppy disk controller busy Bits 3 – 2 Reserved Bit 1 1 Drive 1 is busy Bit 0 1 Drive 0 is busy
03F5h	R/W	Floppy disk controller data register

I/O Port	Read/ Write	Description
03F6h	R	Floppy disk controller control port Bits 7 – 4 Reserved Bit 3　　　0 Reduce write current 　　　　　1 Head select enable Bit 2　　　0 Disable floppy disk reset 　　　　　1 Enable floppy disk reset Bit 1　　　0 Enable floppy disk initialization 　　　　　1 Disable floppy disk initialization Bit 0　　　Reserved
03F7h	R	Floppy disk controller input register. Bits 7 – 1 apply to the floppy drive that is currently selected. Bit 7　　　1 Floppy disk change line Bit 6　　　1 Write gate Bit 5　　　Head select 3/Reduced write current Bit 4　　　Head select 2 Bit 3　　　Head select 1 Bit 2　　　Head select 0 Bit 1　　　Select drive 1 Bit 0　　　Select drive 0
03F7h	W	Floppy disk controller select register for data transfer rate Bits 7 – 2 Reserved Bits 1 – 0 00 500 Kbs mode 　　　　　01 300 Kbs mode 　　　　　00 250 kbs mode
03F8h	W	Transmitter Holding Register (contains the character to be sent). Bit 0, the least significant bit, is sent first. Bits 7 – 0 Contains data bits 7 – 0 when the Divisor Latch Access Bit 　　　　　(DLAB) is 0.
03F8h	R	Receiver Buffer Register (contains the received character). Bit 0, the least significant bit, is received first. Bits 7 – 0 Contains data bits 7 – 0 when the Divisor Latch Access Bit 　　　　　(DLAB) is 0.
03F8h	R/W	Divisor Latch, low byte Both divisor latch registers store the data transmission rate divisor. Bits 7 – 0 Bits 7 – 0 of divisor when DLAB is 1.
03F9h	R/W	Divisor Latch, high byte. Bits 7 – 0 Bits 15 – 8 of data transmission rate divisor when DLAB is 1.
03F9h	R/W	Interrupt Enable Register. Permits the serial port controller interrupts to enable the chip interrupt output signal. Bits 7 – 4 Reserved Bit 3　　　Modem status interrupt enable if set. Bit 2　　　Receiver line status interrupt enable if set. Bit 1　　　Transmitter Holding register empty interrupt enable if set. Bit 0　　　Received data available interrupt enable when DLAB is 0 if 　　　　　set.

I/O Port	Read/ Write	Description

03FAh	R	Interrupt ID Register. Information about a pending interrupt is stored here. When the ID register is addressed, the highest priority interrupt is held and no other interrupts are acknowledged until the microprocessor services that interrupt.
		Bits 7 – 3 Reserved
		Bits 2 – 1 The pending interrupt that has the highest priority.
		    11 Receiver Line Status Interrupt, priority is the highest.
		    10 Received Data Available, second in priority.
		    01 Transmitter Holding Register Empty, third in priority.
		    00 Modem Status Interrupt, fourth in priority.
		Bit 0 Interrupt pending if set to logical 0. If logical 1, no interrupt is pending.

03FBh	R/W	Line Control Register
		Bit 7 Divisor Latch Access Bit (DLAB)
		    0 Access receiver buffer, transmitter holding register, and interrupt enable register.
		    1 Access Divisor Latch of baud rate generator.
		Bit 6 Set Break Control. Serial output is forced to spacing state and remains there if set.
		Bit 5 Stick Parity.
		Bit 4 Even Parity Select.
		Bit 3 Parity Enable.
		Bit 2 Number of Stop Bits per Character.
		    0 One stop bit.
		    1 1½ stop bits if 5-bit word length is selected.
		    2 stop bits if 6, 7, or 8-bit word length is selected.
		Bits 1 – 0 Number of Lines per character
		    00 5-Bit word length.
		    01 6-Bit word length.
		    10 7-Bit word length.
		    11 8-Bit word length.

03FCh	R/W	Modem Control Register Bits 7 – 5 Reserved Bit 4 Loopback mode for diagnostic testing of serial port if set. The output from the transmitter shift register is looped back to the receiver shift register input. Transmitted data is immediately received so the microprocessor can verify the transmit and receive data serial port paths. Bit 3 Force OUT2 interrupt if set. Bit 2 Force OUT1 active if set. Bit 1 Force Request To Send active if set. Bit 0 Force Data Terminal Ready active if set.

I/O Port	Read/ Write	Description
03FDh	R	Line Status Register Bit 7 Reserved Bit 6 Transmitter shift and holding registers empty if set. Bit 5 Transmitter holding register empty if set. The controller is ready to accept a new character to send. Bit 4 Break interrupt if set. The received data input is held in the zero bit state longer than the transmission time of the start bit + data bits + parity bits + stop bits. Bit 3 Framing error if set. The stop bit that follows the last parity or data bit is zero. Bit 2 Parity error if set. The character has incorrect parity. Bit 1 Overrun error if set. A character was sent to the receiver buffer before the previous character in the buffer could be read, which destroys the previous character. Bit 0 Data Ready if set. A complete incoming character has been received and sent to the receiver buffer register.
03FEh	R	Modem Status Register Bit 7 Data Carrier Detect if set. Bit 6 Ring Indicator if set. Bit 5 Data Set Ready if set. Bit 4 Clear To Send if set. Bit 3 Delta Data Carrier Detect if set. Bit 2 Trailing Edge Ring Indicator if set. Bit 1 Delta Data Set Ready if set. Bit 0 Delta Clear To Send if set.
03FFh	R/W	Serial port 1 scratch register
I/O ports 0401h – 04D6h are only used by EISA systems.		
0401h	R/W	DMA channel 0 word count byte 2, high byte
0403h	R/W	DMA channel 1 word count byte 2, high byte
0405h	R/W	DMA channel 2 word count byte 2, high byte
0407h	R/W	DMA channel 3 word count byte 2, high byte

040Ah	W	Extended DMA chaining mode register, channels 0 – 3
		Bits 7 – 5 Reserved
		Bit 4 0 Generate IRQ13
		            1 Generate terminal count
		Bit 3 0 Do not start chaining
		            1 Programming complete
		Bit 2 0 Disable buffer chaining mode (default value)
		            1 Enable buffer chaining mode
		Bits 1 – 0 DMA channel select
		            00 Channel 0
		            01 Channel 1
		            10 Channel 2
		            11 Channel 3

040Ah	R	Channel interrupt (IRQ13) status register Bits 7 – 5 Interrupt on channels 7 – 5 Bit 4 Reserved Bits 3 – 0 Interrupt on channels 3 – 0

I/O Port	Read/ Write	Description

040Bh	W	DMA extended mode register for channels 0 – 3
		Bit 7 0 Enable stop register
		Bit 6 0 Terminal count is an output for this channel (default)
		Bits 5 – 4 DMA cycle timing
		           00 ISA-compatible (default)
		           01 Type A timing mode
		           10 Type B timing mode
		           11 DMA burst mode
		Bits 3 – 2 Address mode
		           00 8-bit I/O, count by bytes (default)
		           01 16-bit I/O, count by words, address-shifted
		           10 32-bit I/O, count by bytes
		           11 16-bit I/O, count by bytes
		Bits 1 – 0 DMA channel select

0461h	R/W	Extended NMI status and control register
		Bit 7 1 NI pending from fail-safe timer (read only)
		Bit 6 1 NMI pending from bus timeout NMI status (read only)
		Bit 5 1 NMI pending (read only)
		Bit 4 Reserved
		Bit 3 1 Bus timeout NMI enable (R/W)
		Bit 2 1 Fail-safe NMI enable (R/W)
		Bit 1 1 NMI I/O port enable (R/W)
		Bit 0 RSTDRV. Bus reset (R/W)
		           0 Normal bus reset
		           1 Reset bus asserted

0462h	W	Software NMI register. Writing to this register causes an NMI if NMIs are enabled.
0464h	R	Bus master status latch enable register (slots 1 – 8). Identifies the last bus master to control the bus. Bit 7 0 Slot 8 Bit 6 0 Slot 7 Bit 5 0 Slot 6 Bit 4 0 Slot 5 Bit 3 0 Slot 4 Bit 2 0 Slot 3 Bit 1 0 Slot 2 Bit 0 0 Slot 1
0465h	R	Bus master status latch enable register (slots 9 – 16). Identifies the last bus master to control the bus. Bit 7 0 Slot 16 Bit 6 0 Slot 15 Bit 5 0 Slot 14 Bit 4 0 Slot 13 Bit 3 0 Slot 12 Bit 2 0 Slot 11 Bit 1 0 Slot 10 Bit 0 0 Slot 9
0481h	R/W	DMA channel 3 address byte 3, high byte
0483h	R/W	DMA channel 2 address byte 3, high byte
0485h	R/W	DMA channel 1 address byte 3, high byte

I/O Port	Read/ Write	Description
0487h	R/W	DMA channel 0 address byte 3, high byte
0489h	R/W	DMA channel 6 address byte 3, high byte
048Bh	R/W	DMA channel 7 address byte 3, high byte
048Dh	R/W	DMA channel 5 address byte 3, high byte
04C6h	R/W	DMA channel 5 word count byte 2, high byte
04CAh	R/W	DMA channel 6 word count byte 2, high byte
04CEh	R/W	DMA channel 7 word count byte 2, high byte
04D0h	W	IRQ0 – IRQ7 interrupt edge/level registers Bit 7 1 IRQ7 is level-sensitive Bit 6 1 IRQ6 is level-sensitive Bit 5 1 IRQ5 is level-sensitive Bit 4 1 IRQ4 is level-sensitive Bit 3 1 IRQ3 is level-sensitive Bits 2 – 0 Reserved
04D1h	W	IRQ8 – IRQ15 interrupt edge/level registers Bit 7 1 IRQ15 is level-sensitive Bit 6 1 IRQ14 is level-sensitive Bit 5 Reserved Bit 4 1 IRQ12 is level-sensitive Bit 3 1 IRQ11 is level-sensitive Bit 2 1 IRQ10 is level-sensitive Bit 1 1 IRQ9 is level-sensitive Bit 0 Reserved
04D4h	R	Chaining mode status register Bits 7 – 5 1 Enable Channels 7 – 5 Bit 4 Reserved Bits 3 – 0 1 Enable Channels 3 – 0

04D4h	W	Extended DMA chaining mode register, channels 7 – 4
		Bits 7 – 5 Reserved
		Bit 4 0 Generate IRQ13
		         1 Generate terminal count
		Bit 3 0 Do not start chaining
		         1 Programming complete
		Bit 2 0 Disable buffer chaining mode (default value)
		Bits 1 – 0 Select DMA channel
		         00 Channel 4
		         01 Channel 5
		         10 Channel 6
		         11 Channel 7

04D6h	W	DMA extended mode register for channels 7 – 4. See I/O port 040Bh for the bit settings.
0500h – 07FFh		A copy of all I/O port assignments from 0110h – 03FFh is placed here in EISA systems.
0800h– 08FFh	R/W	I/O port access registers for EISA CMOS RAM
0900h – 0BFFh		A copy of all I/O port assignments from 0110h – 03FFh is placed here in EISA systems.
0C00h	R/W	Page register to write to SRAM or I/O

EISA and ISA I/O Ports, Continued

I/O Port	Read/Write	Description
0C80h	R/W	EISA motherboard ID Bit 7 Reserved. Should be zero. Bits 6 – 2 First letter of manufacturer code. Bits 1 – 0 First two bits of second letter of manufacturer code
0C81h	R/W	EISA motherboard ID Bits 7 – 5 Remaining 3 bits of second letter of manufacturer code. Bits 4 – 0 Third letter of manufacturer code.
0C82h	R/W	EISA motherboard ID Bits 7 – 0 Reserved for use by manufacturer. Often used for manufacturer's product number. American Megatrends EISA motherboards have the serial number in BCD.
0C83h	R/W	EISA motherboard ID Bits 7 – 3 Product Revision Number assigned by EISA motherboard manufacturer. Bits 2 – 0 EISA Bus Version (initial version is 001) 001 is currently the only standard value defined for this field, but, in practice, EISA motherboard and adapter card manufacturers have been using this field. In American Megatrends EISA motherboards: Bits 7 – 4 EISA Configuration file revision number Bit 3 Reserved Bits 2 – 0 EISA bus version
0C84h	R/W	American Megatrends EISA Motherboard ID data Bits 7 – 3 Schematic release (for internal use only) Bits 2 – 0 PCB release (for internal use only)
0C85h	R/W	American Megatrends EISA Motherboard ID data CPU speed in MHz (in BCD)
0D00h – 0FFFh		A copy of all I/O port assignments from 0110h – 03FFh is placed here in EISA systems.
EISA Adapter Card Ports		
In the following rows, *n* can be 1h – Fh and represents EISA expansion slots 1 – 15.		
*n*000 – *n*0FFh		EISA expansion slot *n*.
*n*100 – *n*3FFh		A copy of all I/O port assignments from 0100h – 03FFh.
*n*4000 – *n*4FFh		EISA expansion slot *n*.
*n*500 – *n*7FFh		A copy of all I/O port assignments from 0100h – 03FFh.
*n*800 – *n*8FFh		EISA expansion slot *n*.
*n*900 – *n*BFFh		A copy of all I/O port assignments from 0100h – 03FFh.
*n*C00 – *n*CFFh		EISA expansion slot *n*.
*n*D00 – *n*FFFh		A copy of all I/O port assignments from 0100h – 03FFh.

EISA and ISA I/O Ports, Continued

I/O Port	Read/ Write	Description
n000 – n0FFh		EISA expansion slot n.
n100 – n3FFh		A copy of all I/O port assignments from 0100h – 03FFh.
n4000 – n4FFh		EISA expansion slot n.
n500 – n7FFh		A copy of all I/O port assignments from 0100h – 03FFh.
n800 – n8FFh		EISA expansion slot n.
n900 – nBFFh		A copy of all I/O port assignments from 0100h – 03FFh.
nC00 – nCFFh		EISA expansion slot n.
nD00 – nFFFh		A copy of all I/O port assignments from 0100h – 03FFh.

EISA Adapter Card Compressed ID

I/O Port	Description of Contents
nC80h	Bit 7 Reserved, should be zero. Bits 6 – 2 First letter of manufacturer code. Bits 1 – 0 First two bits of second letter of manufacturer code.
nC81h	Bits 7 – 5 Remaining 3 bits of second letter of manufacturer code. Bits 4 – 0 Third letter of manufacturer code.
nC82h	Bits 7 – 4 First hex digit of product number. Bits 3 – 0 Second hex digit of product number.
nC83h	Bits 7 – 4 First hex digit of revision number. Bits 3 – 0 Second hex digit of revision number.

nC84h	EISA Adapter Card Control Register
	Bits 7 – 3 Reserved, should be zero.
	Bit 2 IOCHKRST (write/only)
	      0 Normal Operation.
	      1 Reset the adapter card after sending an Active High Pulse.
	Bit 1 IOCHKERR (read/only)
	      0 No I/O error pending.
	      1 I/O error detected by adapter card.
	Bit 0 ENABLE (Read/Write)
	      0 Adapter Card Disable.
	      1 Adapter Card Enable.

Video I/O Ports

Some I/O devices (such as the video controllers) also use system memory addresses as well as their assigned I/O port addresses. This technique (memory-mapped I/O) makes the microprocessor think that the devices are part of system memory. Memory-mapped devices are easier to program because they permit more flexible memory instructions. The following table describes the video ports used in the MDA and CGA video standard. The EGA, VGA, Super VGA, and XGA video standards use I/O ports much more extensively, but since the system BIOS does not perform EGA, VGA, or XGA video, they are not discussed here.

MDA I/O Ports

The 6845 CRTC index register is mapped to I/O port 03B4h. The value in port 03B4h controls the register that appears at I/O port 03B5h. The 6845 mode control register is accessed directly via I/O port 03B8h.

I/O Port	Read/ Write	Description
03B4h	W	CRTC index register
03B5h	W	Index 00h Horizontal total
		Index 01h Horizontal displayed
		Index 02h Horizontal sync position
		Index 03h Horizontal sync pulse width
		Index 04h Vertical total
		Index 05h Vertical displayed
		Index 06h Vertical sync position
		Index 07h Vertical sync pulse width
		Index 08h Interlace mode
		Index 09h Maximum scan lines
		Index 0Ah Cursor start
		Index 0Bh Cursor end
		Index 0Ch Start address, high byte
		Index 0Dh Start address, low byte
		Index 0Eh Cursor location, high byte
		Index 0Fh Cursor location, low byte
		Index 10h Light pen, high byte
		Index 11h Light pen, low byte
03B8h	W	Mode control register
03BAh	R	CRT status register

CGA I/O Ports

The 6845 CRTC index register is mapped to I/O port 03D4h. The value
written to 03D4h controls the register that appears in port 03D5h.

I/O Port	Read/ Write	Description	
03D4h	W	CRTC index register	
03D5h	W	Index 00h	Horizontal total
		Index 01h	Horizontal displayed
		Index 02h	Horizontal sync position
		Index 03h	Horizontal sync pulse width
		Index 04h	Vertical total
		Index 05h	Vertical displayed
		Index 06h	Vertical sync position
		Index 07h	Vertical sync pulse width
		Index 08h	Interleaved mode
		Index 09h	Maximum scan lines
		Index 0Ah	Cursor start
		Index 0Bh	Cursor end
		Index 0Ch	Start address, high byte
		Index 0Dh	Start address, low byte
		Index 0Eh	Cursor location, high byte
		Index 0Fh	Cursor location, low byte
		Index 10h	Light pen, high byte
		Index 11h	Light pen, low byte
03D8h	W	Mode control register	
03D9h	W	Palette register	
03DAh	R	CRT status register	
03DBh	W	Clear light pen latch	
03DCh	W	Preset light pen latch	

Chapter 10

Power On Self Test

The first routine that executes in the system BIOS is called the Power On Self Test (POST). POST must execute before any ISA or EISA system can be used.

POST performs diagnostic tests on system memory and key system components. It also initializes BIOS configuration tables. It then boots the operating system.

Starting POST

POST begins in one of several different ways:

Starting POST	What the BIOS Does
Turn the system on.	Jumps to the address pointed to by the processor reset vector (FFFF0h). All POST tests and initializations are then executed. If successful, POST calls INT 19h Bootstrap Loader.
Press the reset button.	Jumps to the address pointed to by the processor reset vector (FFFF0h). All POST tests and initializations are then executed. If successful, POST calls INT 19h Bootstrap Loader.
Press CTRL ALT DEL.	The INT 09h keyboard hardware interrupt service transfers control to POST. POST does not test memory above 64 KB, but all other tests and initializations are performed. POST then calls INT 19h Bootstrap Loader.

POST Functions

Before POST Enables the NMI

NMI and I/O checks are disabled by POST when it begins execution. Before the NMI is enabled, the BIOS POST:

1. Writes data in all motherboard and I/O adapter memory locations to establish that parity is good at all locations.

2. Enables the onboard and 32-bit slot memory parity checks by writing to I/O port 0061h with data bit 2 set to zero.

3. Enables the I/O channel check signal by writing to I/O Port 61h with data bit 3 set to zero.

POST Diagnostic Tests

POST usually performs the following tests in the following order. In some BIOS, the tests are performed in a slightly different sequence. Additional tests and initializations are performed in some BIOS. The errors that can be generated are listed below.

If 0Fh at CMOS RAM location 0Fh (Shutdown Byte) is 00h, POST performs all tests and initializations.

Processor Register Test

The following values are loaded consecutively into all registers: 0555h, 0AAAh, 0CCCh, and 0F0Fh. If any register does not retain any of these values, Beep Code 5 is issued.

ROM BIOS Checksum Test

A checksum is performed on the system BIOS. If it is incorrect, Beep Code 9 is issued.

POST Diagnostics, Continued

Keyboard Controller Test

The BIOS issues a keyboard controller BAT command. If the response is not 55h, Beep Code 6 is issued.

CMOS Shutdown Register Test

The BIOS writes the values 55h, then AAh to 0Fh in CMOS RAM. *CMOS not operational* is displayed and the system halts and must be rebooted if this test fails. The battery probably should be replaced if this test fails.

System Timer Test

The *CH-1 timer error* or *CH-2 timer error* is displayed if this test fails on channel 1 or 2 of the timer. Beep Code 4 is issued if timer channel 1 does not work.

Memory Refresh Test

Timer channels 0 and 1 are tested. Beep Code 1 is issued if either channel does not work.

Base 64 KB Test

An address test, sequential read/write, and random read/write test are performed on the first 64 KB of RAM. Beep Code 3 is issued if any errors, including parity errors, occur.

Cache Memory Test

Memory reads are performed with secondary cache memory enabled. Then memory reads are performed with secondary cache memory disabled. If cache is not performing as expected, *Cache Memory bad, do not enable cache* is displayed.

cont'd

CMOS RAM Battery Test

POST reads the CMOS RAM status register (40:8Dh) to see if the battery is on. POST reads CMOS diagnostic data. POST then calculates the CMOS RAM checksums. The following error messages may be generated: *CMOS battery state low, CMOS system option not set*, or *CMOS checksum error.*

Display Verification

POST does a vertical and horizontal retrace and a sequential read and write of 4 KB in different display modes. Beep Code 8 is issued if there is any error. Other messages that may be issued are: *Display switch setting not proper* or *CMOS display type mismatch.*

Enter Protected Mode

This test issues INT 15h Function 89h. *8042 Gate-A20 error, system halted* is displayed if POST does not successfully switch to protected mode.

Address Line Test

A test pattern is written to both conventional and extended memory. Beep Code 3 is issued if any error occurs.

Conventional and Extended Memory Test

Zeros are written to extended and conventional memory unless ESC is pressed. Sequential and random read/write tests are performed. A running count of the amount of memory tested is displayed. Beep Code 3 or 7 is issued if there are errors.

DMA Controller Test

Several patterns are written to DMA page registers 80h through 8Fh and then DMA registers 0 through 7. The following errors may be generated: *DMA error, system halted, DMA #1 error, system halted*, or *DMA #2 error, system halted.*

Keyboard Test

The keyboard self-test command is issued. A stuck key check is performed. The keyboard interface test is then performed. Possible errors are *Keyboard error* or *KB/Interface error*.

System Configuration Verification

The floppy and hard disk areas are initialized and a Seek command is performed on floppy drive A: or hard disk drive C:. Possible errors are *FDD controller failure, HDD controller error, C: drive failure,* or *D: drive failure*.

The memory size is verified. *CMOS memory size mismatch* is generated if there is an error.

Adaptor ROMs are checked and the timer data area is initialized. Possible errors include: *CMOS time & date not set*.

The parallel and serial ports are configured. *Keyboard is locked* is displayed if the keyboard is locked.

AMIBIOS POST Checkpoint Codes

POST routines are performed by the BIOS each time the system is reset or rebooted. POST routines perform diagnostic tests on many system components and initialize key system peripherals and components.

Each time a POST routine is completed, a POST Checkpoint Code is written to I/O port address 0080h. You can display this code by attaching diagnostic equipment, such as the American Megatrends Diagnostic Kit, to this I/O port.

A list of the AMIBIOS POST Checkpoint Codes that can be displayed via I/O address 0080h follows. Appendix E contains a list of POST checkpoint codes for older AMIBIOS products.

cont'd

ISA AMIBIOS POST Checkpoint Codes

The following ISA and EISA AMIBIOS checkpoint codes are valid for a generic AMIBIOS. However, it is a common practice to customize an AMIBIOS for a specific manufacturer. The checkpoint codes are often modified and new checkpoint codes are often added. This list is not all-inclusive. It is not possible to make an all-inclusive list.

Code	Description
01h	Processor register test about to start. The NMI is disabled next.
02h	The NMI is disabled. The Power-On delay is starting.
03h	Power-On delay has been completed. Initializations required before the keyboard BAT is done are now in progress.
04h	The initializations required before the keyboard BAT are completed. Reading the keyboard SYS bit to check for soft reset or power-on next.
05h	The soft reset or power-on setting has been determined. Next, enabling the ROM and disabling shadow RAM and Cache Memory, if any.
06h	ROM is enabled. Calculating the ROM BIOS checksum and waiting for the keyboard controller input buffer to be free.
07h	The ROM BIOS checksum test passed and the keyboard controller input buffer is free. Issuing a BAT command to the keyboard controller next.
08h	A BAT command has been issued to the keyboard controller. Verifying the BAT command next.
09h	The keyboard controller BAT result was verified. A keyboard controller command byte is to be written next.
0Ah	A keyboard controller command byte code has been issued. Writing the command byte data next.
0Bh	The keyboard controller command byte has been written. Issuing the Pin 23, 24 blocking and unblocking command next.
0Ch	Pin 23, 24 of the keyboard controller has been blocked and unblocked. The keyboard controller NOP command is issued next.
0Dh	The keyboard controller NOP command processing is done. The CMOS RAM shutdown register test is performed next.
0Eh	The CMOS RAM shutdown register Read/Write test passed. Calculating the CMOS RAM checksum and updating the DIAG byte next.
0Fh	The CMOS RAM checksum calculation is done and the DIAG byte is written. CMOS RAM initialization begins next if CMOS RAM is to be initialized during every boot.
10h	CMOS RAM initialization (if any) is done. Next, the CMOS RAM status register is initialized for Date and Time.
11h	The CMOS RAM status register has been initialized. Disabling the DMA and interrupt controllers next.
12h	DMA controllers 1 and 2 and interrupt controllers 1 and 2 are disabled. Disabling the video display and initializing port B next.

Code	Description
13h	The video display is disabled and port B is initialized. Chipset initialization and auto memory detection are about to begin.
14h	Chipset initialization and auto memory detection are done. The 8254 Channel 2 timer test is about to start.
15h	The 8254 Channel 2 timer test is half-completed. The entire 8254 Channel 2 timer test is completed next.
16h	The entire 8254 Channel 2 timer test is done. The 8254 Channel 1 timer test is done next.
17h	The 8254 Channel 1 timer test is done. The 8254 Channel 0 timer test is completed next.
18h	The 8254 Channel 0 timer test is done. About to start memory refresh.
19h	Memory refresh has been started. The memory refresh test is performed next.
1Ah	The memory refresh line is toggling. Checking the 15 μsecond ON/OFF time next.
1Bh	The memory refresh test has been completed. The base 64 KB memory test is about to start.
20h	The base 64 KB memory test has been started. The address line test is to be done next.
21h	The address line test passed. Toggling parity next.
22h	The parity toggle has been completed. Performing a sequential data read/write test next.
23h	The base 64 KB sequential data read/write test passed. Performing any necessary system initialization before interrupt vector initialization.
24h	The system configuration required before vector initialization has been completed. Interrupt vector initialization is about to begin.
25h	Interrupt vector initialization is done. Reading the input port of the 8042 for the turbo switch setting (if any).
26h	The input port of the 8042 has been read. Initializing global data for the turbo switch.
27h	Global data initialization is done. Initialization after the interrupt vector initialization will be done next.
28h	Initialization after interrupt vector initialization is completed. Setting monochrome mode next.
29h	Monochrome mode is set. Setting color mode next.
2Ah	Color mode is set. Toggling parity before the optional Video ROM test next.
2Bh	Parity toggle completed. About to do any system initialization required before the video ROM check.
2Ch	Initialization before video ROM control is done. Looking for video ROM next. Control passed to video ROM next.
2Dh	The video ROM check is done. Next, do processing after the video ROM returns control.
2Eh	Finished processing after the video ROM had control. If an EGA or VGA adapter is not found, the display memory read/write test is next.
2Fh	No EGA or VGA adapter has been found. The display memory read/write test is about to begin.
30h	The display memory read/write test passed. About to look for retrace check.
31h	The display memory read/write test or retrace check failed. About to perform the alternate display memory read/write test.
32h	The alternate display memory read/write test passed. About to look for alternate display retrace checking.

Code	Description
33h	The video display check is completed. Verification of the display type with switch setting and the actual adapter card is next.
34h	Verification of the display adapter is done. The display mode is set next.
35h	The display mode has been set. The BIOS ROM data area is about to be checked.
36h	The BIOS ROM data area check is completed. Setting the cursor for the Power-On message next.
37h	Cursor setting for the Power-On message is done. Displaying the Power-On message next.
38h	The Power-On message has been displayed. Reading the new cursor position next.
39h	The new cursor position has been read and saved. Displaying the BIOS Identification String next.
3Ah	The BIOS Identification String has been displayed. Displaying the "Hit <DEL>..." message next.
3Bh	The "Hit <DEL>..." message has been displayed. The virtual mode memory test is about to start.
40h	Preparing the virtual mode test. Verifying from display memory next.
41h	Returned to POST after verifying from display memory. Preparing the descriptor tables next.
42h	The descriptor tables have been prepared. Entering virtual mode for the memory test next.
43h	Entered virtual mode. Enabling interrupts for diagnostics mode next.
44h	Interrupts are enabled if the diagnostics switch is on. Initializing data to check the memory wraparound at 0:0h next.
45h	Data has been initialized for the memory wraparound check. Checking for memory wraparound at 0:0h and finding the total system memory size next.
46h	The memory wraparound test has been done. The memory size calculation has been done. About to write memory test patterns.
47h	The memory test patterns were written to extended memory. Writing patterns in conventional memory (first 640 KB) next.
48h	The patterns to be tested were written to conventional memory. Finding the amount of memory below 1 MB next.
49h	The amount of memory below 1 MB was found and verified. Finding the amount of memory above 1 MB next.
4Ah	The amount of memory above 1 MB was found and verified. Performing the BIOS ROM data area check next.
4Bh	The BIOS ROM data area check is done. Checking the DEL key status and clearing the memory below 1 MB for a soft reset next.
4Ch	The memory below 1 MB has been cleared via a soft reset. Clearing the memory above 1 MB next.
4Dh	The memory above 1 MB has been cleared via a soft reset. Saving the memory size next.
4Eh	The memory test has started. No soft reset was performed. About to display the first 64 KB memory test.
4Fh	The memory size display has started. This display is updated during the memory test. Running the sequential and random memory test next.

Code	Description
50h	The test of memory below 1 MB completed. Adjusting the memory size for relocation and shadowing next.
51h	The memory size has been adjusted for memory relocation above 1 MB and shadowing options. The test of memory above 1 MB is next.
52h	The test of memory above 1 MB has completed. Preparing for real mode next.
53h	The CPU registers have been saved, including the memory size. Entering real mode next.
54h	Shutdown was successful and the CPU is in real mode. Restoring the registers saved during preparation for shutdown next.
55h	The registers have been restored. Disabling the Gate A20 address line next.
56h	The Gate A20 address line was disabled successfully. Checking the BIOS ROM data area next.
57h	The BIOS ROM data area check is partially completed. Completing the BIOS ROM data area check next.
58h	The BIOS ROM data area check has completed. Clearing the "Hit Del" message next.
59h	The "Hit Del" message has been cleared. About to start the DMA and interrupt controller tests.
60h	The DMA page register test passed. About to verify display memory.
61h	The display memory verification test is done. About to perform the DMA Controller 1 base register test.
62h	The DMA Controller 1 base register test passed. Performing the DMA Controller 2 base register test next.
63h	The DMA Controller 2 base register test passed. Performing the BIOS ROM data area check next.
64h	The BIOS ROM data area check is partially done. The BIOS ROM data area check is completed next.
65h	The BIOS ROM data area check is done. Programming DMA Controllers 1 and 2 next.
66h	DMA Controller 1 and 2 programming was completed. Initializing the 8259 interrupt controller next.
67h	The 8259 initialization is done. Starting the keyboard test next.
80h	The keyboard test has started. Issuing the keyboard reset command next and clearing the output buffer.
81h	The keyboard reset command completed successfully. Next, checking for stuck keys and issuing the interface test command if there was an error.
82h	The keyboard controller interface test is done. About to write a command byte and initialize the circular buffer.
83h	The command byte has been written and the global data initialization is done. About to check for locked keys.
84h	Locked key checking is done. About to check for a memory size mismatch with CMOS RAM data.
85h	The memory size check has been completed. About to display a soft error and check for password or bypass Setup.
86h	The password has been checked. About to do programming before Setup.
87h	The programming before Setup has been completed. Calling the BIOS Setup program next.

Code	Description
88h	Returned from the BIOS Setup program and cleared the screen. Programming after Setup.
89h	The programming after Setup is completed. Displaying the Power-On screen message next.
8Ah	The first screen message has been displayed. About to display the "Wait..." message.
8Bh	The "Wait..." message has been displayed. About to perform system and video BIOS shadowing.
8Ch	System and video BIOS shadowing was successful. About to perform Setup options programming after Standard CMOS Setup.
8Dh	The Setup options are programmed. The mouse check and initialization is done next.
8Eh	The mouse check and initialization is done. Checking the floppy disk next.
8Fh	The floppy disk check indicated that the floppy drive needs to be initialized. Floppy drive configuration is next.
90h	Floppy drive configuration has completed. The test for the presence of a hard disk drive is next.
91h	The hard disk presence test has completed. Hard disk configuration is next.
92h	Hard disk configuration has completed. Checking the BIOS ROM data area next.
93h	The BIOS ROM data area check was partially completed. The entire BIOS ROM data area check is completed next.
94h	The BIOS ROM data area check has fully completed. Setting the base and extended memory sizes next.
95h	The memory size has been adjusted because of mouse support and hard disk type 47. Verifying from display memory next.
96h	Returned after verifying from display memory. Initializing before C800h adaptor ROM control next.
97h	The necessary initialization before control passed to the adaptor ROM at C800h option has completed. The adaptor ROM check and control test is next. Relinquishing control to the adaptor ROM at C800h.
98h	The adaptor ROM control test has been done. About to do required processing after the adaptor ROM returns control.
99h	Any initialization for the option ROM test was done. Configuring the timer data area and the parallel printer base address next.
9Ah	Set the timer data area and the parallel printer base address. Setting the RS-232 base address next.
9Bh	Set the RS-232 base address. Initializing before the coprocessor test next.
9Ch	The required initialization before the coprocessor test has been done. Initializing the coprocesssor next.
9Dh	The coprocessor has been initialized. Performing any initialization after the coprocessor test next.
9Eh	Initialization after the coprocessor test is completed. Checking the Extended Keyboard, Keyboard ID, and Num Lock keyboard settings next.
9Fh	The Extended Keyboard flags have been checked, the Keyboard ID flag set, and Num Lock is set On or Off as specified. The Keyboard ID command is issued next.
A0h	The Keyboard ID command has been issued. The Keyboard ID flag reset is next.

Code	Description
A1h	The Keyboard ID flag reset has been done. The cache memory tests follow.
A2h	The cache memory test has been done. Displaying any soft errors next.
A3h	The soft error display is complete. Setting the keyboard typematic rate next.
A4h	The keyboard typematic rate is set. Programming the memory wait states next.
A5h	Memory wait states programming is done. The screen is cleared next.
A6h	The screen has been cleared. Enabling parity and the NMI next.
A7h	The NMI and parity have been enabled. Performing any initialization required before passing control to the adaptor ROM at E000h next.
A8h	Initialization before E000h adaptor ROM control has been done. The E000h adaptor ROM receives control next.
A9h	Returned from E000h adaptor ROM control. Performing any initialization required after E000h adaptor ROM control next.
A0h	Initialization after E000h adaptor ROM control is completed. Displaying the system configuration next.
00h	The system configuration has been displayed. Passing control to INT 19h Bootstrap Loader next.

cont'd

EISA POST Checkpoint Codes

Code	Description
27h	This is an ISA code, but in an EISA BIOS, F0h executes after it, not checkpoint 28h (executed next in an ISA BIOS).
F0h	Initialization after the interrupt vector is completed. Initializing the EISA slots next.
F1h	EISA slot initialization is completed. Setting up the extended NMI test next.
F2h	Configuration for the extended NMI test has been done. Testing the extended NMI next. After this checkpoint, EISA BIOS POST returns to ISA BIOS POST checkpoint 28h.
28h	This is a standard ISA BIOS checkpoint. The extended NMI test has completed. Setting monochrome mode next.
38h	This is an ISA BIOS checkpoint that is modified in the EISA BIOS. The Power-On message display has completed. Reading the new cursor position next. In an ISA BIOS, the next checkpoint is 39h, but in the EISA BIOS, it is F3h.
F3h	The new cursor position has been read and saved. Displaying any errors that occurred during slot initialization next. The EISA BIOS goes to 39h next, an ISA checkpoint.
67h	This is an ISA BIOS checkpoint. The ISA BIOS goes to 80h next, but the EISA BIOS goes to F4h. 8259 initialization has completed. Programming the 8259 mask registers next.
F4h	The 8259 mask register programming has completed. About to enable the extended NMI. EISA BIOS POST now goes back to a standard ISA BIOS checkpoint, 80h.
80h	This is a standard ISA BIOS checkpoint that EISA BIOS POST returns to. The process of enabling extended source is done. About to start the keyboard test. Clearing the output buffer. Checking for stuck keys. About to issue the keyboard reset command.
8Dh	This is a standard ISA BIOS checkpoint. The ISA BIOS goes to 8Eh next but EISA BIOS POST goes to F5h.
F5h	The Wait message is displayed. About to program the interrupt controller for edge or level sensitivity for a PS/2-type mouse. About to start the mouse check and mouse initialization. EISA BIOS POST now returns to the standard ISA BIOS checkpoint, 8Bh.
8Eh	The mouse check and initialization has completed. About to perform system and video BIOS shadowing.

POST Error Handling

One of the primary POST functions is to find and indicate any system conditions that prevent proper operation. POST looks for system errors and reports them. Errors are reported in one of two ways:

If...	Then...
the error occurs before the display device is initialized,	a series of beeps sound. Beep codes indicate that a fatal error has occurred. AMIBIOS Beep Codes are described on page 451.
the error occurs after the display device is initialized,	the error message is displayed. Displayed BIOS messages are described on page 452. A prompt to press F1 can also appear.

Beep Codes

Beep codes occur when the BIOS cannot successfully configure the display. They indicate a serious problem. Errors that cause beep codes occur during POST. POST is performed every time the system is powered on.

All errors except Beep Code 8 are fatal. Fatal errors do not allow the system to continue. Beep codes are described on page 451.

Displayed Errors

If POST is able to configure the system display, it can display errors on the screen. In general, these errors are not as serious as the beep codes. Displayed POST messages are described on page 452.

POST Diagnostic Codes

POST also produces a series of diagnostic codes that indicate specific milestones that have been passed in the POST code. These codes are described beginning on page 159. POST codes are accessible via the Manufacturing Test Port (I/O Port 80h).

POST Memory Test

Normally, the only visible POST routine is the memory test. A screen such as the following appears when the system is powered on:

```
AMIBIOS (C) 1993 American Megatrends Inc.

xxxxx KB OK

Hit <DEL> if you want to run SETUP




(C) American Megatrends Inc.
XX-XXXX-XXXXXX-XXXXXXXX-XXXXXX-XXXX-X
```

BIOS Identification String

A BIOS Identification string is displayed at the left bottom corner of the screen. The BIOS Identification Strings show the options installed in the Hi-Flex AMIBIOS.

Displaying Additional BIOS ID Strings

Step	Action
1	Enable *Wait for <F1> If any Error* in Advanced CMOS Setup to *Enabled* before freezing the screen.
2	When a problem occurs, freeze the screen by powering on the system and holding a key down on the keyboard to cause a *Keyboard Error* message.
3	Press INS during system boot to display two additional BIOS Identification strings.
4	Press F1 to continue the boot process.

See page 469 for a complete description of the contents of all three AMIBIOS Identification Strings.

BIOS Configuration Summary Screen

AMIBIOS displays the BIOS Configuration Summary screen (see the sample screen below) when the POST routines complete successfully. This screen may be slightly different in your computer. AMIBIOS manufactured before 12/15/1988 do not display this screen.

```
System Configuration (C) Copyright 1985-1991 American Megatrends Inc.

Main Processor        : 80486      Base Memory Size   : 640 KB
Numeric Coprocessor   : Present    Ext. Memory Size   : 7808 KB
Floppy Drive A:       : 1.2 MB 5¼  Hard Disk C: Type  : 44
Floppy Drive B:       : 1.44 MB 3½ Hard Disk D: Type  : None
Display Type:         : VGA or EGA Serial Port(s)     : 3F8
ROM-BIOS Date:        : 07/07/91   Parallel Port(s)   : 378

Memory Found                      Memory Configured

Bank 1=1 MB Bank 2=1 Meg          Bank 1=1 MB Bank 2=1 Meg

Shadow RAM      F000=Enable               Cache Memory=64K

C000=Enable     C400=Enable     C800=Enable     CC00=Enable
D000=Disable    D400=Disable    D800=Disable    DD00=Disable
E000=Disable    E400=Disable    E800=Disable    EC00=Disable
```

ROM Extensions

An adaptor ROM on an adapter card is an optional extension to the system BIOS. Extension ROMs can either replace existing ROM BIOS device service routines or add new service routines. Examples of ROM extensions include an ESDI hard disk drive BIOS or a SCSI BIOS. POST detects ROM extensions and allows them to initialize themselves, test, and initialize the devices that they control. The ROM extensions then return control to POST.

Handling ROM Extensions

By convention, ROM extensions can appear on any 2 KB boundary between C0000h and FFFFFh. The BIOS can handle any ROM extension at these locations. POST searches the memory from C0000h through FFFFFh in 2 KB increments for ROM extensions. Any ROM found at E0000h must be 64 KB in length.

cont'd

ROM Extensions, Continued

Identifying a ROM Extension

ROM Extensions must have a standard header. The data in the header indirectly identifies the type of device and its use. The following table lists the most important parts of a ROM extension header:

Offset	Contents	Description
0	55AAh	ROM extension header identifier.
1		Length code. The length in 512-byte (½K) units. A 64 KB ROM extension has a length code of 128.
2		Three-byte instruction. Normally, this field has a one-byte FAR RETURN instruction or a three-byte JMP instruction.
5	Varies	The header contains a number of other fields.
Last	00h	Usually 00h.

System Boot

If...	and...	then...
The *System Boot Up Sequence* option is A:, C:,	a bootable floppy disk is in drive A:,	INT 19h reads the boot sector on the floppy disk and places its contents at 7C00h.
The boot sequence is A:, C:,	drives A: and C: have no bootable disk,	INT 19h invokes INT 18h.
The boot sequence is A:, C:,	the floppy disk in drive A: is not bootable, but drive C: is bootable,	INT 19h reads the boot sector on drive A: and places its contents at 7C00h.
The *System Boot Up Sequence* option is C:, A:,	a boot sector is found on drive C:,	INT 19h reads the boot sector on drive C: and places its contents at 7C00h.
The boot sequence is C:, A:,	drive C: has no boot sector (the hard disk is not formatted for boot) but drive A: does,	INT 19h reads the boot sector on drive A: and places its contents at 7C00h.
The boot sequence is C:, A:,	neither drive C: or A: has a boot sector,	INT 19h invokes INT 18h.

If INT 19h does not find a boot sector, INT 18h is invoked. INT 18h can be vectored to a routine that takes over the boot process. Booting over a network can be done in this manner. INT 18h is initialized to point to a routine that displays *No Boot Device Available* and transfers control to INT 18h if INT 19h fails.

Chapter 11

Using Interrupts

The interrupt is the method used in ISA and EISA systems to access BIOS services. Both software programs and peripheral devices use interrupts:

- hardware peripheral devices use interrupts to report an event or request that an action be performed.

- software programs use the INT mnemonic to request certain actions from a peripheral device.

What an Interrupt Does

An interrupt essentially stops other microprocessor operations. The number specified with software interrupts instructs the BIOS to perform an operation using a specific peripheral device.

Requesting a Software Interrupt

Invoke a software interrupt from any assembler language program. Place the interrupt number after the assembler mnemonic INT. The microprocessor executes the instructions identified by the interrupt number when it finds an INT mnemonic. These instructions make up an interrupt service routine (or device service routine).

cont'd

Microprocessor Interrupt Handling

The microprocessor stops all other activity and activates a subroutine stored in system memory when it receives an interrupt signal.

If the signal indicates a software interrupt, it also contains an interrupt number. These subroutines are either interrupt service routines (ISRs) or device service routines (DSRs). The ISR or DSR is keyed to the interrupt number (either software or hardware). The ISR or DSR contains the code that executes the task or routine requested by the INT mnemonic and interrupt number.

Using Registers to Further Define the Interrupt

Before a software interrupt is invoked, special prespecified codes and parameters may have to be placed in processor registers (AX, BX, CX, DX to maintain 8088-compatibility) to further specify the operation that the interrupt routine is to perform. The interrupt routine output is usually returned in the microprocessor registers or flags.

Types of Interrupts

Type	Description	Range
Processor	Generated or processed by the microprocessor.	00h – 04h
Hardware	Generated by hardware devices. Eight are hardwired to the processor or motherboard. IRQs 2, 8, 9, and 11–15 are reserved.	08h – 0Fh 70h – 77h
Software	Handled by the BIOS. INTs 05h, 10h through 1Ah, and 40h, 41h, 42h, 43h, 46h, and 4Ah are reserved.	40h – 5Fh
DOS	Only available when DOS is active. INTs 20h through 3Fh are reserved for DOS.	20h – 3Fh
BASIC	Reserved	80h – BFh
User	INT 67h is used for EMS. All others can be revectored to user-written routines.	60h – 6Fh

This book does not discuss DOS, Basic, or user interrupts.

Processor Interrupts

Processor interrupts (00 – 04) are invoked by the CPU because of an unusual program result. For example, an INT 00h occurs when a program tries to divide a value by 0. When a divide by zero happens, the CPU generates INT 00h and halts.

Hardware Interrupts

A hardware device sends a signal or instruction to the microprocessor requesting a certain service or task when it needs to be serviced. Peripheral devices invoke hardware interrupts by setting an assigned Interrupt Request (IRQ) line. In EISA systems, the end user can assign IRQs to peripheral devices via the EISA Configuration Utility (ECU). or example, when a key is pressed on the keyboard, the keyboard generates a hardware interrupt (IRQ), which is vectored to an Interrupt Service Routine (ISR) in the BIOS (09h). INTs 08h – 0Fh and 70h – 77h are reserved for hardware interrupts.

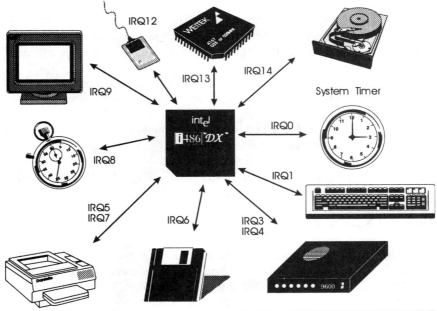

cont'd

Hardware Interrupt Priorities

The priority for hardware interrupts is: NMI, IRQ0, IRQ1, IRQ2 (which cascades the second Interrupt Controller — IRQ8, IRQ9, IRQ10, IRQ11, IRQ12, IRQ13, IRQ14, IRQ15), then back to the first Interrupt Controller for IRQ3, IRQ4, IRQ5, IRQ6, and IRQ7. Hardware interrupts IRQ0 – IRQ7 correspond to software interrupts 00h – 07h. Hardware interrupts IRQ8 – IRQ15 correspond to software interrupts 70h – 77h. See the BIOS Interrupt Summary Table on page 180 for more information about interrupts.

The Nonmaskable interrupt (NMI) is a special case. Generated by hardware devices to demand immediate attention from the microprocessor, it often signals an emergency, such as a low voltage condition or a memory error. The BIOS generates INT 02h to handle the NMI. See page 183 for additional information about the Nonmaskable Interrupt and INT 02h.

Software Interrupts

Software Interrupts are invoked via the Intel x86 assembly language INT mnemonic. Most software interrupts are vectored to device service routines (DSRs) in the ROM BIOS or operating system. Exceptions are:

- INTs 1Dh, 1Eh, 1Fh, 41h, 42h, 43h, and 46h do not service a device, but return ROM-resident hardware parameter tables.

- INTs 20h – 3Fh are software interrupts that are only used by the operating system, by convention.

- INTs 05h, 10h – 1Ah, 1Dh – 1Fh, 40h, 41h, 42h, 43h, 44h, and 46h can only be used by the system BIOS.

Interrupt Numbers

Every interrupt is assigned a unique number. To maintain IBM BIOS compatibility, certain ranges of interrupts are reserved for special use: INTs 60 – 67h are used for user software interrupts. INTs 20h – 3Fh are reserved for the operating system.

Interrupt Numbers and Interrupt Vectors

The originator of the interrupt does not need to know the memory address of the required interrupt handler. It only needs to know the interrupt number. The interrupt number points to the interrupt vector table, a table in low memory that contains the segmented address of the interrupt handling subroutine.

Each interrupt number is associated with a specific interrupt vector. The interrupt vector is the doubleword segment:offset address of the routine assigned to an interrupt number. Interrupt vectors are stored in a table that begins at 0:0000h. The vector for INT 00h is stored at address 0:0h through 0:03h. The vector for INT 02h is stored at 0:08h to 0:0Bh, the vector for INT 03h is stored at 0:0Ch to 0:0Fh, and so on.

The interrupt vector table is normally supervised by the BIOS and DOS. The programmer either uses an existing interrupt number and vector or assigns a new one when new interrupt handling routines are created.

POST, described on page 155, writes the interrupt vectors to low memory and initializes the vector address of all interrupts used by the BIOS. The operating system initializes all operating system-specific interrupt vectors when it boots. Applications programs that add their own interrupt routines are responsible for initializing the interrupt vectors for their own interrupts.

Next Sequential Instruction Processed after an Interrupt

Interrupts automatically save the contents of the CS and IP registers on the stack, so the system can return after the interrupt is processed. The IRET instruction performs this function. IRET also restores the flags, CS, and EIP. The interrupt process also saves the flag register on the stack and clears the interrupt flag (IF), temporarily preventing additional interrupts. It is a convention when writing interrupt routines to turn interrupts back on as soon as possible.

cont'd

Initializing the Interrupt Vector Table

Each time the BIOS initializes the system, it creates the interrupt vector table, which contains vectors (pointers) to the location (address) of the entry point. The interrupt vector table is at 0:0000h in this format:

Byte	Description
First	Least significant byte of offset
Second	Most significant byte of offset
Third	Least significant byte of segment
Fourth	Most significant byte of segment

For example, if the four-byte entry for an interrupt is stored in the interrupt vector table as 7D EA 00 F0, the interrupt entry point address is F000:EA7Dh.

Using the Interrupt Vector Table

By replacing the existing vector in an Interrupt Vector table entry with a pointer to your own BIOS routine, you can add a new BIOS service or replace an existing service. An entry for each BIOS interrupt number from 00h through BFh appears in the interrupt vector table. Counting in hex by fours, you can easily determine the address of the interrupt vector table to be added or replaced. For example, the interrupt vector table entry for INT 10h is at 0:0040h (4 times 10h). The interrupt vector table entry for INT 47h (an interrupt that is available for use by end users) is 0:011Ch.

Unexpected Interrupt Handler

The BIOS initializes unused interrupt vectors to the BIOS unexpected interrupt handler. The unexpected interrupt handler routine processes all interrupts that are either user-defined processes (INT 1Ch and INT 4Ah), or not meaningful to the BIOS (INT 73h, for example).

If an unexpected interrupt occurs, the BIOS either returns to the caller with CF set to 1 and all registers preserved, or revectors the interrupt to a caller-supplied interrupt processing routine.

Replacing an Interrupt Routine

The best way to add BIOS code is to revector a vector in the Interrupt Vector Table at address 0:0000h to your own routine. You must initialize the interrupt vector for your routine at every boot.

Changing an Interrupt Vector

You must write a routine that performs the tasks that the BIOS interrupt service routine you are replacing performs, as well as the additional tasks that you want to add to the BIOS ISR. DOS provides a function that does this, as shown below:

```
old     DD                              ;define a dword for old value
...     ...
        MOV     AL,16h                  ;define the interrupt to read
        MOV     AH,35h                  ;set the DOS function call
        INT     21h                     ;invoke DOS interrupt
        MOV     OLD,BX                  ;offset of interrupt handler
        MOV     OLD[2],ES               ;segment of interrupt handler
        ...     ...
NEW     PROC    FAR
        IRET
        ENDP

        MOV     BX,CS                   ;DS points to code segment
        MOV     DS,BX                   ;
        MOV     DX,OFFSET NEW           ;offset to new code in DX
        MOV     AL,16h                  ;set interrupt number
        MOV     AH,25h                  ;set function
        INT     21h                     ;call DOS interrupt
```

The new interrupt handler (NEW) replaces the previous interrupt handler. DS:DX is a doubleword pointer to the new handler. If this code is not located in the same code segment as the old interrupt handler, the MOV instructions for CS via BX to DS won't work.

Adding an Interrupt Routine

Several INT 15h System Service functions can be used to add additional interrupt routines. INT 15h Functions 80h, 81h, 82h, 85h, 90h, and 91h are basically empty shells just waiting for a programmer to write a routine for them. Entire interrupt service routines can be added by a programmer. Interrupts 60h – 6Fh are available for use. See the table on pages 180 through 181 for a list of available interrupts. AMIDiag Version 4.0 or later lists all interrupt assignments in the system. If you add an interrupt service routine, you must make sure that the interrupt vector for this routine is initialized after every system boot or the BIOS does not know what to do with it.

BIOS Register Conventions

Input to BIOS Interrupt Function Calls

The Intel x86 processor registers are used as follows to input values to a BIOS device service routine:

Register	Conventional Use
CS and IP	Automatically loaded, reserved, and restored as part of the interrupt process.
DS and ES	Preserved by the interrupt services.
SS	Not changed by the interrupt services.
SP	Preserved because, by coding convention, all BIOS device service routines leave the stack clean before returning.
AX	The contents of this register may be changed by the BIOS.
BX	The contents of this register may be changed by the BIOS.
CX	The contents of this register may be changed by the BIOS.
DX	The contents of this register may be changed by the BIOS.
SI and DI	The contents of this register may be changed by the BIOS.

Output from BIOS Interrupt Function Calls

The Intel x86 processor registers are used in the following manner for output values from a BIOS device service routine:

Register	Conventional Use
AH	Used to return error information.
AL	Sometimes used to return error information.
CF	The Carry Flag (CF) is set if an error occurred when the Interrupt request was processed.
FLAG Bits	All flag bits might be changed by the BIOS service. You cannot depend on any bit to be the same.

Chapter 12

BIOS Software Interrupts

The system interrupts supported in BIOS are routines used to access
I/O devices without directly accessing the hardware.

The system interrupts supported by the BIOS are described in this
chapter.

How Interrupts are Used

Interrupts are mainly associated with specific peripheral devices. Most
interrupts have functions selected by placing a value in AH. The
functions specify the activity to be performed by the interrupt service.
Functions are described under each interrupt heading. The functions
that the interrupt performs are described and the required input and
output values are listed.

Types of Interrupts

The BIOS interrupts are all software interrupts. See page 171 for a
complete description of the types of interrupts.

BIOS Interrupt Summary

INT Code	Type	Function	Turn to
00h	Processor	Divide by Zero	Page 182
01h	Processor	Single Step	Page 182
02h	Processor	Nonmaskable Interrupt (NMI)	Page 183
03h	Processor	Breakpoint	Page 184
04h	Processor	Arithmetic Overflow	Page 184
05h	Software	Print Screen	Page 184
06h	Processor	Invalid Op Code	Page 185
07h	Processor	Coprocessor Not Available	Page 185
08h	Hardware	Timer	Page 186
09h	Hardware	Keyboard Controller Output Buffer Full Interrupt	Page 187
0Ah	Hardware	IRQ2 Cascade from Second Interrupt Controller	Page 189
0Bh	Hardware	IRQ3 Serial Port (COM2 or COM4)	Page 189
0Ch	Hardware	IRQ4 Serial Port (COM1 or COM3)	Page 189
0Dh	Hardware	IRQ5 Parallel Printer (LPT2)	Page 189
0Eh	Hardware	IRQ6 Floppy Controller	Page 189
0Fh	Hardware	IRQ7 Parallel Printer (LPT1)	Page 189
10h	Software	Video Service	Page 190
11h	Software	Equipment List Service	Page 201
12h	Software	Return Memory Size Service	Page 201
13h	Software	Hard and Floppy Disk Service	Page 202
14h	Software	Serial Communications Service	Page 224
15h	Software	Systems Services	Page 237
16h	Software	Keyboard Service	Page 299
17h	Software	Parallel Printer Service	Page 319
18h	Software	ROM Basic	Page 321
19h	Software	Bootstrap Loader	Page 321
1Ah	Software	Real Time Clock Service	Page 336
1Bh	Software	Ctrl Break	Page 408
1Ch	Software	User Timer Tick	Page 408
1Dh	Software	Video Control Parameter Table	Page 408
1Eh	Software	Floppy Disk Base Table	Page 408
1Fh	Software	Video Graphics Table	Page 409
20h – 3Fh	Software	DOS interrupts	*
40h	Software	Floppy Disk Revector	*
41h	Software	Hard Disk C: Parameter Table	*
42h	Software	EGA Default video driver	*
43h	Software	Video Graphics Characters	*

INT Code	Type	Function	Turn to
44h	Software	Novell NetWare API	*
45h	Software	Available	*
46h	Software	Hard Disk D: Parameter Table	*
47h – 49h	Software	Available	*
4Ah	Software	User Alarm	*
4Bh – 5Bh	Software	Available	*
5Ch	Software	NetBIOS	*
5Dh – 63h	Software	Available	
64h	Software	IPX (Novell NetWare)	
65h – 66h	Software	Available	*
67h	Software	EMS	*
68h – 6Fh	Software	Available	*
70h	Hardware	IRQ8 Real Time Clock	Page 410
71h	Hardware	IRQ 9 Redirect Interrupt Cascade	*
72h – 73h	Hardware	IRQ10-12 Reserved. Do not use.	*
74h	Hardware	IRQ12 PS/2 Mouse	
75h	Hardware	IRQ13 Math Coprocessor	Page 411
76h	Hardware	IRQ14 Hard Drive Controller	Page 411
77h	Hardware	IRQ15 Power Management BIOS	Page 411
78h – 79h	Software	Available	*
7Ah	Software	(IPX) Novell NetWare API	*
78h – BFh	Software	Available	*

*   Not described in this book.

BIOS Stack Area

The BIOS uses 30:0000h – 30:00FFh (on top of the interrupt vector table) as a stack area. This area is used for BIOS calculations and temporary storage. The addresses for INTs C0h through FFh, not supported in the AMIBIOS, would ordinarily occupy this space.

INT 00h through INT 07h

The first eight interrupts (00h through 07h) are called by the processor directly, but they can also be called via any software program using the INT instruction. See the INT 05h example below. All processors in the Intel x86 family handle the INT mnemonic.

INT 00h Divide by Zero

Input: None

Output: None

Description:

INT 00h is a logical or processor interrupt. INT 00h is generated by the microprocessor to handle any division operation that has a denominator value of zero. The exact behavior is dependent on the operating system or application program in use when the interrupt occurs. Most programs display an error message, such as "Divide By Zero" and then terminate.

INT 01h Single Stepping

Input: Trap bit = 1

Output: None

Description:

INT 01h is a logical or processor interrupt. INT 01h traces the execution of each instruction in a software program. Most debugging utility programs use this interrupt.

INT 02h Nonmaskable Interrupt (NMI)

Input: None

Output: None

Description:

An NMI is a hardware interrupt. The BIOS generates INT 02h, an interrupt service routine that handles the NMI. The hardware NMI is used primarily to halt the system when memory errors occur. You can prevent the execution of all software interrupts by invoking CLI, with the exception of INT 02h, which handles the NMI. The NMI cannot be masked by CLI, but the NMI can be turned off.

The operating system resets the interrupt vector that corresponds to the NMI to its own routine when it boots. The operating system NMI routine calls the BIOS INT 02h NMI handling routine when an NMI-generating error occurs. The BIOS NMI handling routine displays a message that describes the hardware error that caused the NMI.

Disabling the NMI

The NMI can be disabled by writing to I/O port 70h with data bit 7 set and enabled by writing to I/O port 70h with data bit 7 reset.

Why an NMI Occurs

An NMI can be generated by:

- an onboard dynamic RAM parity failure,
- a 32-bit adapter card memory parity failure,
- an error reported by the I/O channel adapter card through the I/O channel check (-IOCHCK) signal,
- a bus timeout on an EISA slot,
- when a program sets bit 7 of I/O Port 462h (EISA only),
- a fail-safe timer NMI (EISA only), or
- when an EISA card is enabled or disabled.

NMI Source Indicator

The status bits (I/O port 61h) indicate whether the NMI was caused by a memory parity check or I/O check.

INT 03h Breakpoint

Input: None

Output: None

Description: INT 03h is a logical or processor interrupt. INT 03h provides a single-byte instruction (CCh) that halts the execution of a program so that the programmer can evaluate the microprocessor registers and other areas of memory. INT 03h is useful in debugging and is used in many commercial debuggers.

INT 04h Overflow Error

Input: Overflow bit of FLAGS register = 1

Output: None

Description: INT 04h is a logical or processor interrupt. The Overflow bit in the FLAGS register is set to 1 when a numeric overflow occurs after a mathematical operation. The INTO instruction (INTerrupt on Overflow) calls INT 04h when executed afterwards. If INT 04h is invoked, the Overflow bit is not read. INT 04h is not used often, so most operating systems set it to an IRET.

INT 05h Print Screen

Input: None

Output: None

Description: INT 05h is a software interrupt. The system dumps the contents of the screen to a printer attached to the system when the PRINT SCREEN key is pressed. By using the INT instruction, programmers can also accomplish the same task. INT 05h only works in text modes. It does not dump graphics screens.

INT 06h Invalid Op Code

Input: None

Output: None

Description: INT 06h is a logical or processor interrupt called after
the processor generates an Invalid Op Code Exception
Error. You can replace the interrupt vector table entry
for INT 06h with your own routine.

INT 07h Coprocessor Not Available

Input: None

Output: None

Description: INT 07h is a logical or processor interrupt. If the
emulation bit (EM) in the processor control register is
set and an ESC instruction is encountered, INT 07h is
called by the processor. Programs that use coprocessor
emulation can trap this interrupt and provide another
routine to be executed when this interrupt occurs.

Interrupts 08h Through 0Fh

INTs 08h – 0Fh are generated by the interrupt controller and
correspond to IRQs 0 – 7. INTs 08h – 0Fh are vectors that handle IRQs
08h – 0Fh, respectively. Since these interrupts are not generated by the
CPU directly, the interrupt controller sets the corresponding IRQ line
to request that the CPU generate the appropriate interrupt (08h – 0Fh)
when invoked.

IRQs have a fixed priority: NMI, 0, 1, 2, 8, 9, 10, 11, 12, 13, 14, 15, 3, 4,
5, 6, and 7. When it receives a signal on an IRQ line, the interrupt
controller decides which interrupt request has the highest priority and
then forwards that request to the CPU. All ISA and EISA systems have
two interrupt controllers and sixteen IRQ lines. The IRQ 2 line
cascades the second interrupt controller to the first interrupt controller.

INT 08h Timer Interrupt (IRQ0)

Input: None

Output: None

Description:

Hardware INT 08h can be used to measure time increments independent of the system clock frequency. INT 08h is called approximately 18.2 times per second. INT 08h increments the system time count at location 40:6Ch through 40:6Eh every time it is called. If the system time count (40:6Ch) exceeds 24 hours, the Timer Overflow Flag (40:70h) is set, the date is incremented by the BIOS, and the system time count is reset to 0. INT 08h also decrements the floppy disk motor count at 40:40h. INT 08h turns the floppy drive motor off when the count reaches 0.

INT 08h also issues an INT 1Ch Timer Tick interrupt every time it is called. Programmers can revector INT 1Ch to their own routines and use the clock feature for timed events. The following graphic illustrates how the system timer is used with the BIOS.

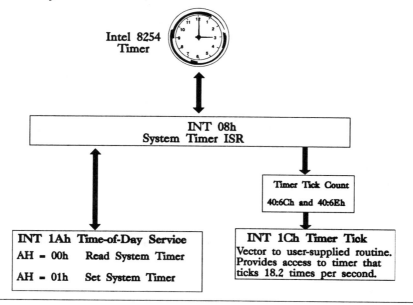

INT 09h Keyboard Interrupt (IRQ1)

Input: None

Output: None

Description:

ISA systems generally use 8042 processors to control the keyboard and keyboard registers. If a key is pressed, released, or pressed and held, the 8042 issues an interrupt signal to the interrupt controller. The interrupt controller sets an IRQ line (IRQ1) so the microprocessor can issue an interrupt. The BIOS INT 09h routine is then called. INT 09h reads the character from the keyboard and stores it in a buffer. The following graphic illustrates this process:

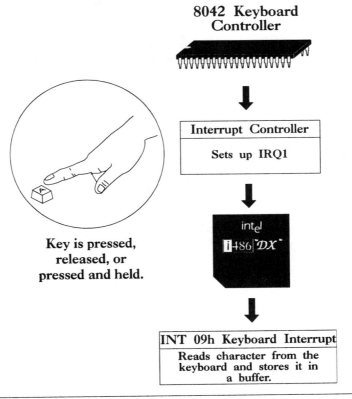

cont'd

Keyboard Key Processing

When...	the BIOS...
The BIOS receives the ASCII Scan code for any key.	The ASCII scan code is read from port 60h and is placed in the 32-byte keyboard buffer (40:1Eh).
CTRL, SHIFT, or ALT is pressed.	The Keyboard Control flags (40:17h and 40:18h) and the Keyboard Extended Mode State and Type flag (40:96h) are updated.
CTRL ALT DEL is pressed.	The reset flag (40:72h) is set to 1234h and the routine jumps to the POST tests, followed by a system reboot. This allows POST to skip the memory test it usually performs.
PAUSE is pressed.	The system enters a wait loop until a valid ASCII character key is pressed.
PRINT SCREEN is pressed.	The BIOS issues an INT 05h call.
CTRL BREAK is pressed.	The BIOS issues an INT 1Bh call.
SYSREQ is pressed.	INT 15h Function 85h is called. This routine is initialized by the BIOS to do nothing. Other software programs can trap this interrupt and provide an interrupt handler for SYSREQ.

Testing for a Keystroke

After reading the scan code from I/O port 60h, an INT 15h Function 4Fh is issued. This function is initialized by the BIOS to do nothing. Other software programs can trap this interrupt and provide an interrupt handler that will execute when a specified key or keychord is pressed.

INTs 0Ah Through 0Fh Miscellaneous Interrupts

Input: None

Output: None

Description:

These interrupts are defined by other external peripheral devices attached to the system.

In ISA systems, interrupts 0Ah – 0Fh are attached to the following IRQ lines. The corresponding IRQ line is enabled, alerting the microprocessor that the attached device needs servicing when these interrupts are called.

Interrupt	Hardware Interface
0Ah	IRQ2 Cascade to second interrupt controller
0Bh	IRQ3 Serial port 2 or 4
0Ch	IRQ4 Serial port 1 or 3
0Dh	IRQ5 Parallel port 2
0Eh	IRQ6 Floppy disk drive
0Fh	IRQ7 Parallel port 1

The above IRQ assignments are not fixed. They can vary from system to system. AMIDiag Version 4.0 or later lists the hardware interrupt assignments for your system.

EISA systems are even more flexible. The EISA Configuration Utility (ECU) allows you to assign IRQs in any order to any EISA adapter card, with few restrictions.

INT 10h Video Service

INT 10h, the video interrupt routine, has seventeen functions supported by the system BIOS. The system BIOS only supports two video display adapters: monochrome display adapter (MDA) and color graphics adapter (CGA). The BIOS support for EGA, VGA, and XGA display adapters is provided by the video adapter. If EGA is used, INT 42h points to the BIOS Video Service Routine. Both the EGA and VGA video BIOS reside at C0000h.

INT 10h Functions

Function	Title
00h	Set Video Mode
01h	Set Cursor Type
02h	Set Cursor Position
03h	Return Cursor Position
04h	Return Light Pen Position
05h	Set Current Video Page
06h	Scroll Text Upward
07h	Scroll Text Downward
08h	Return Character or Attribute
09h	Write Character or Attribute
0Ah	Write Character
0Bh	Subfunction BH = 00h Set Palette Subfunction BH = 01h Set Color Palette
0Ch	Write Graphic Pixel
0Dh	Read Graphic Pixel
0Eh	Write a Character
0Fh	Return Video Display Mode
13h	Write Character String

Note: The IBM BIOS does not preserve registers AX, BX, SI, DI, or BP after INT 10h calls. AMIBIOS does.

Function 00h Set Video Mode

Input: AH   =   00h
            AL   =   Video Mode
              00h 40 x 25 text mode, monochrome with CGA card
              01h 40 x 25 text mode, color with CGA card
              02h 80 x 25 text mode, monochrome with CGA card
              03h 80 x 25 text mode, color with CGA card
              04h 320 x 200 four-color graphics with CGA card
              05h 320 x 200 monochrome with CGA card
              06h 640 x 200 monochrome with CGA card
              07h 80 x 25 monochrome with monochrome card

Output: No registers set.

Description:

Function 00h sets the video mode. Only the video modes supported in the MDA and CGA video standards are supported by the system BIOS. This function programs the CRTC, selects a default color palette, and clears the video buffer if the proper flag is set in the save area.

Video Modes

Mode	Adapter	Resolution	Type	Colors	Lines and Rows	Array	Max. Pages	Buffer
0, 1	CGA	320 x 200	Text	16/256K	40x25	8x8	8	B8000h
2, 3	CGA	640 x 200	Text	16/256K	80x25	8x8	4	B8000h
4, 5	CGA	320 x 200	Graphics	4/256K	40x25	8x8	1	B8000h
6	CGA	640 x 200	Graphics	2/256K	80x25	8x8	1	B8000h
7	MDA	720 x 350	Text	None	80x25	9x14	1	B0000h

cont'd

Function 01h Set Cursor Type

Input: AH = 01h

CH = Starting Cursor Line (bits 4 to 0) — Cursor is
disabled if 20h

CL = Ending Cursor Line (bits 4 to 0)

Output: No registers set. 40:60h is updated.

Description: Function 01h sets the type of cursor. If the system has
an MDA, the range for starting cursor line and ending
cursor line is 0 to 13. Using a CGA, the range for both
values is 0 to 7. If CH is set to 20h, the cursor is
disabled. This function programs the CRTC to display
the text cursor type. The BIOS default values are:

CH – Starting Cursor Line Default	CL – Ending Cursor Line
Monochrome (MDA) 11	Monochrome (MDA) 12
Color (CGA) 6	Color (CGA) 7

Only one cursor type is maintained for each video page.

Function 02h Set Cursor Position

Input: AH = 02h

BH = Video Page Number

DH = Line on Screen

DL = Column on Screen

Output: No registers set. 40:50h is updated.

Description: Function 02h positions the cursor on one of the
available video pages. The line parameter can be 0 – 24.
The column parameter can be 0 – 39 in 40-column
mode, and 0 – 79 in 80-column mode. If the current
video page number is in BH, the CRTC is updated to
the current cursor position on the specified page.

Function 03h Return Cursor Position

Input: AH = 03h
BH = Video Page Number

Output: CH = Beginning Line of the Blinking Cursor
CL = Ending Line of the Blinking Cursor
DH = Line on Screen
DL = Column on Screen

Description:

Function 03h reads the current cursor position on the specified video page. This function is used only in text mode.

Function 04h Return Light Pen Position

Input: AH = 04h

Output: AH = 00h   Position is Unreadable
01h   Position is Readable
04h   Light pen disabled or no valid light pen address.
BX = Column on Graphic Screen (Pixel)
CH = Line on Graphic Screen (Raster Line)
CL = Raster line if resolution of mode is less than 200 lines.
DH = Line on Text Screen
DL = Column on Text Screen

Description:

This function can be used to determine the position of the light pen. This routine is not accurate in graphics mode and is ineffective when used on monochrome monitors with long image-retention phosphors. The raster line value is always a multiple of two, and depending on graphic screen size, the pixel value is a multiple of four (in 320 x 200 mode) or a multiple of eight (in a 640 x 200 mode).

cont'd

Function 05h Set Current Video Page

Input: AH   = 05h
              AL   = Video Page Number

Output: None

Description:

This function sets the video system to use a new video page or selects the portion of the video buffer to be displayed by setting AL to the appropriate video page number. This function is ignored if CGA is used because CGA uses the entire 16K video buffer. The BIOS programs the CRTC Start Address Registers in video modes 0 – 3.

The BIOS maintains the current cursor location in as many as eight video pages at 40:50h. When a different video page is selected, the BIOS moves the cursor to the position that the cursor was at the last time the requested video page was displayed.

Function 06h Scroll Text Upward

Input: AH   = 06h
              AL   = Number of Scrolling Lines
              BH   = Color or Attribute for Scrolling Lines
              CH   = Line Number of Upper Left Corner of Window
              CL   = Column Number of Upper Left Corner of Window
              DH   = Line Number of Lower Right Corner of Window
              DL   = Column Number of Lower Right Corner of Window

Output: None

Description:

Function 06h creates a window defined by values specified in CH, CL, DH, and DL. It scrolls the number of lines specified in AL upward through the window. The color or attribute of the new lines is in BH. If AL is 00h, the window is cleared.

Function 07h Scroll Text Downward

Input: AH = 07h
        AL = Number of Scrolling Lines
        BH = Color or Attribute of Scrolling Lines
        CH = Line Number of Upper Left Corner of Window
        CL = Column Number of Upper Left Corner of Window
        DH = Line Number of Lower Right Corner of Window
        DL = Column Number of Lower Right Corner of Window

Output: None

Description:

Function 07h creates a window (defined by values in CH, CL, DH, and DL) and scrolls a number of window lines downward through the window. The number of lines to be scrolled is in AL, and the color or attribute of the new lines is in BH. If AL is set to 00h, the window is cleared.

Function 08h Return Character or Attribute

Input: AH = 08h
        BH = Video Page Number

Output: AH = Color or Attribute of Character
        AL = ASCII Code of Character

Description:

Function 08h retrieves the ASCII code of the character at the current cursor location on the video page specified in BH. The function returns the character attribute or color in AH.

cont'd

Function 09h Write Character or Attribute

Input: AH = 09h

AL = ASCII Code of Character to be Written

BH = Video Page Number (or background pixel value if in 320 x 200 x 256 color mode)

BL = Attribute or Color of Character (or background pixel value in graphics mode)

CX = Number of Repetitions

Output: None

Description:

Function 09h writes a character(s) to the current cursor position on the video page specified in BH. You can also specify the character attribute or color and the number of times the character is to be written. The new cursor position is not changed.

Function 0Ah Write Character

Input: AH = 0Ah

AL = ASCII Code of Character to be Written

BH = Video Page Number (Background pixel value if in 320 x 200 x 256 color mode)

BL = Foreground pixel value (in graphics mode only)

CX = Number of Repetitions

Output: None

Description:

Function 0Ah writes a character(s) to the current cursor position on the video page specified in BH. You can also specify the number of times the character is to be written. The new cursor position is not changed.

Function 0Bh Subfunction 00h Set Palette

Input: AH = 0Bh
BH = 00h
BL = Screen Border and Background Color

Output: No registers set. 40:66h is updated.

Description:

Function 0Bh subfunction 00h sets the screen background and border color. If the system is running in text mode, only the screen border color is defined. If the system is running in graphics mode, both the background color and the screen border color are defined. Use INT 10h Function 10h instead of this function if the system is using EGA or VGA.

Function 0Bh Subfunction 01h Set Color Palette

Input: AH = 0Bh
BH = 01h
BL = Number of Color Palette

Output: No registers set. 40:66h is updated.

Description:

Function 0Bh subfunction 01h is valid only in 320 x 200 graphics mode. It also sets the screen color palette. The two palettes in 320 x 200 mode are:

Palette	Colors
Palette 0	Green, Red, and Yellow
Palette 1	Cyan, Magenta, and White

cont'd

Function 0Ch Write Graphic Pixel

Input: AH = 0Ch
        AL = Pixel Color Number
        BH = Video Page Number (you can only use this in video
               modes that permit multiple pages)
        CX = Screen Column Number
        DX = Screen Line Number

Output: None

Description:

Function 0Ch draws a color graphic pixel at the specified coordinates
in CX and DX. Specify the video page in BH and the pixel color
number in AL. The BH value is ignored in 320 x 200 with 256 colors
mode. If VGA or EGA is used, the BH value is ignored in 320 x 200
with 4 colors mode.

Function 0Dh Read Graphic Pixel

Input: AH = 0Dh
        BH = Video Page Number (you can only use this in video
               modes that permit multiple pages)
        CX = Screen Column Number
        DX = Screen Line Number

Output: AL = Pixel Color Number

Description:

Function 0Dh reads the color of the pixel specified in CX and DX. The
current video page is specified in BH.

Function 0Eh Write Character

Input: AH = 0Eh
AL = ASCII Code of the Character
BH = Active page
BL = Foreground color of character if using graphics mode.

Output: No registers set. 40:50h is updated.

Description: Function 0Eh writes a character to the current video page at the current cursor position. The cursor column position is incremented after writing the character. If the end of a line is reached, the cursor row position is also incremented and the column position is set to zero. Certain ASCII codes are interpreted as control characters when input to this function: 07h = beep, 08h = backspace, 0Ah = line feed, and 0Dh = carriage return.

Function 0Fh Return Video Display Mode

Input: AH = 0Fh

Output: AH = Number of Display Columns
AL = Video mode
00h 40 x 25 text mode, monochrome with CGA card
01h 40 x 25 text mode, color with CGA card
02h 80 x 25 text mode, monochrome with CGA card
03h 80 x 25 text mode, color with CGA card
04h 320 x 200 four-color graphics with CGA card
05h 320 x 200 monochrome with CGA card
06h 640 x 200 monochrome with CGA card
07h 80 x 25 monochrome with monochrome card
BH = Current Video Page

Description: Function 0Fh returns the current video mode in AL, the current page number in BH, and the number of columns allowed in this video mode in AH.

cont'd

Function 13h Write Character String

Input:	AH	=	13h

AL = Output Mode:

00h   Attribute in BL, do not update cursor position.
01h   Attribute in BL, update cursor position.
02h   Attribute in string buffer, do not update cursor position.
03h   Attribute in string buffer, update cursor position.

	BH	=	Video page number
	BL	=	Attribute of all characters in character string
	CX	=	Number of characters in buffer
	DH	=	Screen line number
	DL	=	Screen column number
	ES:BP	=	Segment:Offset address of string buffer

Output: No registers set. 40:50h is updated.

Description:

Function 13h writes character strings to the video screen and wraps the string to the next line if it is too long for the current text line. Specify the video page number in BH, the screen line number in DH, and the screen column number in DL where the string is to be displayed. The string should be stored in a buffer in RAM. The segment part of the buffer address is in ES and the offset in BP. The number of characters to be displayed from the buffer should be in CX.

If output modes 0 or 2 are used, this function does not change the cursor position. If output modes 1 or 3 are used, this function sets the final cursor position to the next position past the last character displayed.

If the output mode is 0 or 1, the attribute for all characters in the string is determined by the value in BL. In modes 2 and 3, the string consists of sets of two bytes. The first byte is the ASCII value of the character and the second byte is the attribute of the character.

INT 11h Equipment List Service

Input: None

Output: AX = Configuration Code:

Bits 15–14	Number of parallel ports installed.	
Bit 13	Reserved	
Bit 12	Internal modem present if set (if not using serial port).	
Bits 11–9	Number of serial ports installed.	
Bit 8	Reserved	
Bits 7–6	00	One floppy disk drive.
	01	Two floppy disk drives.
Bits 5–4	00b	Reserved
	01b	Video mode is 40x25 CGA.
	10b	Video mode is 80x25 CGA.
	11b	Video mode is 80x25 MDA.
	All video modes are monochrome.	
Bit 3	Reserved	
Bit 2	PS/2 mouse present if set.	
Bit 1	Math coprocessor installed if set.	
Bit 0	One or more floppy disk drives if set.	

Description: INT 11h reads the system configuration code. The video mode reported by INT 11h is the mode used when the system was initially booted. Use INT 10h Function 0Fh to find the current video mode.

INT 12h Return Memory Size Service

Input: None

Output: AX = Memory size in kilobytes

Description: INT 12h returns the amount of real mode memory installed on the system. Real mode memory is memory from 0 – 1024 KB. Use INT 15h Function 88h to find the amount of memory beyond the first megabyte.

INT 13h Hard Disk Service

INT 13h Hard Disk Service Functions

The INT 13h functions discussed in this chapter are:

Function	Title
00h	Reset Hard Disk Drive
01h	Return Hard Disk Drive Status
02h	Read Disk Sectors
03h	Write Disk Sectors
04h	Verify Disk Sectors
05h	Format Disk Cylinder
06h	Format Disk Track and Mark Lead Sectors
07h	Format Entire Disk Starting at Specified Cylinder
08h	Return Disk Parameters
09h	Initialize Hard Disk Controller
0Ah	Read Hard Disk Sectors and Error Correction Codes
0Bh	Write Hard Disk Sectors and Error Correction Codes
0Ch	Seek Hard Disk Cylinder
0Dh	Reset Hard Disk Controller
10h	Test Unit Ready
11h	Recalibrate Hard Disk
14h	Perform Internal Controller Diagnostic
15h	Return Drive Type

INT 13h Hard Disk Service, Continued

INT 13h Hard Disk Service Error Codes

For most hard disk drive functions, the following error codes are returned through register AH. All error codes appear in AH.

Code	Description	Code	Description
00h	No error	0Dh	Invalid number of sectors for format on hard disk drive
01h	Function invalid	0Eh	Control data address mark found on hard disk drive
02h	Address mark not found	0Fh	DMA arbitration level out of range
03h	Write attempted on write protected floppy disk	10h	Read error (uncorrectable CRC or ECC)
04h	Sector not found	11h	ECC data error corrected on hard disk drive
05h	Hard disk drive reset failed	20h	Error in floppy disk controller
06h	Floppy disk replaced	40h	Track not found on seek
07h	Hard disk drive parameter is corrupt	80h	Timeout, drive not responding
08h	DMA overflow occurred	AAh	Hard disk drive not ready
09h	DMA crossed 64 KB segment boundary	BBh	Unknown error on hard disk drive
0Ah	Hard disk drive bad sector flag	CCh	Hard disk drive write error occurred
0Bh	Hard disk drive bad track flag	E0h	Hard disk drive status register error
0Ch	Floppy disk media type not found	FFh	Hard disk drive sense operation failed

cont'd

INT 13h Hard Disk Service Coding Conventions

For most INT 13h functions, the sector number is placed in CL and the cylinder number in CH.

On a hard disk drive, the cylinder number consists of 10 bits. The lower 8 bits are placed in CH (cylinder number), and the upper 2 bits are placed in CL. The lower 6 bits of CL contain the beginning sector number.

INT 40h Revector for Floppy Functions

INT 13h handles both floppy disk and hard disk drive BIOS functions. If the system has a hard disk drive, the floppy disk device service routine actually resides at INT 40h. All BIOS floppy functions are revectored to INT 40h and then executed.

Function 00h Reset Disk Drive

Input: AH   = 00h
             DL   = 80h Hard Disk Drive C:
                    81h – FFh are valid. 81h = D:, 82h = E:, etc.

Output: AH   = 00h No error
                 = Any other value is an error code (see page 203).
            CF   = 0 No error
                 = 1 Error

Description:

Function 00h should be used when an error follows a disk operation. Function 00h resets the disk controller and recalibrates the hard drives attached to the controller. If Function 00h is issued for a hard disk drive, the floppy controller is reset and then the hard disk drive controller is reset.

Function 01h Return Hard Drive Status

Input: AH = 01h
DL = 80h Hard Disk Drive C:
81h – FFh are valid. 81h = D:, 82h = E:, etc.

Output: AH = 00h No error
= Any other value is an error code (see page 203).
CF = 0 No error
= 1 Error

Description:

Function 01h can be used to read the status of the last operation.

Function 02h Read Disk Sectors

Input: AH = 02h
AL = Number of Sectors to Read
CH = Cylinder Number (low 8 bits)
CL = High two bits of cylinder number in bits 7–6
DH = Head Number
DL = 80h Hard Disk Drive C:
81h – FFh are valid. 81h = D:, 82h = E:, etc.
ES:BX = Buffer Segment:Offset Address

Output: AH = 00h No error
= Any other value is an error code (see page 203).
CF = 0 No error
= 1 Error

Description:

Function 02h reads the specified number of sectors from a specified track on one side of a disk. The sector(s) are read from the disk and then stored in a buffer at address ES:BX.

cont'd

Function 03h Write Disk Sectors

Input: AH = 03h
        AL = Number of Sectors to Write
        CH = Cylinder Number (low 8 bits)
        CL = High two bits of cylinder number in bits 7–6
        DH = Head Number
        DL = 80h Hard Disk Drive C:
             81h – FFh are valid. 81h = D:, 82h = E:, etc.
    ES:BX = Buffer Offset:Segment Address

Output: AH = 00h No error
           = Any other value is an error code (see page 203).
        CF = 0 No error
           = 1 Error

Description: Function 03h writes the number of sectors in AL to the cylinder number in CH using the disk drive head specified in DH. The beginning sector number is in CL. The data written to the sectors comes from the buffer starting at the address in ES:BX.

Function 04h Verify Disk Sectors

Input: AH = 04h
        AL = Number of Sectors to Verify
        CH = Cylinder Number (low 8 bits)
        CL = High two bits of cylinder number in bits 7–6
        DH = Head Number
        DL = 80h Hard Disk Drive C:
             81h – FFh are valid. 81h = D:, 82h = E:, etc.

Output: AH = 00h No error
           = Any other value is an error code (see page 203).
        CF = 0 No error
           = 1 Error

Description: Function 04h verifies that the ECC code after each sector is correct for the data contained in that sector.

INT 13h Hard Disk Service, Continued

Function 05h Format Disk Cylinder

Input: AH = 05h
      AL = Interleave Factor
      CH = Cylinder Number (low 8 bits)
      CL = High two bits of cylinder number in bits 7–6
      DL = 80h Hard Disk Drive C:
           81h – FFh are valid. 81h = D:, 82h = E:, etc.
  ES:BX = Buffer Segment:Offset Address

Output: AH   = 00h No error
        = Any other value is an error code (see page 203).
      CF = 0 No error
        = 1 Error

Description: Function 05h formats an entire track or cylinder on a disk. A buffer containing sector information is passed in ES:BX. The buffer contains a two-byte record:

Byte 0	00h for a good sector, 80h for a bad sector
Byte 1	Sector Number

Function 06h Format Track and Mark Lead Sectors

Input: AH = 06h
      AL = Interleave Factor
      CH = Cylinder Number (low 8 bits)
      CL = High two bits of cylinder number in bits 7–6
      DH = Head Number
      DL = 80h Hard Disk Drive C:
           81h – FFh are valid. 81h = D:, 82h = E:, etc.

Output: AH   = 00h No error
        = Any other value is an error code (see page 203).
      CF = 0 No error
        = 1 Error

Description: Formats an entire track or cylinder and marks bad sectors. See Function 05h for more on formatting.

cont'd

Function 07h Format Entire Disk Starting at Specified Cylinder

Input: AH = 07h
        AL = Interleave Factor
        CH = Cylinder Number (low 8 bits)
        CL = High two bits of cylinder number in bits 7–6
        DL = 80h Hard Disk Drive C:
               81h – FFh are valid. 81h = D:, 82h = E:, etc.

Output: AH = 00h No error
           = Any other value is an error code (see page 203).
        CF = 0 No error
           = 1 Error

Description: Formats an entire hard disk, starting at the cylinder number specified in CH and CL and marks bad sectors. See Function 05h for more on formatting.

Function 08h Return Disk Parameters

Input: AH = 08h
        DL = 80h Hard Disk Drive C:
               81h – FFh are valid. 81h = D:, 82h = E:, etc.

Output: AH = 00h No error
           = Any other value is an error code (see page 203).
        AL = 00h
        CF = 0 No error
           = 1 Error
        CH = Lower 8 bits of last cylinder number
        CL = High two bits of last cylinder number and six bits for last sector number
        DH = Last head number
        DL = Number of hard disk drives
    ES:DI = Address of disk parameter table from BIOS

Description: Function 08h retrieves the parameters for a hard disk drive from the BIOS.

Function 09h Initialize Hard Disk Controller

Input: AH = 09h

DL = 80h Hard Disk Drive C:.

= 81h – FFh are valid. 81h = D:, 82h = E:, etc.

Output: AH = 00h No error

= Any other value is an error code (see page 203).

CF = 0 No error

= 1 Error

Description:

Function 09h initializes the hard disk controller with the values in the BIOS hard disk parameter table. The vector address for INT 41h points to the drive C: disk parameters and the vector for INT 46h points to the drive D: parameters. On an ISA system, these blocks are 16 bytes long, in the following format:

Offset	Description
00h – 01h	Number of cylinders. Byte 01h is the most significant byte.
02h	Number of heads
03h – 04h	Reserved
05h – 06h	Starting write precompensation cylinder. Byte 06h is the MSB.
07h	ECC burst length
08h	Control Byte Bits 7–6 Enable or Disable Retries 00h Enable retries. All other values disable retries. Bit 5 Set if defect map is located at last cylinder plus one. Bit 4 Reserved, always set to zero. Bit 3 Set if more than 8 heads. Bits 2–0 Reserved, always set to zero.
09h – 0Bh	Reserved
0Ch – 0Dh	Landing Zone
0Eh	Number of Sectors per Track
0Fh	Reserved

cont'd

INT 13h Hard Disk Service, Continued

Function 0Ah Read Hard Disk Sectors and Error Correction Codes

Input: AH   = 0Ah
AL   = Number of Sectors to Read
CH   = Lower eight bits of last cylinder number
CL   = Highest two bits of last cylinder number and six bits
for beginning sector number
DH   = Head Number
DL   = 80h Hard Disk Drive C:
= 81h – FFh are valid. 81h = D:, 82h = E:, etc.
ES:BX = Buffer Segment:Offset Address

Output: AH   = 00h No error
= Any other value is an error code (see page 203).
CF   = 0 No error
= 1 Error

Description:

Function 0Ah reads the number of sectors in AL from the hard disk
specified in DL and the location specified in CH and CL using the
head number specified in DH and stores it to memory. It also reads a
four-byte ECC code for each sector.

INT 13h 02h also reads sectors from the hard disk, but terminates the
operation when a read error occurs.

Function 0Ah does not terminate on error.

Function 0Bh Write Hard Disk Sectors and Error Correction Codes

Input: AH = 0Bh
AL = Number of Sectors to Write
CH = Lower eight bits of last cylinder number
CL = Highest two bits of last cylinder number and six bits for beginning sector number
DH = Head Number
DL = 80h Hard Disk Drive C:
= 81h – FFh are valid. 81h = D:, 82h = E:, etc.
ES:BX = Buffer Segment:Offset Address

Output: AH = 00h No error
= Any other value is an error code (see page 203).
CF = 0 No error
= 1 Error

Description:

Function 0Bh writes the number of sectors specified in AL to the hard disk specified in DL using the head number specified in DH. It also writes a four-byte Error Correction Code (ECC) for each sector. The four-byte ECC must follow the data to be written to each sector.

The data to be written to the drive is stored at the location pointed to in ES:BP. The buffer must contain 512 bytes of data followed by a four-byte ECC, then another 512 bytes of data and another four-byte ECC, and so on.

cont'd

Function 0Ch Seek Hard Disk Cylinder

Input: AH = 0Ch
          CH = Cylinder Number (lower eight bits)
          CL = Cylinder Number (upper two bits)
          DH = Head Number
          DL = 80h Hard Disk Drive C:
              = 81h – FFh are valid. 81h = D:, 82h = E:, etc.

Output: AH = 00h No error
              = Any other value is an error code (see page 203).
          CF = 0 No error
              = 1 Error

Description:

Function 0Ch moves the hard disk heads to the specified cylinder but does not transfer data. It is not necessary to call this function before calling Functions 0Ah Read or 0Bh Write because Functions 0Ah and 0Bh contain an implicit Seek command.

Function 0Dh Reset Hard Disk Controller

Input: AH = 0Dh
          DL = 80h Hard Disk Drive C:
              = 81h – FFh are valid. 81h = D:, 82h = E:, etc.

Output: AH = 00h No error
              = Any other value is an error code (see page 203).
          CF = 0 No error
          CF = 1 Error

Description:

Function 0Dh resets the specified hard disk drive. Unlike Function 00h, it does not reset the floppy controller.

Function 10h Test Unit Ready

Input: AH = 10h

DL = 80h Hard Disk Drive C:

= 81h – FFh are valid. 81h = D:, 82h = E:, etc.

Output: AH = 00h No error

= Any other value is an error code (see page 203).

CF = 0 No error. Hard Disk Drive Ready

= 1 Error. Hard Disk Drive Not Ready

Description:

Function 10h determines if the hard disk drive specified in DL is ready.

Function 11h Recalibrate Hard Disk

Input: AH = 11h

DL = 80h Hard Disk Drive C:

= 81h – FFh are valid. 81h = D:, 82h = E:, etc.

Output: AH = 00h No error

= Any other value is an error code (see page 203).

CF = 0 No error

= 1 Error

Description:

Function 11h recalibrates the specified hard disk drive, places the read/write head at cylinder 0, and returns the drive status in AH.

cont'd

INT 13h Hard Disk Service, Continued

Function 14h Perform Internal Controller Diagnostic

Input: AH = 14h
          DL   = 80h Hard Disk Drive C:
               = 81h – FFh are valid. 81h = D:, 82h = E:, etc.

Output: AH = 00h No error
               = Any other value is an error code (see page 203).
          CF   = 0 No error
               = 1 Error

Description:

Function 14h executes a diagnostic self-test routine built into ISA hard disk controllers. This diagnostic routine returns the status and results in AH.

Function 15h Return Drive Type

Input: AH = 15h
          DL   = 80h Hard Disk Drive C:
               = 81h – FFh are valid. 81h = D:, 82h = E:, etc.

Output: AH = 00h No drive present
               = 03h Drive is a hard disk drive
          CF   = 00h No error
               = 1 Error
    CX:DX = Number of 512 byte sectors

Description:

If AH is 03h, the drive is a hard disk drive and CX:DX contains the number of 512-byte sectors.

INT 13h Floppy Disk Service

INT 13h Floppy Disk Service Functions

The INT 13h Floppy Disk functions discussed in this chapter are:

Function	Title
00h	Reset Floppy Disk Drive
01h	Return Drive Status
02h	Read Floppy Disk Sectors
03h	Write Disk Sectors
04h	Verify Disk Sectors
05h	Format Disk Track
08h	Return Disk Parameters
15h	Return Drive Type
16h	Disk Media Change Status
17h	Set Floppy Disk Type
18h	Set Floppy Disk Type before Format

cont'd

INT 13h Floppy Disk Service, Continued

INT 13h Floppy Disk Service Error Codes

For most floppy and hard disk drive functions, the following error codes are returned through register AH. All error codes appear in AH.

Code	Description	Code	Description
00h	No error	0Dh	Invalid number of sectors for format on hard disk drive
01h	Function invalid	0Eh	Control data address mark found on hard disk drive
02h	Address mark not found	0Fh	DMA arbitration level out of range
03h	Write attempted on write protected floppy disk	10h	Read error (uncorrectable CRC or ECC)
04h	Sector not found	11h	ECC data error corrected on hard disk drive
05h	Hard disk drive reset failed	20h	Error in floppy disk controller
06h	Floppy disk replaced	40h	Track not found on seek
07h	Hard disk drive parameter is corrupt	80h	Timeout, drive not responding
08h	DMA overflow occurred	AAh	Hard disk drive not ready
09h	DMA crossed 64 KB segment boundary	BBh	Unknown error on hard disk drive
0Ah	Hard disk drive bad sector flag	CCh	Hard disk drive write error occurred
0Bh	Hard disk drive bad track flag	E0h	Hard disk drive status register error
0Ch	Floppy disk media type not found	FFh	Hard disk drive sense operation failed

INT 13h Floppy Disk Service Coding Conventions

For most INT 13h functions, the sector number is placed in CL and the
cylinder number in CH.

INT 40h Revector for Floppy Functions

INT 13h handles both floppy disk and hard disk drive BIOS functions.
If the system has a hard disk drive, the floppy disk service routine
actually resides at INT 40h. All BIOS floppy functions are revectored
to INT 40h and then executed.

Function 00h Reset Floppy Disk Drive

Input: AH = 00h
            DL = 00h Floppy Drive A:
                   01h Floppy Drive B:

Output: AH = 00h No error
                = Any other value is an error code (see page 216).
            CF = 0 No error
                = 1 Error

Description:

Function 00h should be used when an error follows a disk operation.
Function 00h resets the disk controller and recalibrates the floppy
drives attached to the floppy controller. If Function 00h is issued for a
hard disk drive, both the floppy controller and the hard disk drive
controller are reset, in that order.

cont'd

Function 01h Return Drive Status

Input: AH   = 01h
         DL   = 00h Floppy Drive A:
                 01h Floppy Drive B:

Output: AH   = 00h No error
                 = Any other value is an error code (see page 216).
         CF   = 0 No error
                 = 1 Error

Description:

Function 01h can be used to read the status of the last disk operation.

Function 02h Read Disk Sectors

Input: AH   = 02h
         AL   = Number of Sectors to Read
         CH   = Track Number
         CL   = Beginning Sector Number
         DH   = Side 0 or 1
         DL   = 00h Floppy Drive A:
                    01h Floppy Drive B:
         ES:BX = Buffer Segment:Offset Address

Output: AH   = 00h No error
                    = Any other value is an error code (see page 216).
         AL   = Number of sectors actually read
         CF   = 0 No error
                    = 1 Error

Description:

Function 02h reads the specified number of sectors from a specified track on one side of a disk. The sector(s) are read from the disk and then stored in a buffer at address ES:BX.

INT 13h Floppy Disk Service, Continued

Function 03h Write Disk Sectors

Input: AH = 03h
              AL = Number of Sectors to Write
              CH = Track Number
              CL = Beginning Sector Number
              DH = Floppy Side 0 or 1
              DL = 00h Floppy Drive A: 01h Floppy Drive B:
              ES:BX = Buffer Offset:Segment Address

Output: AH = 00h No error
                  = Any other value is an error code (see page 216).
              AL = Number of sectors actually written
              CF = 0 No error
                  = 1 Error

Description: Function 03h writes the number of sectors in AL to the
                  track in CH on one side (in DH) of a floppy disk. The
                  beginning sector number is in CL. The data written to
                  the sectors is from the buffer at address ES:BX.

Function 04h Verify Disk Sectors

Input: AH = 04h
              AL = Number of Sectors to Verify
              CH = Track Number
              CL = Sector Number
              DH = Floppy Side 0 or 1
              DL = 00h Floppy Drive A: 01h Floppy Drive B:

Output: AH = 00h No error
                  = Any other value is an error code (see page 216).
              AL = Number of sectors actually read and verified.
              CF = 0 No error
                  = 1 Error

Description: Function 04h verifies that the ECC code after each
                  sector is correct for the data contained in that sector.

cont'd

Function 05h Format Disk Track

Input: AH = 05h
         AL = Number of Sectors to Format
         CH = Track Number
         DH = Floppy Side 0 or 1
         DL = 00h Floppy Drive A:
              01h Floppy Drive B:
   ES:BX = Buffer Segment:Offset Address

Output: AH = 00h No error
            = Any other value is an error code (see page 216).
        CF = 0 No error
           = 1 Error

Description:

Function 05h formats an entire track or cylinder on a disk. A buffer containing sector information is passed through ES:BX.

The buffer contains a four-byte record for each sector in the track, in the following format:

Byte 0 Track number
Byte 1 Head number
Byte 2 Logical sector number
Byte 3 Number of bytes per sector:
      0 128 bytes per sector
      1 256 bytes per sector
      2 512 bytes per sector (ISA and EISA Standard)
      3 1024 bytes per sector

Call INT 13h function 17h or 18h to set the floppy disk media type before invoking this function.

INT 13h Floppy Disk Service, Continued

Function 08h Return Disk Parameters

Input: AH   = 08h
         DL   = 00h Floppy Drive A:
               01h Floppy Drive B:

Output: AH   = 00h Error Code
             = Any other value is an error code (see page 216).
         BL   = Drive type (for floppy drives)
               01h for 360 KB, 40 track 5¼"
               02h for 1.2 MB, 80 track 5¼"
               03h for 720 KB, 80 track 3½"
               04h for 1.44 MB, 80 track 3½"
               05h for 2.88 MB, 80 track 3½"
         CF   = 0 No error
             = 1 Error
         CH   = Lower 8 bits of last cylinder number
         CL   = High two bits of last cylinder number and low six
               bits for last sector number
         DH   = Last head number
         DL   = Number of disk drives
      ES:DI = Address of disk parameter table from BIOS

Description:

Function 08h retrieves the parameters for a floppy disk drive from the ROM BIOS. 00h is returned in BL when: the drive type is known but CMOS RAM data is invalid or not present, the CMOS RAM battery is low, or the CMOS RAM checksum value is corrupt.

If the specified drive is not installed, all returned values are 00h. AX, ES, BX, CX, DH, and DI are 0. DL is the number of drives present if: the drive number is invalid, or the drive type is unknown and CMOS RAM is not present, or the CMOS RAM battery is low or the CMOS RAM checksum is invalid, or the drive type in CMOS RAM is invalid.

cont'd

Function 15h Return Drive Type

Input: AH = 15h
        DL = 00h Floppy Drive A:
              01h Floppy Drive B:

Output: AH = 00h No drive present
            = 01h Drive does not have change line support
            = 02h Drive does have change line support
        CF = 0 No error
            = 1 Error

Description:

Function 15h indicates if floppy disk change line information is available.

Function 16h Disk Media Change Status

Input: AH = 16h
        DL = 0 Floppy Drive A:
            = 1 Floppy Drive B:

Output: AH = 00h No floppy disk (media) change
            = 01h Invalid floppy disk parameter
            = 06h Floppy disk was changed since last access
            = 80h Floppy disk drive not ready
            = Any other value is an error code (see page 216).

Description:

Function 16h indicates if a media change was made since the last floppy disk access.

INT 13h Floppy Disk Service, Continued

Function 17h Set Floppy Disk Type

Input: AH = 17h
          AL   = Floppy disk Format
               = 01h   320 or 360 KB floppy in 320 or 360 KB drive
               = 02h   360 KB floppy in 1.2 MB floppy drive
               = 03h   1.2 MB floppy in 1.2 MB floppy drive
               = 04h   720 KB floppy in 720 KB floppy drive
          DL   = 00h Floppy Drive A:
                01h Floppy Drive B:

Output: AH = 00h No error
               = Any other value is an error code (see page 216).
          CF   = 0 No error
               = 1 Error

Description:

Function 17h sets the format of a disk in a floppy drive and sets the data rate and media type if the drive supports the disk change line.

Function 18h Set Floppy Disk Type before Format

Input: AH = 18h
          CH   = Maximum number of tracks
          CL   = Sectors per track
          DL   = 00h Floppy Drive A:
                01h Floppy Drive B:

Output: AH = 00h Specified track and sector data is supported
               = Any other value is an error code (see page 216).
          CF   = 0 No error
               = 1 Error
      ES:DI = Pointer to drive parameter table if AH is 00h.

Description: Use Function 18h to set the media type before a formatting a floppy disk. Call Function 18h before INT 13h Function 05h is called.

INT 14h Serial Communications Service

INT 14h accesses and controls the serial ports. Most systems have two serial ports, attached to IRQ3 (COM2 or COM4) and IRQ4 (COM1 or COM3). AMIBIOS permits up to four serial ports to be configured. These serial ports are initialized to the following starting I/O port addresses:

COM1 3F8h,
COM2 2F8h,
COM3 3E8h, and
COM4 2E8h.

Additional serial ports can be configured in a customized BIOS.

The default values for the serial I/O port addresses used in a Hi-Flex AMIBIOS can be modified via AMIBCP.

INT 14h Functions

Functions 00h through 03h are defined in ISA standards. Functions 04h and 05h are defined in PS/2 standards and are only available in an AMIBIOS dated 080891 (August 8, 1991) or later.

Function	Title
00h	Initialize Serial Port
01h	Send Character to Serial Port
02h	Receive Character from Serial Port
03h	Read Serial Port Status
04h	Extended Initialize Serial Port
05h	Extended Serial Port Control

Serial Port I/O Addresses

The Serial I/O ports consists of eight contiguous I/O ports, in the following format:

I/O Port	Read and Write Status	Description
Base	Write	Transmitter Holding Register (contains the character to be sent). Bit 0, the least significant bit, is sent first. Bits 7–0 Contains data bits 7–0 when the Divisor Latch Access Bit (DLAB) is 0.
Base	Read	Receiver Buffer Register (contains the received character). Bit 0, the least significant bit, is received first. Bits 7–0 Contains data bits 7–0 when the Divisor Latch Access Bit (DLAB) is 0.
Base	Read and Write	Divisor Latch, low byte Both divisor latch registers store the data transmission rate divisor. Bits 7–0 Bits 7–0 of divisor when DLAB is 1.
Base + 1	Read and Write	Divisor Latch, high byte. Bits 7–0 Bits 15–8 of data transmission rate divisor when DLAB is 1.
Base + 1	Read and Write	Interrupt Enable Register. Permits the serial port controller interrupts to enable the chip interrupt output signal. Bits 7–4 Reserved Bit 3 Modem status interrupt enable if set. Bit 2 Receiver line status interrupt enable if set. Bit 1 Transmitter Holding register empty interrupt enable if set. Bit 0 Received data available interrupt enable when DLAB is 0 if set.

Base + 2	Read	Interrupt ID Register. Information about a pending interrupt is stored here. When the ID register is addressed, the highest priority interrupt is held and no other interrupts are acknowledged until the microprocessor services that interrupt.
		Bits 7–3 Reserved
		Bits 2–1 The pending interrupt that has the highest priority.
		   11b Receiver Line Status Interrupt, priority is the highest.
		   10b Received Data Available, second in priority.
		   01b Transmitter Holding Register Empty, third in priority.
		   00b Modem Status Interrupt, fourth in priority.
		Bit 0 0 Interrupt pending
		              1 No interrupt is pending.

I/O Port	Read and Write Status	Description

Base + 3	Read and Write	Line Control Register
		Bit 7 Divisor Latch Access Bit (DLAB)
		     0 Access receiver buffer, transmitter holding register, and interrupt enable register.
		     1 Access Divisor Latch of baud rate generator.
		Bit 6 Set Break Control. Serial output is forced to spacing state and remains there if set.
		Bit 5 Stick Parity if set.
		Bit 4 Even Parity Select if set.
		Bit 3 Parity Enable if set.
		Bit 2 Number of Stop Bits per Character.
		     0 One stop bit.
		     1 $1\frac{1}{2}$ stop bits if 5-bit word length is selected.
		          2 stop bits if 6, 7, or 8-bit word length is selected.
		Bits 1–0 Number of Lines per character
		     00b 5-Bit word length.
		     01b 6-Bit word length.
		     10b 7-Bit word length.
		     11b 8-Bit word length.

Base + 4	Read and Write	Modem Control Register Bits 7–5 Reserved Bit 4 Loopback mode for diagnostic testing of serial port if set. The output from the transmitter shift register is looped back to the receiver shift register input. Transmitted data is immediately received so the microprocessor can verify the transmit and receive data serial port paths. Bit 3 Force OUT2 interrupt if set. Bit 2 Force OUT1 active if set. Bit 1 Force Request To Send active if set. Bit 0 Force Data Terminal Ready active if set.

I/O Port	Read and Write Status	Description
Base + 5	Read Only	Line Status Register
		Bit 7 Reserved
		Bit 6 Transmitter shift and holding registers empty if set.
		Bit 5 Transmitter holding register empty if set. The controller is ready to accept a new character to send.
		Bit 4 Break interrupt if set. The received data input is held in the zero bit state longer than the transmission time of the start bit + data bits + parity bits + stop bits.
		Bit 3 Framing error if set. The stop bit that follows the last parity or data bit is zero.
		Bit 2 Parity error if set. The character has incorrect parity.
		Bit 1 Overrun error if set. A character was sent to the receiver buffer before the previous character in the buffer could be read, which destroys the previous character.
		Bit 0 Data Ready if set. A complete incoming character has been received and sent to the receiver buffer register.
Base + 6	Read Only	Modem Status Register
		Bit 7 Data Carrier Detect if set.
		Bit 6 Ring Indicator if set.
		Bit 5 Data Set Ready if set.
		Bit 4 Clear To Send if set.
		Bit 3 Delta Data Carrier Detect if set.
		Bit 2 Trailing Edge Ring Indicator if set.
		Bit 1 Delta Data Set Ready if set.
		Bit 0 Delta Clear To Send if set.
Base + 7	Read and Write	Reserved

cont'd

Function 00h Initialize Serial Port

Input: AH = 00h

AL = Parameter byte

Bits 7–5 Data transmission rate

000b	110
001b	150
010b	300
011b	600
100b	1200
101b	2400
110b	4800
111b	9600

Bits 4–3 Parity

00b	No parity
01b	Odd parity
10b	No parity
11b	Even parity

Bit 2   Number of stop bits

0	One bit
1	Two bits

Bits 1–0 Data length

10b	Seven bits
11b	Eight bits

DX = Serial Port Number. Index to serial port base table at 40:00h.

00h	COM 1	01h	COM 2
02h	COM 3	03h	COM 4

Function 00h Initialize Serial Port, cont'd

Output: AH = Line Status
           Bit 7 Timeout if set.
           Bit 6 Transmit Shift Register is empty if set.
           Bit 5 Transmit Holding Register is empty if set.
           Bit 4 Break signal detected if set.
           Bit 3 Framing error detected if set.
           Bit 2 Parity error detected if set.
           Bit 1 Data overrun error detected if set.
           Bit 0 Receive data ready if set.

      AL = Modem Status
           Bit 7 Receive line signal detected if set.
           Bit 6 Ring indicator if set.
           Bit 5 Data set ready if set.
           Bit 4 Clear to send if set.
           Bit 3 Delta receive line signal detect if set.
           Bit 2 Trailing edge ring indicator if set.
           Bit 1 Delta data set ready if set.
           Bit 0 Delta clear to send if set.

Description:

Function 00h initializes the specified serial port with the parameters in the parameter byte (AL). It returns the line status in AH and the modem status in AL.

cont'd

Function 01h Send Character to Serial Port

Input: AH = 01h

AL = Character to be sent

DX = Serial port number. Index to serial port base table at 40:00h.

00h COM 1   01h COM 2

02h COM 3   03h COM 4

Output: AH = Line Status

Bit 7 Timeout error if set.

Bit 6 Transmit Shift and Holding Register empty if set.

Bit 5 Transmit Holding Register empty if set.

Bit 4 Break Interrupt if set.

Bit 3 Framing Error if set.

Bit 2 Parity Error if set.

Bit 1 Data overrun error detected if set.

Bit 0 Receive data ready if set.

AL = Character Sent

Description:

Function 01h sends a character to the serial port. It returns the line status in AH.

Function 02h Receive Character from Serial Port

Input: AH = 02h

DX = Serial Port Number. Index to serial port base table at 40:00h.

00h COM 1	01h COM 2
02h COM 3	03h COM 4

Output: AH = Line Status

Bit 7 Timeout error if set.

Bit 6 Transmit Shift and Holding Register empty if set.

Bit 5 Transmit Holding Register empty if set.

Bit 4 Break Interrupt if set.

Bit 3 Framing Error if set.

Bit 2 Parity Error if set.

Bit 1 Data overrun error detected if set.

Bit 0 Receive data ready if set.

AL = Character Received

Description:

Function 02h receives a character in AL from the serial port. Function 02h also returns the port status in AH.

cont'd

Function 03h Return Serial Port Status

Input: AH   =   03h
         DX   =   Serial Port Number. Index to serial port base table at
                  40:00h.
                  00h COM 1   01h COM 2
                  02h COM 3   03h COM 4

Output: AH   =   Line Status
                 Bit 7 Timeout error if set.
                 Bit 6 Transmit Shift and Holding Register empty if
                        set.
                 Bit 5 Transmit Holding Register empty if set.
                 Bit 4 Break Interrupt if set.
                 Bit 3 Framing Error if set.
                 Bit 2 Parity Error if set.
                 Bit 1 Data overrun error detected if set.
                 Bit 0 Receive data ready if set.
        AL   =   Modem Status
                 Bit 7 Receive line signal detected if set.
                 Bit 6 Ring indicator if set.
                 Bit 5 Data set ready if set.
                 Bit 4 Clear to send if set.
                 Bit 3 Delta receive line signal detect if set.
                 Bit 2 Trailing edge ring indicator if set.
                 Bit 1 Delta data set ready if set.
                 Bit 0 Delta clear to send if set.

Description:

Function 03h returns the status of the specified serial port. Function
03h differs from function 00h. Function 03h has no initialization
process, but Function 00h does.

Function 04h Extended Initialize Serial Port

Input: AH = 04h

        AL = 00h No break signal
                 01h Break signal

        BH = 00h No parity
                 01h Odd parity
                 02h Even parity
                 03h Stick parity odd
                 04h Stick parity even

        BL = 00h 1 Stop bit
                 01h 2 Stop bits if data length is 6, 7, or 8 bits
                 10h 1½ Stop bits if data length is 5 bits

        CH = 00h Data length is 5 bits
                 01h Data length is 6 bits
                 02h Data length is 7 bits
                 03h Data length is 8 bits

        CL = 00h   110 bps
                 01h   150 bps
                 02h   300 bps
                 03h   600 bps
                 04h 1200 bps
                 05h 2400 bps
                 06h 4800 bps
                 07h 9600 bps
                 08h 19200 bps

        DX = Serial port number. Index to serial port base table at 40:00h.

00h COM 1	01h COM 2
02h COM 3	03h COM 4

cont'd

Function 04h Extended Initialize Serial Port, cont'd

Output: AH = Line Status

             Bit 7 Timeout if set.

             Bit 6 Transmit Shift Register is empty if set.

             Bit 5 Transmit Holding Register is empty if set.

             Bit 4 Break signal detected if set.

             Bit 3 Framing error detected if set.

             Bit 2 Parity error detected if set.

             Bit 1 Data overrun error detected if set.

             Bit 0 Receive data ready if set.

      AL = Modem Status

             Bit 7 Receive line signal detected if set.

             Bit 6 Ring indicator if set.

             Bit 5 Data set ready if set.

             Bit 4 Clear to send if set.

             Bit 3 Delta receive line signal detect if set.

             Bit 2 Trailing edge ring indicator if set.

             Bit 1 Delta data set ready if set.

             Bit 0 Delta clear to send if set.

Description:

Function 04h initializes the specified serial port with the parameters in the parameter byte (AL). Function 04h returns the line and modem status (if a modem is attached).

Function 04h differs from Function 00h in that different input parameters are required.

**Function 05h Extended Serial Port Control Subfunction AL = 00h
Read from Modem Control Register**

Input: AH   = 05h

           AL   = 00h Read from Modem Control Register

           DX   = Serial Port Number. Index to serial port base table at 40:00h.

                             00h COM 1   01h COM 2

                             02h COM 3   03h COM 4

Output: AH   = Line Status

                      Bit 7   Timeout if set.

                      Bit 6   Transmit Shift Register is empty if set.

                      Bit 5   Transmit Holding Register is empty if set.

                      Bit 4   Break signal detected if set.

                      Bit 3   Framing error detected if set.

                      Bit 2   Parity error detected if set.

                      Bit 1   Data overrun error detected if set.

                      Bit 0   Receive data ready if set.

           AL   = Modem Status

                      Bit 7   Receive line signal detected if set.

                      Bit 6   Ring indicator if set.

                      Bit 5   Data set ready if set.

                      Bit 4   Clear to send if set.

                      Bit 3   Delta receive line signal detect if set.

                      Bit 2   Trailing edge ring indicator if set.

                      Bit 1   Delta data set ready if set.

                      Bit 0   Delta clear to send if set.

           BL   = Modem Control Register

                      Bits 7–5 Reserved

                      Bit 4   Loop for testing if set.

                      Bit 3   OUT2 if set.

                      Bit 2   OUT1 if set.

                      Bit 1   Request to send if set.

                      Bit 0   Data terminal ready if set.

Description: Function 05h Subfunction 00h reads the modem control register for the specified serial port.

cont'd

Function 05h Extended Serial Port Control Subfunction AL = 01h Set Modem Control Register

Input: AH = 05h
      AL   = 01h Set Modem Control Register
      DX = Serial Port Number. Index to serial port base table at
            40:00h.

00h COM 1	01h COM 2
02h COM 3	03h COM 4

Output: AH = Line Status

Bit 7	Timeout if set.
Bit 6	Transmit Shift Register is empty if set.
Bit 5	Transmit Holding Register is empty if set.
Bit 4	Break signal detected if set.
Bit 3	Framing error detected if set.
Bit 2	Parity error detected if set.
Bit 1	Data overrun error detected if set.
Bit 0	Receive data ready if set.

      AL   = Modem Status

Bit 7	Receive line signal detected if set.
Bit 6	Ring indicator if set.
Bit 5	Data set ready if set.
Bit 4	Clear to send if set.
Bit 3	Change in receive line signal detect if set.
Bit 2	Trailing edge ring indicator if set.
Bit 1	Change in data set ready if set.
Bit 0	Change in clear to send if set.

      BL   = Modem Control Register

Bits 7–5	Reserved
Bit 4	Loop for testing if set.
Bit 3	OUT2 if set.
Bit 2	OUT1 if set.
Bit 1	Request to send if set.
Bit 0	Data terminal ready if set.

Description: Function 05h Subfunction 01h sets the modem control register for the specified serial port.

INT 15h Systems Services

INT 15h provides a variety of services:

Category	Description and INT 15h Functions
EISA Support	INT 15h Function D8h, subfunctions 00h through 04h, are defined only in the EISA specifications and are supported in the EISA BIOS.
Multitasking Services	The BIOS provides six hooks that can be used by programmers: INT 15h Functions 80h, 81h, 82h, 85h, 90h, and 91h are defined in the ISA standard and are available in the BIOS but do not perform any service. Software developers can trap or redirect the vectors of these interrupt functions to point to programmer-supplied service routines. No routines for these functions are provided in the BIOS.
Protected Mode Services	Function 87h Move Block provides a way to move large blocks of information from conventional to extended memory. Function 89h switches to protected mode.
Wait Routines	Functions 83h and 86h provide wait control. Function 86h does not return control to the calling program until a specified interval completes. Function 83h returns control to the caller immediately but sets a bit when a predetermined wait period is finished.
System Information	Function C1h returns the extended BIOS data area address. Function C0h returns system configuration data. Function 88h returns the extended memory size.
Advanced Power Management	Function 53h provides power management functions that conform to the Microsoft/Intel APM specification for systems that have power management functions.
PS/2 Support	Functions 4Fh, C1h, and C2h are defined in the PS/2 specification. AMIBIOS supports some PS/2-defined operations, including all PS/2 mouse operations. The programmer can invoke these mouse functions if the system includes the necessary hardware as well as the appropriate American Megatrends Keyboard Controller BIOS (version KF or later). Function C2h PS/2 Mouse Support is supported in all AMIBIOS dated August 8, 1991 (080891) or later.
Tape Cassette Services	INT 15h only handled the cassette tape I/O interface on the IBM PC. In the AMIBIOS, these functions (00h, 01h, 02h, and 03h) are not supported. If called, the BIOS sets the Carry Flag in the FLAGS register and returns AH = 86h (no cassette present). You can trap Functions 00h – 03h and substitute your own code.
Joystick support	Function 84h provides joystick support for up to two joysticks.

cont'd

INT 15h Functions

Function	Title
4Fh	Keyboard Intercept
53h	Advanced Power Management AL = 00h APM Installation Check AL = 01h APM Real Mode Interface Connect AL = 02h APM 16-Bit Protected Mode Interface Connect AL = 03h APM 32-Bit Protected Mode Interface Connect AL = 04h APM Interface Disconnect AL = 05h CPU Idle AL = 06h CPU Busy AL = 07h Set Power State AL = 08h Enable Power Management AL = 09h Restore BIOS Power-On Defaults AL = 0Ah Get Power Status AL = 0Bh Get PM Event AL = 0Ch Get Power State AL = 0Dh Enable Device Power Management AL = 80h OEM-Defined APM Functions BH = 7Fh APM Installation Check BH = 00h-7Eh; 80h-FFh OEM-Defined Function
80h	Device Open (replaced by BIOS user routine)
81h	Device Close (replaced by BIOS user routine)
82h	Program Termination (replaced by BIOS user routine)
83h	Set Event Wait Interval
84h	Joystick Support DX = 001h Read Current Switch Settings DX = 01h Read Resistive Inputs
85h	System Request Key (replaced by BIOS user routine)
86h	Wait
87h	Move Block
88h	Return Extended Memory Size
89h	Switch to Protected Mode
90h	Device Busy Loop (replaced by BIOS user routine)
91h	Interrupt Complete (replaced by BIOS user routine)
C0h	Return System Configuration Parameters
C1h	Return Address of Extended BIOS Data Area
C2h	PS/2 Mouse Support
C3h	Fail-Safe Timer
D8h	EISA Support

Function 4Fh PS/2 Keyboard Intercept

Input: AH = 4Fh
        AL = Scan Code

Output: AL = Scan Code
       CF = 0 Scan Code processed but should not go to keyboard buffer.
          = 1 Scan Code processed or modified and should go to keyboard buffer.

Description:

INT 09h calls this function each time a key is pressed. Function 4Fh can be used to search the data from a keyboard. If the specified scan code is found, the routine provided by the programmer is executed. This routine can modify the scan code.

cont'd

Function 53h Subfunction AL = 00h APM Installation Check

Mode: Real Mode

Input: AH   = 53h
             AL   = 00h
             BX   = Power Device ID
                   = 0000h BIOS

Output: AH   = 1 APM major version number (in BCD)
             AL   = 1 APM minor version number (in BCD)
             BH   = P (in ASCII)
             BL   = M (in ASCII)
             CF   = 0 APM is supported by the BIOS.
                   = 1 APM is not supported by the BIOS.
             CX   = APM Flags
                     Bit 3 1 BIOS Power Management is disabled.
                     Bit 2 0 A *CPU Idle* call does not slow the processor
                            clock speed or stop the clock.
                     Bit 1 1 The 32-bit protected mode interface is
                            supported.
                     Bit 0 1 The 16-bit protected mode interface is
                            supported.

Description:

This subfunction allows the APM driver (the calling program) to
ascertain the APM specification version that is supported. It also
specifies if the system BIOS supports APM.

Function 53h Subfunction AL = 01h APM Real Mode Interface Connect

Mode: Real Mode

Input: AH = 53h
AL = 01h
BX = Power Device ID
= 0000h BIOS

Output: AH = Error code if unsuccessful
= 02h   A real mode interface connection is already established.
= 05h   A 16-Bit protected mode interface connection is already established.
= 07h   A 32-Bit protected mode interface connection is already established.
= 09h   Device ID unrecognized.
CF = 0 Successful
= 1 Unsuccessful
CX = APM 16-bit data segment (real mode segment base address)

Description:

This subfunction initializes the interface between the APM Driver (the calling program) and the BIOS. Before the interface is established, the BIOS provides OEM-defined power management. Once the interface is defined, the APM driver and the BIOS coordinate power management activities.

cont'd

Function 53h Subfunction AL = 02h APM 16-Bit Protected Mode Interface Connect

Mode: Real Mode

Input: AH = 53h
           AL = 02h
           BX = Power Device ID
               = 0000h BIOS

Output: AH = 00h Successful
               = Error code if unsuccessful
               = 02h A real mode interface connection is already established.
               = 05h A 16-Bit protected mode interface connection is already established.
               = 06h The 16-bit protected mode interface is not supported.
               = 07h A 32-Bit protected mode interface connection is already established.
               = 09h Device ID unrecognized
           AX = APM 16-bit code segment or the real mode segment base address
           BX = Offset of the entry point into the BIOS
           CF = 0 Successful
               = 1 Unsuccessful
           CX = APM 16-bit data segment (real mode segment base address)
           DI = BIOS code segment length
           SI = BIOS data segment length

Description:

This subfunction initializes the 16-bit protected mode interface between the APM Driver (the calling program) and the BIOS. This function must be invoked from real mode. This interface allows a routine making a call in protected mode to invoke BIOS functions without switching into real or Virtual 8086 mode.

Function 53h Subfunction AL = 02h APM 16-Bit Protected Mode Interface Connect, cont'd

Initializing Descriptors

The APM 16-bit protected mode interface uses two consecutive segment/selector descriptors as a 16-bit code and data segment.

The calling program must initialize these descriptors with the segment base and length information returned by this call. The selectors can be in the GDT or LDT and must be valid when the BIOS is called in protected mode.

The code segment descriptor must specify protection level 0. The BIOS function must be invoked with CPL = 0 so the BIOS can execute privileged instructions.

The calling program invokes the BIOS using the 16-bit interface by making a FAR call to the code segment selector that the calling program initialized and the offset returned in BX from this call.

The calling program must supply a stack that can handle both the BIOS and potential interrupt handlers.

The calling program's stack becomes active when interrupts are enabled in the BIOS functions. The BIOS does not switch stacks when interrupts are enabled, including the NMI.

The BIOS 16-bit protected mode interface must be called with a 16-bit stack.

When a BIOS function is called in protected mode, the current I/O permission bitmap must permit access to the I/O ports that the BIOS uses.

cont'd

Function 53h Subfunction AL = 03h APM 32-Bit Protected Mode Interface Connect

Mode: Real Mode

Input:	AH	=	53h
	AL	=	03h
	BX	=	Power Device ID
		=	0000h BIOS

Output:	AH	=	00h	Successful
		=		Error code if unsuccessful
		=	02h	A real mode interface connection is already established.
		=	05h	A 16-Bit protected mode interface connection is already established.
		=	07h	A 32-Bit protected mode interface connection is already established.
		=	08h	The 32-bit protected mode interface is not supported.
		=	09h	Device ID unrecognized
	AX	=		APM 32-bit code segment or the real mode segment base address
	EBX	=		Offset of the entry point into the BIOS
	CF	=		0 Successful
		=		1 Unsuccessful
	CX	=		APM 16-bit data segment (real mode segment base address)
	DI	=		BIOS code segment length
	DX	=		APM data segment (real mode segment base address)
	SI	=		BIOS data segment length

Description: This subfunction initializes the 32-bit protected mode interface between the APM Driver (the calling program) and the BIOS. This function must be invoked from real mode. This interface allows a routine making a call in protected mode to invoke BIOS functions without switching into real or Virtual 8086 mode.

Function 53h Subfunction AL = 03 APM 32-Bit Protected Mode Interface Connect, cont'd

Initializing Descriptors

The APM 32-bit protected mode interface uses three consecutive segment/selector descriptors as 32-bit code, 16-bit code, and data segment. Both the 32-bit and 16-bit code segment descriptors are needed because the BIOS 32-bit interface can call other BIOS routines.

The calling program must initialize these descriptors with the segment base and length information returned by this call. The selectors can be in the GDT or LDT and must be valid when the BIOS is called in protected mode.

The code segment descriptor must specify protection level 0. The BIOS function must be invoked with CPL = 0 so the BIOS can execute privileged instructions.

The calling program invokes the BIOS using the 32-bit interface by making a FAR call to the 32-bit code segment selector that the calling program initialized and the offset returned in EBX from this call.

The calling program must supply a stack that can handle both the BIOS and potential interrupt handlers.

The calling program's stack becomes active when interrupts are enabled in the BIOS functions. The BIOS does not switch stacks when interrupts are enabled, including the NMI.

The BIOS 32-bit protected mode interface must be called with a 32-bit stack.

When a BIOS function is called in protected mode, the current I/O permission bitmap must permit access to the I/O ports that the BIOS uses.

cont'd

Function 53h Subfunction AL = 04h APM Interface Disconnect

Mode: Real Mode, 16-Bit Protected Mode, 32-Bit Protected Mode

Input: AH   = 53h
            AL   = 04h
            BX   = Power Device ID
                 = 0000h BIOS

Output: AH   = Error code if unsuccessful
                 = 03h Interface disconnected
                 = 09h Device ID unrecognized
            CF   = 0 Successful
                 = 1 Unsuccessful

Description:

This subfunction:

- disconnects the BIOS and the APM driver,
- restores the BIOS default functions, and
- returns control of power management to the BIOS.

All power management parameters in effect when APM is
disconnected will remain in effect.

Function 53h Subfunction AL = 05h CPU Idle

Mode: Real Mode, 16-bit Protected Mode, 32-bit Protected Mode

Input: AH = 53h
             AL = 05h
             BX = Power Device ID
                 = 0000h BIOS

Output: AH = Error code if unsuccessful
                 = 03h Interface disconnected
             CF = 0 Successful
                 = 1 Unsuccessful

Description:

Call this function to inform the BIOS that the system is idle. The BIOS will suspend the system until the next system event, which is usually an interrupt. This function permits the BIOS to implement power-saving actions, such as a CPU HLT instruction or slowing the CPU clock.

cont'd

Function 53h Subfunction AL = 06h CPU Busy

Mode: Real Mode, 16-bit Protected Mode, 32-bit Protected Mode

Input: AH = 53h
AL = 06h
BX = Power Device ID
= 0000h BIOS

Output: AH = Error code if unsuccessful
= 03h Interface disconnected
CF = 0 Successful
= 1 Unsuccessful

Description:

You only need to invoke this subfunction if *INT 15h AH = 53h Subfunction AL = 05h CPU Idle* was previously invoked. Check bit 2 in CX after invoking *Function 53h Subfunction AL = 00h APM Installation Check* to determine if the BIOS will slow the clock during an *INT 15h AH = 53h Subfunction AL = 05h CPU Idle* call.

This subfunction tells the BIOS that the system is busy. The BIOS restores the CPU clock speed to full speed.

Do not call this function when the CPU is already operating at full speed. While it is not illegal to do so, it adds system overhead.

Function 53h Subfunction AL = 07h Set Power State

Mode: Real Mode, 16-bit Protected Mode, 32-bit Protected Mode

Input: AH   =   53h
AL   =   07h
BX   =   Power Device ID
=   0001h All devices under APM
=   01xxh Display (xx = unit number). Use xx = FF to specify all devices in a class.
=   02xxh Secondary storage
=   03xxh Parallel ports
=   04xxh Serial ports
=   E000h – EFFFh OEM-defined device IDs
CX   =   Power state
0000h APM enabled (not supported for Device ID 0001h)
0001h Standby
0002h Suspend
0003h Off
0004h – 001Fh Reserved system states
0020h – 003Fh OEM-defined system states
0040h – 007Fh OEM-defined device states
0080h – FFFFh Reserved device states

Output: AH   =   Error code if unsuccessful
=   01h Power management disabled
=   03h Interface disconnected
=   09h Device ID unrecognized
=   0Ah Parameter value out of range
=   60h Unable to enter requested state
CF   =   0 Successful
=   1 Unsuccessful

Description:

This subfunction sets the specified power state for the specified device.

cont'd

Function 53h Subfunction AL = 07h Set Power State, cont'd

Examples - System Standby

The following example places the system in Standby State. The calling program invokes this function in response to a *System Standby Request Notification* from the BIOS. The calling program can also invoke this function at any time if it determines that the system is idle and should go to Standby. Standby State is exited when any interrupt occurs.

Input: AH   = 53h
             AL   = 07h
             BX   = 0001h All devices under APM
             CX   = 0001h System standby

Function 53h Subfunction AL = 08h Enable Power Management

Mode: Real Mode, 16-bit Protected Mode, 32-bit Protected Mode

Input: AH = 53h
          AL   = 08h
          BX   = Power Device ID
                = 0001h All devices under APM
                = FFFFh All devices under APM (as specified in the
                    APM 1.0 specification)
          CX = Function code
                = 0000h Disable power management
                = 0001h Enable power management

Output: AH = Error code if unsuccessful
                = 01h Power management disabled
                = 03h Interface disconnected
                = 09h Device ID unrecognized
                = 0Ah Parameter value out of range
          CF   = 0 Successful
                = 1 Unsuccessful

Description:

This subfunction enables (or disables) automatic power down. When disabled, the BIOS does not automatically power devices down, enter Suspend State, enter the Standby State, or perform any power-saving steps in response to Function 53h Subfunction AL = 05h CPU Idle calls.

cont'd

Function 53h Subfunction AL = 09h Restore BIOS Power-On Defaults

Mode: Real Mode, 16-bit Protected Mode, 32-bit Protected Mode

Input: AH = 53h
　　　　　 AL = 09h
　　　　　 BX = Power Device ID
　　　　　　　 = 0001h All devices under APM
　　　　　　　 = FFFFh All devices under APM (as specified in the APM 1.0 documents)

Output: AH = Error code if unsuccessful
　　　　　　　 = 03h Interface disconnected
　　　　　　　 = 09h Device ID unrecognized
　　　　　 CF = 0 Successful
　　　　　　　 = 1 Unsuccessful

Description:

This subfunction reinitializes the BIOS power-on default values.

Function 53h Subfunction AL = 0Ah Get Power Status

Mode: Real Mode, 16-bit Protected Mode, 32-bit Protected Mode

Input: AH = 53h
AL = 0Ah
BX = Power Device ID
= 0001h BIOS

Output: AH = Error code if unsuccessful
= 09h Device ID unrecognized
BH = Line status
= 00h Offline
= 01h Online
= 02h On backup power
= FFh Unknown
BL = Battery status
= 00h High
= 01h Low
= 02h Critical
= 03h Charging
= FFh Unknown
CF = 0 Successful
= 1 Unsuccessful
CL = Remaining battery life (percentage of charge)
= 0 – 100 Percentage of full charge
= 255 Unknown
DX = Remaining battery life (time units)
= Bit 15   0 Time unit is seconds
                  1 Time unit is minutes
= Bits 14-0   Number of seconds or minutes of battery
                life left
                0000h – 7FFFh   Valid number
                FFFFh   Unknown

Description:

This subfunction returns the current system power status.

cont'd

Function 53h Subfunction AL = 0Bh Get PM Event

Mode: Real Mode, 16-bit Protected Mode, 32-bit Protected Mode

Input: AH   = 53h
             AL   = 0Bh

Output: AH   = Error code if unsuccessful
                  = 03h Interface disconnected
                  = 80h No power management events pending
             CF   = 0 Successful
                  = 1 Unsuccessful

Description:

This subfunction returns the next power management event or indicates that no power management events are pending. Power management events can apply to a device or to the APM system.

This subfunction should be invoked until no power management events are pending or an error occurs.

Function 53h Subfunction AL = 0Ch Get Power State

Mode: Real Mode, 16-bit Protected Mode, 32-bit Protected Mode

Input: AH = 53h

          AL = 0Ch

          BX = Power Device ID

               = 0001h All devices under APM

               = 01xxh Display (xx is the unit number). Specify xx = FF to include all devices in a class.

               = 02xxh Secondary storage (xx is the unit number).

               = 03xxh Parallel ports (xx is the unit number).

               = 04xxh Serial ports (xx is the unit number).

               = E00h – EFFFh OEM-defined power device IDs.

Output: AH = Error Code if unsuccessful

               = 01h Power management disabled

                  09h Device ID unrecognized

          CF = 0 Successful

               = 1 Unsuccessful

          CX = 0000h APM enabled

               = 0001h Standby

               = 0001h Suspend

               = 0003h Off

               = 0004h – 001Fh Reserved system states

               = 0020h – 003Fh OEM-defined system states

               = 0040h – 007Fh OEM-defined device states

               = 0080h – FFFFh Reserved device states

Description:

This subfunction returns the device power state for a specific Device ID. *0001h All devices under APM* or *all devices in a class* (*x*FF*x*h) is returned for the specified Power Device ID when that device has been used in an *AL = 07h Set Power State* call. When the power device ID has not been used in an *AL = 07h Set Power State* call, this function is unsuccessful and returns AH = 09h Device ID unrecognized. Use this subfunction to find out if BIOS power management is enabled for a device. This subfunction returns AH = 01h if BIOS power management is disabled for a device.

cont'd

Function 53h Subfunction AL = 0Dh Enable Device Power Management

Mode: Real Mode, 16-bit Protected Mode, 32-bit Protected Mode

Input: AH = 53h
        AL = 0Dh
        BX = Power Device ID
            = 0001h All devices under APM
            = 01xxh Display (xx is the unit number). Specify xx = FF to include all devices in a class.
            = 02xxh Secondary storage (xx is the unit number).
            = 03xxh Parallel ports (xx is the unit number).
            = 04xxh Serial ports (xx is the unit number).
            = E00h – EFFFh OEM-defined power device IDs.
        CX = Function code
            = 0000h Disable power management
            = 0001h Enable power management

Output: AH = Error code if unsuccessful
            = 01h Power management disabled
            = 03h Interface disconnected
            = 09h Device ID unrecognized
            = 0Ah Parameter value out of range
        CF = 0 Successful
            = 1 Unsuccessful

Description:

This subfunction enables (or disables) automatic power down for the specified device. When disabled, the BIOS does not automatically power the device down.

Function 53h Subfunction AL = 80h BH = 7Fh APM Installation Check (OEM-Defined APM Functions)

Mode: Real Mode, 16-bit Protected Mode, 32-bit Protected Mode

Input: AH   =   53h
             AL   =   80h
             BH   =   7Fh OEM APM installation check

Output: AH   =   Error code if unsuccessful
                  =   03h Interface disconnected
             BX   =   OEM ID
             CF   =   0 Successful
                  =   1 Unsuccessful
             CX   =   Optional OEM-Specific information
             DX   =   Optional OEM-Specific information

Description:

Call this subfunction to find out if the BIOS supports OEM hardware-dependent functions.

cont'd

Function 53h Subfunction AL = 80h BH = OEM-Defined Function Code

Mode: Real Mode, 16-bit Protected Mode, 32-bit Protected Mode

Input: AH   =   53h
            AL   =   80h
            BH   =   00h – 7Eh OEM-Defined function code
                 =   80h – FFh OEM-Defined function code

Output: AH   =   Error code if unsuccessful
                 =   03h Interface disconnected
            CF   =   0 Successful
                 =   1 Unsuccessful
            CX   =   Optional OEM-Specific information
            DX   =   Optional OEM-Specific information

Description:

Call this subfunction to access OEM product-specific APM functions.

INT 15h Systems Services, Continued

INT 15h Power Management Error Codes

These error codes appear in AH after a function call.

AH	Description	Generated by
01h	Power management disabled	AL = 07h Set Power State AL = 08h Enable Power Management AL = 0Ah Get Power Status AL = 0Dh Enable Device Power Management
02h	Real mode interface connection already established	AL = 01h APM Real Mode Interface Connect AL = 02h APM 16-Bit Protected Mode Interface Connect AL = 03h APM 32-Bit Protected Mode Interface Connect
03h	Interface disconnected	AL = 04h APM Interface Disconnect AL = 05h CPU Idle AL = 06h CPU Busy AL = 07h Set Power State AL = 08h Enable Power Management AL = 09h Restore BIOS Power-On Defaults AL = 0Bh Get PM Event AL = 0Dh Enable Device Power Management AL = 80h OEM APM Function
05h	16-bit protected mode interface already established	AL = 01h APM Real Mode Interface Connect AL = 02h APM 16-Bit Protected Mode Interface Connect AL = 03h APM 32-Bit Protected Mode Interface Connect
06h	16-bit protected mode interface not supported	AL = 02h APM 16-Bit Protected Mode Interface Connect
07h	32-bit protected mode interface already established	AL = 01h APM Real Mode Interface Connect AL = 02h APM 16-Bit Protected Mode Interface Connect AL = 03h APM 32-Bit Protected Mode Interface Connect
08h	32-bit protected mode interface not supported	AL = 03h APM 32-Bit Protected Mode Interface Connect

INT 15h Systems Services, Continued

AH	Description	Generated by
09h	Device ID Unrecognized	AL = 01h APM Real Mode Interface Connect AL = 02h APM 16-Bit Protected Mode Interface Connect AL = 03h APM 32-Bit Protected Mode Interface Connect AL = 04h APM Interface Disconnect AL = 07h Set Power State AL = 08h Enable Power Management AL = 09h Restore BIOS Power-On Defaults AL = 0Ah Get Power Status AL = 0Ch Get Power State AL = 0Dh Enable Device Power Management
0Ah	Parameter values out of range	AL = 07h Set Power State AL = 08h Enable Power Management AL = 0Dh Enable Device Power Management
60h	Unable to enter requested state	AL = 07h Set Power State
80h	No power management events pending	AL = 0Bh Get PM Event
86h	Reserved. No APM present.	

Function 80h Device Open

Input: AH = 80h
         BX = Device ID
         CX = Process ID

Output: Programmer-defined

Description: Function 80h can be used by multiprocessing systems.
         The system program manager traps this function and
         provides a routine for INT 15h Function 80h that
         attaches a logical device to a specified process.

Function 81h Device Close

Input: AH = 81h
         BX = Device ID
         CX = Process ID

Output: Programmer-defined

Description: Function 81h can be used by multiprocessing systems.
         The system program manager traps this function and
         provides a routine for INT 15h Function 81h that
         detaches a logical device from a specified process.

Function 82h Process Termination

Input: AH = 82h
         BX = Process ID

Output: Programmer-defined

Description: Function 82h can be used by multiprocessing systems.
         The system program manager traps this function and
         provides a routine for INT 15h Function 82h that
         terminates a process.

cont'd

Function 83h Event Wait

Input: AH   = 83h
        AL   = 00h Request Wait or 01h Cancel Wait
        CX:DX = Number of μseconds to delay
        ES:BX = Pointer to a Flag

Output: AH   = 00h
        AL   = Value written to CMOS RAM Register B if
                successful.
             = 00h Function is busy
        CF   = 0 No error
             = 1 Function is busy

Description: Function 83h sets a flag after a specified number of
              μseconds has elapsed. Bit 7 of the byte at address ES:BX
              is set after the wait has expired. The number of
              μseconds to delay should be a multiple of 976.

Function 84h Joystick Support

Input: AH   = 84h
        DX   = 00h Read Current Switch Settings
                01h Read Resistive Inputs

Output: *If DX was set to 0:*
        AL   = Bits 7–4 Switch Settings
                Bits 3–0 Reserved
                If DX was set to 1:
        AX   = Joystick A x coordinate
        BX   = Joystick A y coordinate
        CX   = Joystick B x coordinate
        DX   = Joystick B y coordinate
        CF   = 0 No error
             = 1 Value in DX is incorrect

Description: Function 84h reads the switches and inputs of a joystick
              attached via a game adapter. If a game adapter is not
              installed, 00h is returned in AH.

Function 85h SysReq Key Handler

Input: AH   = 85h
         AL   = 00h Key Make (Depressed)
                01h Key Break (Released)

Output: Programmer-defined

Description:

A multitasking operating system can use Function 85h to see when SYSREQ is pressed or released. The programmer can trap this function and provide another service routine. The BIOS returns AH = 00h and the Carry Flag is set to 0.

Function 86h Wait Function

Input: AH   = 86h
         CX:DX = Number of μseconds to Wait

Output: CF   = 0 No error
             = 1 Error

Description:

Function 86h delays the system for a specified number of μseconds.

cont'd

Function 87h Move Extended Memory Block

Input: AH = 87h
        CX = Number of Words to Move
    ES:SI = Address of Descriptor Table

Output: AH = 00h No error
             = 01h RAM Parity Error (Parity Error Cleared)
             = 02h Exception INT Error
             = 03h Gate Address 20 (GA20) Failed
        CF = 0 No error
             = 1 Error

Description:

Function 88h moves data between conventional (DOS) memory and extended memory. It uses a Global Descriptor Table (GDT) in the following format (all offsets are with respect to ES:SI):

Offset	Entry Description
00h – 07h	Dummy entry, should be all zeros.
08h – 0Fh	GDT entry (ES:SI)
10h – 17h	Source GDT entry
18h – 1Fh	Destination GDT entry
20h – 27h	Temporary BIOS CS entry
28h – 2Fh	Temporary SS area

Initialize the source GDT and destination GDT entries. All other entries should be initialized to zero. Interrupts are disabled while this function is performed.

Function 88h Return Extended Memory Size

Input: AH = 88h

Output: AX = Number of contiguous 1 KB Blocks of Extended
                     Memory

Description: Function 88h returns the size of extended memory
                  (memory above 1 MB) installed on the system. The
                  number of 1 KB blocks of extended memory is specified
                  in AX.

Function 89h Switch to Protected Mode

Input: AH   = 89h
          BH   = Offset to Interrupt Descriptor Table that points to the
                      beginning of the first eight hardware interrupts.
          BL   = Offset to Interrupt Descriptor Table that points to the
                      beginning of the next eight hardware interrupts.
       ES:SI = Address of Descriptor Table.

Output: AH   = 00h No error
               = FFh Error
         CF   = 0 No error
               = 1 Error

Description:

Function 89h switches the microprocessor to protected mode from real
mode. In the *IBM PC/AT Technical Reference Manual,* protected mode
was called virtual mode.

cont'd

Function 89h Switch to Protected Mode. cont'd

Global Descriptor Table

Initialize a Global Descriptor Table (GDT) as follows. All offsets are with respect to ES:SI.

Offset	Table Entry
00h – 07h	Dummy entry, should be all zeros.
08h – 0Fh	Pointer to GDT.
10h – 17h	Interrupt Descriptor Table (IDT) entry.
18h – 1Fh	Programmer-defined DS entry.
20h – 27h	Programmer-defined ES entry.
28h – 2Fh	Programmer-defined SS entry.
30h – 37h	Programmer-defined CS entry.
38h – 3Fh	Temporary BIOS CS entry.

Setting Values and Initializing

The programmer should initialize the GDT, IDT, DS, ES, SS, and CS entries. The temporary BIOS CS entry should be zero. The dummy entry should be all zeros.

The entry at offset 08h is actually a pointer to the GDT table. Its value consists of the physical address derived from ES:SI (pointer to GDT = ((ES * 10) + SI)) and the segment limit (length of the GDT).

For additional information on Global Descriptor Tables, see the *Intel i486 Programmer's Reference Manual*.

INT 15h Systems Services, Continued

Function 90h Device Busy Loop

Input: AH   = 90h
         AL   = Device Type Code
                00h Hard disk drive
                01h Floppy disk drive
                02h Keyboard
                03h PS/2-type mouse
                80h Network
                FCh Hard disk reset
                FDh Floppy disk drive motor
                FEh Printer
         ES:BX = Pointer to a request block if AL = 80h–FFh (a
                 reentrant device).

Output: Programmer-defined

Description:

Function 90h is provided for system-level device drivers to perform a wait for I/O completion. The service routine is provided by the drivers.

Serially reusable devices must be given device types from 00h – 7Fh.

Reentrant devices must have a device type between 80h and BFh.

Wait-only calls that have no corresponding INT 15h Function 91h Interrupt Complete call must have device types C0h – FFh.

cont'd

Function 91h Interrupt Complete

Input: AH   = 91h
       AL   = Device Type Code
                 00h Hard disk drive
                 01h Floppy disk drive
                 02h Keyboard
                 03h PS/2-type mouse
                 80h Network
                 FCh Hard disk reset
                 FDh Floppy disk drive motor
                 FEh Printer
   ES:BX = Points to a request block if AL = 80h – FFh (a reentrant device).

Output: Programmer-defined

Description:

Function 91h is provided for system-level device drivers to signal that I/O has been completed. The service routine is provided by the drivers.

Function C0h Return Configuration Parameter

Input: AH   = C0h

Output: AH   = 00h No error
       AH   = 86h
       CF   = 0 No error
    ES:BX = Address of Configuration Parameter Table

Function C0h Return Configuration Parameter, cont'd

Description:

Function C0h returns a pointer to the System Configuration Table. The format of this table is:

Offset	Initial Value	Description
00h – 01h		Number of Bytes in this table (must be at least 8)
02h	FCh	Model Byte (always FCh)
03h	01h	Submodel Byte (always 01h)
04h		BIOS Revision Level
05h		Feature Information Byte Bit 7 DMA channel 3 used if set Bit 6 Interrupt controllers cascaded if set Bit 5 Real time clock available if set Bit 4 Keyboard intercept (INT 15h Function 4Fh) available if set Bits 3–0 Reserved, should be zeros.
06h – 09h		Reserved

In all ISA and EISA systems, byte 02h is always FCh and byte 03h is always 01h.

Function C1h Return Address of Extended BIOS Data Area

Input: AH = C1h

Output: CF   = 0 No error
               = 1 Error
        ES = Segment of Extended BIOS Data Area

Description:

Function C1h returns the segment of the extended BIOS data area.

cont'd

Function C2h PS/2 Mouse Support

Function C2h, originally defined in the PS/2 specification, controls a PS/2-type mouse or pointing device. Support for a PS/2-type mouse is provided by the AMIBIOS if the system has the proper hardware and an American Megatrends Keyboard Controller BIOS version F (KF) or later. See page 431 for more information about the American Megatrends Keyboard Controller BIOS.

Function C2h Subfunction 00h Enable Mouse

Input:	AH	=	C2h
	AL	=	00h
	BH	=	00h Disable
		=	01h Enable
Output:	AH	=	00h No error
		=	01h Invalid subfunction number
		=	02h Invalid input values
		=	03h Mouse interface error
		=	04h Resend required
		=	05h Far call is not installed
	CF	=	0 No error
		=	1 Error

Description:

Function C2h Subfunction 00h enables or disables the mouse.

Function C2h Subfunction 01h Reset Mouse

Input: AH = C2h
           AL = 01h

Output: AH = 00h No error
               = 01h Invalid subfunction number
               = 02h Invalid input values
               = 03h Mouse interface error
               = 04h Resend required
               = 05h Far call is not installed
           CF = 0 No error
               = 1 Error

Description:

Function C2h Subfunction 01h resets the mouse and sets the sample rate, resolution, and other attributes to the default values. The mouse is also disabled by default.

The default settings are:

Parameter	Disabled State
Mouse	Disabled
Sample Rate	100 samples per second
Resolution	4 counts per millimeter
Data package size	unchanged
Scaling	1:1

cont'd

Function C2h Subfunction 02h Set Sample Rate

Input: AH = C2h
       AL = 02h
       BH = 00h 10 samples per second
              01h 20 samples per second
              02h 40 samples per second
              03h 60 samples per second
              04h 80 samples per second
              05h 100 samples per second (default)
              06h 200 samples per second

Output: AH = 00h No error
           = 01h Invalid subfunction number
           = 02h Invalid input values
           = 03h Mouse interface error
           = 04h Resend required
           = 05h Far call is not installed
       CF = 0 No error
           = 1 Error

Description:

Function C2h Subfunction 02h sets the mouse sample rate. The default sample rate is 100 samples per second.

Function C2h Subfunction 03h Set Resolution

Input: AH = C2h
AL = 03h
BH = 00h 1 count per millimeter
01h 2 counts per millimeter
02h 4 counts per millimeter (default)
03h 8 counts per millimeter

Output: AH = 00h No error
= 01h Invalid subfunction number
= 02h Invalid input values
= 03h Mouse interface error
= 04h Resend required
= 05h Far call is not installed
CF = 0 No error
= 1 Error

Description: Function C2h Subfunction 03h sets the mouse resolution rate. The default is 4 counts per millimeter.

Function C2h Subfunction 04h Return Mouse Type

Input: AH = C2h
AL = 04h

Output: AH = 00h No error
= 01h Invalid subfunction number
= 02h Invalid input values
= 03h Mouse interface error
= 04h Resend required
= 05h Far call is not installed
BH = Device ID
CF = 0 No error
= 1 Error

Description: Function C2h Subfunction 04h returns the mouse device ID number.

cont'd

Function C2h Subfunction 05h Initialize Mouse Interface

Input: AH = C2h
        AL = 05h
        BH = Data Packet Size (1 to 8, representing 1 – 8 bytes)

Output: AH = 00h No error
             = 01h Invalid subfunction number
             = 02h Invalid input values
             = 03h Mouse interface error
             = 04h Resend required
             = 05h Far call is not installed
        CF = 0 No error
             = 1 Error

Description:

Function C2h Subfunction 05h performs the same operations as Subfunction 01h, but it also sets the data packet size of the mouse interface. The default values specified in subfunction 01h are used here also and the packet size must be in BH. The default settings are:

Parameter	Disabled State
Mouse	Disabled
Sample Rate	100 samples per second
Resolution	4 counts per millimeter
Data package size	Unchanged
Scaling	1:1

Function C2h Subfunction 06h Mouse Status or Set Scaling Factor

Input:	AH	= C2h
	AL	= 06h
	BH	= 00h Return mouse status
		= 01h Set 1:1 scaling factor
		= 02h Set 2:1 scaling factor

Output:	AH	= 00h No error
		= 01h Invalid subfunction number
		= 02h Invalid input values
		= 03h Mouse interface error
		= 04h Resend required
		= 05h Far call is not installed
	BL	= Status Byte *(If BH was 00h, BL is the status byte)*
		Bit 7 Reserved
		Bit 6 0 Stream mode is used
		1 Remote mode is used
		Bit 5 0 Mouse disabled
		1 Mouse enabled
		Bit 4 0 1:1 scaling is used
		1 2:1 scaling is used
		Bit 3 Reserved
		Bit 2 1 Left button pressed
		Bit 1 Reserved
		Bit 0 1 Right button pressed
	CF	= 0 No error
		= 1 Error
	CL	= Resolution rate
		00h 1 count per millimeter
		01h 2 counts per millimeter
		02h 4 counts per millimeter
		03h 8 counts per millimeter

cont'd

Function C2h Subfunction 06h Mouse Status or Set Scaling Factor, cont'd

Output:, cont'd

> DL = Sample rate
> > 0Ah   10 samples per second
> > 14h   20 samples per second
> > 28h   40 samples per second
> > 3Ch   60 samples per second
> > 50h   80 samples per second
> > 64h 100 samples per second
> > C8h 200 samples per second

Description:

Function C2h Subfunction 06h can be used to ascertain the mouse status or to set the mouse scaling factor.

Function C2h Subfunction 07h Set Mouse Handler Address

Input: AH   = C2h
             AL   = 07h
             ES:BX = Address of Programmer Routine

Output: AH   = No error
                   = 01h Invalid subfunction number
                   = 02h Invalid input values
                   = 03h Mouse interface error
                   = 04h Resend required
                   = 05h Far call is not installed
             CF   = 0 No error
                   = 1 Error

Description:

Function C2h Subfunction 07h attaches a programmer-supplied mouse routine to the BIOS mouse service routine such that each time the BIOS routine receives data from the mouse, the programmer-supplied routine is called by the BIOS. Four parameters must be placed on the stack before this subfunction is invoked.

Address	Description
SS:SP + 0Ah	Status word Bits 15–8 Reserved Bit 7 y coordinate has overflowed if set to 1 Bit 6 x coordinate has overflowed if set to 1 Bit 5 y coordinate is negative if set to 1 Bit 4 x coordinate is negative if set to 1 Bits 3–2 Reserved. Bit 3 should be 1 and Bit 2 should be zero. Bit 1 Right button pressed if set to 1 Bit 0 Left button pressed if set to 1
SS:SP + 08h	x coordinate
SS:SP + 06h	y coordinate
SS:SP + 04h	z coordinate (should be 00h)

The programmer-supplied routine should exit via a far return and must not remove the parameters from the stack.

cont'd

INT 15h Systems Services, Continued

Function C3h Fail-Safe Timer Control

Input: AH = C3h
AL = 00h Disable fail-safe timer
= 01h Enable fail-safe timer
BX = Fail-safe timer value

Output: CF = 0 No error
= 1 Error

Description:

Function C3h enables or disables the EISA fail-safe timer. The value in BX becomes the timer count value when enabled. The fail-safe timer is placed in mode 0 operation, the fail-safe timer NMI is enabled, and the value in BX is copied to the BIOS extended data area. CF is set if there is an invalid input.

The fail-safe timer value in the BIOS extended data area is cleared when disabled.

Function D8h EISA Support

Function D8h configures EISA controllers and stores values in EISA
Extended CMOS RAM. This function is the only way in which EISA
Extended CMOS RAM should be accessed.

This function has four subfunctions that are primarily used by the
EISA Configuration Utility (ECU) with the Configuration (CFG) files
supplied by EISA product manufacturers with EISA adapter cards and
motherboards.

All EISA subfunctions (00h/80h through 04h/84h) are described in this
section. Functions 00 – 04h are used for 16-bit cards. Functions 80h –
84h are used for 32-bit cards. Improper use of these subfunctions could
cause an EISA system to operate erratically.

EISA Extended CMOS RAM

EISA-specific configuration data is stored in I/O-mapped EISA
Extended CMOS RAM. There must be at least 4 KB of EISA Extended
CMOS RAM, in addition to the required 64 bytes of ISA CMOS RAM.

EISA Devices

Any controller in an EISA system can be called an EISA device. There
can be up to 64 devices in an EISA system: 16 physical devices and 48
virtual (logical) devices.

EISA Devices and Slots

EISA controllers and EISA devices are essentially the same. EISA slots
are used as addresses in EISA systems and are the actual physical
expansion slots on the EISA motherboard. EISA devices are addressed
by their physical or logical slot number. The EISA motherboard is
always Slot 0. The physical slots are 1 – 15.

cont'd

EISA Device Number

A physical device resides in an actual expansion slot on the EISA motherboard and is numbered 1 – 15. This number is the EISA device number.

Embedded Devices

The motherboard can have one or more devices on it that are called embedded devices, which are also EISA devices. Embedded device numbers begin after the last physical device number. If the last physical device is 7, then the first embedded device is 8.

Virtual Devices

A virtual device is often a software device driver that uses system resources but does not physically exist. ISA devices on the motherboard can be virtual devices. Virtual devices are numbered sequentially after the last physical or embedded device. If the last physical or embedded device is 6, then the first virtual device is 7.

Device Functions

A device can have more than one function. Some standard functions are: memory, serial port, parallel port, floppy disk, and hard disk.

Function D8h Subfunction 00h (80h) Read Slot Configuration Information

Input: AH = D8h
              AL = 00h (for 16-bit addressing)
                   = 80h (for 32-bit addressing)
              CL = Slot Number (virtual and embedded devices included)
                        00h Motherboard
                        01h   Slot 1
                        ...   ...
                        0Fh   Slot 15

Function D8h Subfunction 00h (80h) Read Slot Configuration Information, cont'd

Output: AH = 00h No error
            = 80h Invalid slot number
            = 81h Invalid function number
            = 82h EISA Extended CMOS RAM is corrupt
            = 83h Slot is empty
            = 86h Invalid BIOS call
            = 87h Invalid system configuration

AL = CFG and Slot Status

Bit 7	0	Duplicate CFG ID not found.
	1	Duplicate CFG ID found.
Bit 6	0	Product ID was readable.
	1	Product ID was not readable.
Bits 5–4	00b	Slot is an expansion slot.
	01b	Slot is an embedded device.
	10b	Slot is a virtual device.
	11b	Reserved
Bits 3–0	0000b	No duplicate CFG ID found.
	0001b	First duplicate CFG ID used.
	0010b	Second duplicate CFG ID used.
	... ...	
	1111b	Fifteenth duplicate CFG ID used.

BH = Major Revision Level of ECU
BL   = Minor Revision Level of ECU
CF   = 0 No error
       = 1 Error
CH = MSB of CFG Checksum
CL   = LSB of CFG Checksum
DH = Number of Device Function

cont'd

Function D8h Subfunction 00h (80h) Read Slot Configuration Information, cont'd

Output: DL = Combined Function Information Byte
Bits 7–6 Reserved
Bit 5   Slot has one or more port initialization entries if this bit is set.
Bit 4   Slot has one or more port range entries if this bit is set.
Bit 3   Slot has one or more DMA entries if this bit is set.
Bit 2   Slot has one or more IRQ entries if this bit is set.
Bit 1   Slot has one or more memory entries if this bit is set.
Bit 0   Slot has one or more function type entries if this bit is set.

DI (LSB) = Byte 0 of compressed ID
DI (MSB) = Byte 1 of compressed ID
SI (LSB) = Byte 2 of compressed ID
SI (MSB) = Byte 3 of compressed ID

Description:

Function D8h Subfunction 00h returns EISA configuration information for a specified slot by reading information directly from EISA Extended CMOS RAM. The slots can be the motherboard, an adapter card, an embedded device, or a virtual device. Each slot has a corresponding CFG file that is used by the ECU to configure the slot properly.

Duplicate CFG Files

If the system finds that more than one CFG file exists for the specified slot, a duplicate ID condition occurs and bit 8 of AL is set. Bits 3 to 0 of AL indicate the duplicate ID that was used.

**Function D8h Subfunction 00h (80h) Read Slot Configuration
Information,** cont'd

Device ID Number

DI and SI contain a four-byte compressed ID number pertaining to the
device installed in the specified slot. This number identifies the
manufacturer of the device, the device product number, and the
product revision number.

Product ID	Description
DI (LSB)	Bit 7 Reserved, should be zero. Bits 6–2 First character of the manufacturer code. Bits 1–0 First two bits of second character of the manufacturer code.
DI (MSB)	Bits 7–5 Remaining three bits of second character of the manufacturer code. Bits 4–0 Third character of the manufacturer code.
SI (LSB)	Adapter card: Bits 7–4 First hex digit of the manufacturer's product number. Bits 3–0 Second hex digit of the manufacturer's product number. Motherboard: Bits 7–0 Reserved for manufacturer.

SI (MSB)	Adapter card:
	Bits 7–4 Third hex digit of the manufacturer's product number.
	Bits 3–0 Product revision number
	
	Motherboard:
	Bits 7–3 Reserved for manufacturer's use.
	Bits 2–0 EISA bus version number (001 in initial version).
	              001 is currently the only standard value defined for this
	              field, but, in practice, EISA motherboard and adapter card
	              manufacturers have been using this field for their own
	              purposes.

cont'd

**Function D8h Subfunction 01h (81h) Read Function Configuration
Information**

Input: AH = D8h
      AL = 01h (for 16-bit addressing)
           = 81h (for 32-bit addressing)
      CH = Function Number (from 0 through $m - 1$, where m = the contents of DH from Subfunction 00h)
      CL = Slot Number (virtual and embedded devices included)
           00h   EISA Motherboard
           01h   Slot 1
           02h   Slot 2
           ...   ...
           ...   ...
           0Fh   Slot 15
  DS:SI = Address of Data Buffer (16-bit addressing)
  DS:ESI = Address of Data Buffer (32-bit addressing)

Output: AH = 00h No error
          = 80h Invalid slot number
          = 81h Invalid function number
          = 82h EISA Extended CMOS RAM is corrupt
          = 83h Slot is empty
          = 86h Invalid BIOS call
          = 87h Invalid system configuration
      CF = 0   No error
          = 1   Error
  DS:SI = Return data buffer address (if 16-bit call)
  DS:ESI = Return data buffer address (if 32-bit call)

INT 15h Systems Services, Continued

Function D8h Subfunction 01h (81h) Read Function Configuration Information, cont'd

Description:

Function D8h Subfunction 01h reads the specified function information directly from CMOS RAM. The calling software can find the number of functions for a particular device using subfunction 00h (80h).

With subfunction 01h (81h), the caller receives information about each specific device function. This subfunction reads a 320-byte table and then writes this table to the memory buffer address specified in DS:SI. Each block of a variable-length data field describes an individual EISA adapter card. The table format is:

Offset	Description
00h	First Byte of Compressed ID Bit 7 Reserved, should be zero. Bits 6 – 2 First character of the manufacturer code. Bits 1 – 0 First two bits of second character of the manufacturer code.
01h	Second Byte of Compressed ID Bits 7 – 5 Remaining three bits of second character of the manufacturer code. Bits 4 – 0 Third character of the manufacturer code.
02h	Third Byte of Compressed ID Adapter card: Bits 7 – 4 First hex digit of the manufacturer's product number. Bits 3 – 0 Second hex digit of the manufacturer's product number. Motherboard: Bits 7 – 0 Reserved for manufacturer's use.
03h	Fourth Byte of Compressed ID Adapter card: Bits 7 – 4 Third hex digit of the manufacturer's product number. Bits 3 – 0 Product revision number Motherboard: Bits 7 – 3 Reserved for manufacturer's use. Bits 2 – 0 EISA bus version number (001 is initial version).

Offset	Description

04h – 05h	ID and Slot Information
	Byte 0
	Bit 7 0 No duplicate ID is present.
	        1 Duplicate ID found.
	Bit 6 0 ID is readable.
	        1 ID is unreadable.
	Bits 5 – 4 Device Type
	    00b Expansion device
	    01b Embedded device
	    10b Virtual device
	Bits 3 – 0 Number of Duplicate CFG filenames
	    0000b No duplicate CFG
	    0001b First duplicate CFG
	    ... ...
	    1110b Fourteenth duplicate CFG
	    1111b Fifteenth duplicate CFG
	Byte 1
	Bit 7 0 Configuration is successful.
	        1 Configuration is unsuccessful.
	Bits 6 – 2 Reserved, should be zeros.
	Bit 1 0 EISA IOCHKERR not supported.
	        1 EISA IOCHKERR supported.
	Bit 0 0 EISA ENABLE not supported (adapter card cannot be enabled or disabled).
	        1 EISA ENABLE supported (adapter card can be enabled or disabled).
	The EISA specification allows EISA adapter cards to be enabled or disabled via software. If bit 0 of byte 1 above is set, external software can disable the adapter card. Similarly, the availability of IOCHKERR allows external software to check expansion slots for pending errors.

06h – 07h	Revision levels of the CFG overlay files used for a specified slot. Both bytes are 0 if no overlay file exists. Byte 0 Minor revision level of the CFG overlay file. Byte 1 Major revision level of the CFG overlay file.
08h – 21h	Selections made by the system ECU. The possible choices for the specified slot function are counted here. The actual names of the choices are specified in the CFG file. Byte 0 Selection 1 Byte 1 Selection 2 ... ... Byte 24 Selection 25 Byte 25 Selection 26
22h	Slot function information Bit 7 0 Slot function is enabled. 1 Slot function is disabled. Bit 6 CFG is using free form data if set. Bit 5 Port initialization entry(s) follows if set. Bit 4 Port range entry(s) follows if set. Bit 3 DMA entry(s) follows if set. Bit 2 IRQ entry(s) follows if set. Bit 1 Memory entry(s) follows if set. Bit 0 Type and Subtype string follows if set.

Offset	Description
23h – 62h	80-character ASCII string describing the slot device. The string has types and subtypes. The manufacturer determines the type and subtype format, but the following conventions are often used: **Type** **String** COM Communications device KEY Keyboard MEM Memory card MFC Multifunction card MSD Mass storage device NET Network card NPX Math coprocessor OSE Operating system or environment OTH Other PAR Parallel port PTR Pointing device SYS Motherboard VID Video adapter card , Delimiter for Type string fragments ; End of Type string and beginning of Subtype string 0 End of Subtype strings The unused part of the 80-character string should be zero (not including the Subtype delimiter).

73h – B1h	Memory Configuration Section. Nine seven-byte entries:
	Byte 0 Memory Configuration Byte
	Bit 5 0 Memory is not shared
	           1 Memory is shared
	Bits 4 – 3 00b SYS (base/extended memory)
	           01b EXP (expanded memory)
	           10b VIR (virtual memory)
	           11b OTH (other memory)
	Bit 1 0 Memory is not cached
	           1 Memory is cached
	Bit 0 0 Memory is ROM (read only)
	           1 Memory is RAM (read and write)
	Byte 1 Memory Data Size
	Bits 3 – 2 Decode Size
	           00b 20 address lines
	           01b 24 address lines
	           10b 32 address lines
	Bits 1 – 0 Data Access Size
	           00b Byte
	           01b Word (16 bits)
	           10b Doubleword (32 bits)
	Bytes 2 – 4 Starting Memory Address divided by 100h
	Bytes 5 – 6 Memory Size divided by 400. If 0000h, memory size is 64 MB. Size is specified in 1024 byte increments.

Offset	Description

B2h – BFh	Hardware Interrupt Configuration Section. Seven two-byte entries:
	Byte 0
	    Bit 6 0 Interrupt is not shared
	                    1 Interrupt is shared
	    Bit 5 0 Interrupt is edge-triggered
	                    1 Interrupt is level-triggered
	    Bits 3 – 0 Interrupt number
	                    0000b IRQ0
	                    0001b IRQ1
	                    ... ...
	                    1110b IRQ14
	                    1111b IRQ15
	Byte 1 Reserved, should be zero.

C0h – C7h	DMA Channel Description Section. Four two-byte entries:
	Byte 0
	    Bit 6 0 DMA channel is not shared
	                    1 DMA channel is shared
	    Bits 5 – 3 Reserved, should be zeros.
	    Bits 2 – 0 DMA Channel Number
	                    000b Channel 0
	                    001b Channel 1
	                    ... ...
	                    110b Channel 6
	                    111b Channel 7
	Byte 1
	    Bits 7 – 6 Reserved, should be zeros.
	    Bits 5 – 4 DMA Timing
	                    00b ISA-compatible timing
	                    01b Type A timing
	                    10b Type B timing
	                    11b Type C (Burst) timing
	    Bits 3 – 2 DMA Transfer Size
	                    00b Byte transfers
	                    01b Word transfers (16 bits)
	                    10b Doubleword transfers (32 bits)
	    Bits 1 – 0 Reserved, should be zeros.

C8h – 103h	I/O Port Information consists of 20 three-byte entries:
	Byte 0
	    Bit 6 0 Port is not shared
	                    1 Port is shared
	    Bit 5 Reserved, should be zero.
	    Bits 4 – 0 Number of Ports (starting at 0)
	                    00000b One port
	                    00001b Two sequential ports
	                    00010b Three sequential ports
	                    ... ...
	                    11110b Thirty-one sequential ports
	                    11111b Thirty-two sequential ports
	Byte 1 LSB of I/O Port Address
	Byte 2 MSB of I/O Port Address

Offset	Description
104h – 13Fh	I/O Port Initialization Data Section. Entries vary in length.
	Byte 0 Initialization Type
	Bits 6 – 3 Reserved, should be zeros.
	Bit 2 0 Write value to port
	1 Use both mask and value
	Bits 1 – 0 Data Access Size
	If Byte 0, bit 2 is 0, the following format is used:
	00b Byte 3 is the initialization value.
	01b Byte 3 is the LSB of the initialization value. Byte 4 is the MSB of the initialization value.
	10b Byte 3 is the LSB of the initialization value. Byte 4 is the second byte of the initialization value. Byte 5 is the third byte of the initialization value. Byte 6 is the MSB of the initialization value.
	If Byte 0, bit 2 is 1, the following format is used:
	00b Byte 3 is the initialization value. Byte 4 is mask value.
	01b Byte 3 is the LSB of the initialization value. Byte 4 is the MSB of the initialization value. Byte 5 is the LSB of the mask value. Byte 6 is the MSB of the mask value.
	10b Byte 3 is the LSB of the initialization value. Byte 4 is the second byte of the initialization value. Byte 5 is the third byte of the initialization value. Byte 6 is the MSB of the initialization value. Byte 7 is the LSB of the mask value. Byte 8 is the second byte of the mask value. Byte 9 is the third byte of the mask value. Byte 10 is the MSB of the mask value.
	Byte 1 LSB of Port Address
	Byte 2 MSB of Port Address

Note: If bit 6 of the Function Information Section (22h) is set, the table is not in the table format described above, but uses free-form data. Entries through Type and Subtype (23h) are the same, but starting at 73h, the data in the table is in the board manufacturer's proprietary format.

cont'd

Function D8h Subfunction 02h (82h) Clear EISA CMOS RAM

Input: AH = D8h
          AL   = 02h (for 16-bit addressing)
               = 82h (for 32-bit addressing)
          BH = Major Revision Number of ECU
          BL = Minor Revision Number of ECU

Output: AH = 00h
               = 84h Error while clearing CMOS RAM
               = 86h Invalid BIOS call
               = 88h ECU is not supported
          AL   = Major Revision Number of ECU supported by BIOS
                 (if AH = 88h).
          CF = 0 Error
               = 1 No error

Description:

Function D8h Subfunction 02h clears EISA Extended CMOS RAM. This routine does not clear the ISA CMOS RAM, which contains the date, time, hard disk drive type, and basic system configuration.

Function D8h Subfunction 03h (83h) Write to EISA CMOS RAM

Input: AH = D8h
        AL   = 03h (if CS specifies 16-bit addressing)
             = 83h (if CS specifies 32-bit addressing)
        CX = Length of table (if 0, then slot is empty)
    DS:SI = Address of data buffer (16-bit addressing)
   DS:ESI = Address of data buffer (32-bit addressing)

Output: AH = 00h No error
            = 84h Error writing to EISA Extended CMOS RAM
            = 85h CMOS RAM is full
            = 86h Invalid BIOS call
            = 87h EISA configuration is locked
       CF = 0 No error
           = 1 Error

Description:

Function D8h Subfunction 03h writes the configuration data specified in the data buffer pointed to by DS:SI to EISA Extended CMOS RAM. This function does not write to ISA CMOS RAM, which contains the basic system parameters. The data to be written to EISA Extended CMOS RAM should begin at address DS:SI (DS:ESI if using 32-bit addressing) for the length specified in CX. The last two bytes in the table are reserved for the checksum of the CFG file to be used.

EISA Configuration Data Table

The format for the EISA configuration data at DS:SI (DS:ESI) is:

Offset	Description
00h	First Byte of Compressed ID Bit 7 Reserved, should be zero. Bits 6 – 2 First character of the manufacturer code. Bits 1 – 0 First two bits of second character of the manufacturer code.
01h	Second Byte of Compressed ID Bits 7 – 5 Remaining three bits of second character of the manufacturer code. Bits 4 – 0 Third character of the manufacturer code.

Offset	Description
02h	Third Byte of Compressed ID Adapter card: Bits 7 – 4 First hex digit of the manufacturer's product number. Bits 3 – 0 Second hex digit of the manufacturer's product number. Motherboard: Bits 7 – 0 Reserved for manufacturer's use.
03h	Fourth Byte of Compressed ID Adapter card: Bits 7 – 4 Third hex digit of the manufacturer's product number. Bits 3 – 0 Product revision number Motherboard: Bits 7 – 3 Reserved for manufacturer's use. Bits 2 – 0 EISA bus version number (001 is initial version).
04h – 05h	ID and Slot Information Byte 0 Bit 7 0 No duplicate ID is present. 1 Duplicate ID found. Bit 6 0 ID is readable. 1 ID is unreadable. Bits 5 – 4 Device Type 00 Expansion device 01 Embedded device 10 Virtual device Bits 3 – 0 Number of Duplicate CFG filenames 0000b No duplicate CFG 0001b First duplicate CFG ... ... 1110b Fourteenth duplicate CFG 1111b Fifteenth duplicate CFG Byte 1 Bit 7 0 Configuration is successful. 1 Configuration is unsuccessful. Bits 6 – 2 Reserved, should be zeros. Bit 1 0 EISA IOCHKERR not supported. 1 EISA IOCHKERR supported. Bit 0 0 EISA ENABLE not supported (adapter card cannot be enabled or disabled). 1 EISA ENABLE supported (adapter card can be enabled or disabled). The EISA specification allows EISA adapter cards to be enabled or disabled via software. If bit 0 of byte 1 above is set, external software can disable the adapter card. Similarly, the availability of IOCHKERR allows external software to check expansion slots for pending errors.

INT 15h Systems Services, Continued

Offset	Description
06h – 07h	Revision levels of the CFG overlay files used for a specified slot. Both bytes are 0 if no overlay file exists. Byte 0 Minor revision level of the CFG overlay file. Byte 1 Major revision level of the CFG overlay file.
The rest of this table is repeated once for every EISA function in the system. There can be *1 through n* EISA functions. Most EISA Adapter Cards have more than one function. The last function is empty and has a length of 0. All functions must fit in 340 bytes.	
2 bytes, but they do not count as part of the function length.	Function Length. The length does not include these two bytes or the checksum at the end of EISA CMOS RAM. The last function must be set to length 0. Byte 0 LSB of the length of the following function entry. Byte 1 MSB of the length of the following function entry.
2 to 27 bytes for each function.	Selections made by the system ECU. The possible choices for the specified slot function are counted here. The actual names of the choices are specified in the CFG file. Byte 0 Selection 1 Byte 1 Selection 2 ... ... Byte 24 Selection 25 Byte 25 Selection 26
1 byte for each function.	Slot function information Bit 7 0 Slot function is enabled. 1 Slot function is disabled. Bit 6 CFG is using free form data if set. Bit 5 Port initialization entry(s) follows if set. Bit 4 Port range entry(s) follows if set. If not set, the port range section is length 0. Bit 3 DMA entry(s) follows if set. If not set, the DMA entry section is length 0. Bit 2 IRQ entry(s) follows if set. If not set, the IRQ entry section is length 0. Bit 1 Memory entry(s) follows if set. If not set, the Memory section is length 0. Bit 0 Type and Subtype string follows if set.

Offset	Description
2 – 81 bytes for each function.	Byte 0 Length of the following field Bytes 1 - 80 A 1 - 80-character ASCII string describing the slot device. The string has types and subtypes. For example, TYPE=COM, AMI; COM1 would be: 0ChCOM,AMI;COM1 The manufacturer determines the type and subtype format, but the conventions are: **Type** **String** COM Communications device KEY Keyboard MEM Memory card MFC Multifunction card MSD Mass storage device NET Network card NPX Math coprocessor OSE Operating system or environment OTH Other PAR Parallel port PTR Pointing device SYS Motherboard VID Video adapter card , Delimiter for Type string fragments ; End of Type string and beginning of Subtype string 0 End of Subtype strings The unused part of the 80-character string should be zero (not including the Subtype delimiter).

Offset	Description

7 to 63 bytes for each function.	Memory Configuration Section. 0 to Nine seven-byte entries:
	
	Byte 0 Memory Configuration Byte
	
	Bit 7 0 Last entry
	           1 More entries follow
	Bit 6 Reserved, should be zero.
	Bit 5 0 Memory is not shared
	           1 Memory is shared
	Bits 4 – 3 00 SYS (base/extended memory)
	           01 EXP (expanded memory)
	           10 VIR (virtual memory)
	           11 OTH (other memory)
	Bit 1 0 Memory is not cached
	           1 Memory is cached
	Bit 0 0 Memory is ROM (read only)
	           1 Memory is RAM (read and write)
	
	Byte 1 Memory Data Size
	Bits 7 - 4 Reserved, should be zeros.
	Bits 3 – 2 Decode Size
	           00b 20 address lines
	           01b 24 address lines
	           10b 32 address lines
	Bits 1 – 0 Data Access Size
	           00b Byte
	           01b Word (16 bits)
	           10b Doubleword (32 bits)
	
	Bytes 2 – 4 Starting Memory Address divided by 100h
	Bytes 5 – 6 Memory Size divided by 400. If 0000h, memory size is 64 MB. Size is specified in 1024 byte increments.

2 - 14 bytes for each function.	IRQ Configuration Section. 1 to 7 two-byte entries.
	
	Byte 0
	Bit 7 0 Last entry
	          1 More entries follow
	Bit 6 0 Interrupt is not shared
	          1 Interrupt is shared
	Bit 5 0 Interrupt is edge-triggered
	          1 Interrupt is level-triggered
	Bit 4 Reserved (should be 0)
	Bits 3 – 0 Interrupt number
	           0000b IRQ0
	           0001b IRQ1
	           ... ...
	           1110b IRQ14
	           1111b IRQ15
	Byte 1 Reserved; should be zero.

Offset	Description
0 - 4 entries for each function. 2 - 8 bytes for each entry.	DMA Channel Description Section. 0 – 4 two-byte entries.
	Byte 0
	Bit 7 0 Last entry
	1 More entries follow
	Bit 6 0 DMA channel is not shared
	1 DMA channel is shared
	Bits 5 – 3 Reserved, should be zeros.
	Bits 2 – 0 DMA Channel Number
	000b Channel 0
	001b Channel 1
	... ...
	110b Channel 6
	111b Channel 7
	Byte 1
	Bits 7 – 6 Reserved, should be zeros.
	Bits 5 – 4 DMA Timing
	00b ISA-compatible timing
	01b Type A timing
	10b Type B timing
	11b Type C (Burst) timing
	Bits 3 – 2 DMA Transfer Size
	00b Byte transfers
	01b Word transfers (16 bits)
	10b Doubleword transfers (32 bits)
	Bits 1 – 0 Reserved, should be zeros.
1 to 20 entries for each function. 3 to 60 bytes for each entry.	I/O Port Information consists of 0 to 20 three-byte entries:
	Byte 0
	Bit 7 0 Last entry
	1 More entries follow
	Bit 6 0 Port is not shared
	1 Port is shared
	Bit 5 Reserved, should be zero.
	Bits 4 – 0 Number of Ports (starting at 0)
	00000b One port
	00001b Two sequential ports
	00010b Three sequential ports
	... ...
	11110b Thirty-one sequential ports
	11111b Thirty-two sequential ports
	Byte 1 LSB of I/O Port Address
	Byte 2 MSB of I/O Port Address

Offset	Description

0 - 60 bytes for each function. 0 - 20 entries for each function.	I/O Port Initialization Data Section. Entries vary in length.
	
	Byte 0 Initialization Type
	Bit 7 0 Last entry
	                1 More entries follow
	Bits 6 – 3 Reserved, should be zeros.
	Bit 2 0 Write value to port
	                1 Use both mask and value
	Bits 1 – 0 Data Access Size
	If Byte 0, bit 2 is 0, the following format is used:
	            00b Byte 3 is the initialization value.
	            01b Byte 3 is the LSB of the initialization value. Byte 4 is the MSB of the initialization value.
	            10b Byte 3 is the LSB of the initialization value. Byte 4 is the second byte of the initialization value. Byte 5 is the third byte of the initialization value. Byte 6 is the MSB of the initialization value.
	If Byte 0, bit 2 is 1, the following format is used:
	            00b Byte 3 is the initialization value. Byte 4 is mask value.
	            01b Byte 3 is the LSB of the initialization value. Byte 4 is the MSB of the initialization value. Byte 5 is the LSB of the mask value. Byte 6 is the MSB of the mask value.
	            10b Byte 3 is the LSB of the initialization value. Byte 4 is the second byte of the initialization value. Byte 5 is the third byte of the initialization value. Byte 6 is the MSB of the initialization value. Byte 7 is the LSB of the mask value. Byte 8 is the second byte of the mask value. Byte 9 is the third byte of the mask value. Byte 10 is the MSB of the mask value.
	
	Byte 1 LSB of Port Address
	Byte 2 MSB of Port Address

The following field is not included in the entries for each function. It only occurs once at the very end of this table.	
2 bytes	Checksum of the CFG file that configured this table Byte 0 LSB of the EISA configuration file checksum. Byte 1 MSB of the EISA configuration file checksum.

Note: If bit 6 of the Function Information Section (22h) is set, the table is not in the table format described above, but uses free-form data. Entries through the Type and Subtype field are the same, but starting with the Memory Configuration field, the motherboard manufacturer's proprietary format is used.

cont'd

Function D8h Subfunction 04h (84h) Read Slot Device Compressed ID

Input:	AH	= D8h
	AL	= 04h (for 16-bit addressing)
		= 84h (for 32-bit addressing)
	CL	= Slot Number (virtual and embedded devices included)

00h	Motherboard
01h	Slot 1
02h	Slot 2
...	...
...	...
0Fh	Slot 15

Output:	AH	= 00h No error
		= 80h Invalid slot number
		= 83h Slot is empty
		= 86h Invalid BIOS call
		= 87h Invalid system configuration
	CF	= 0 No error
		= 1 Error
	DI (LSB)	= Byte 0 of Compressed ID
	DI (MSB)	= Byte 1 of Compressed ID
	SI (LSB)	= Byte 2 of Compressed ID
	SI (MSB)	= Byte 3 of Compressed ID

Description:

Function D8h Subfunction 04h (84h) returns the compressed ID from the device installed in the specified slot. The slot can be the motherboard, an adapter card, an embedded device, or a virtual device.

DI and SI contain a four-byte compressed ID number of the device installed in the specified slot. The compressed ID format is described on page 283.

INT 16h Keyboard Service

INT 16h controls the system keyboard. Functions 00h through 02h are used with XT-compatible keyboards (83- and 84-key) only.

Functions 10h through 12h are used with AT enhanced keyboards (101- and 102-key) only. Functions 03h, 05h, F0h, F1h, and F4h can be used with either type of keyboard.

INT 16h Functions

Function	Description
00h	Read Character
01h	Return Keyboard Status
02h	Return Keyboard Flags
03h	Set Keyboard Typematic Rate Parameters
05h	Push Character and Scan Code to Buffer
10h	Enhanced Keyboard Read Character
11h	Enhanced Keyboard Write Character
12h	Enhanced Keyboard Return Keyboard Flags
E0h	Flash EPROM Programming
F0h	Set CPU Speed
F1h	Read CPU Speed
F4h	Cache Controller Status

Function 00h Read Character

Input: AH = 00h

Output: AH = Scan code or character ID if special character.
AL = ASCII code

Description:

Function 00h reads a character from the keyboard and returns the scan and ASCII codes for that character.

cont'd

Function 01h Return Keyboard Status

Input: AH   = 01h

Output: AH   = Scan code of character ID if special character (only if
                ZF is 0).
         AL   = ASCII code or character translation
         ZF   = 0   Character waiting
              = 1   No character waiting

Description:

Function 01h determines if a character is waiting for input. If so, it
returns the character and its scan code. Function 01h does not remove
the character from the keyboard buffer. The character must be read
using INT 16h Function 00h if is to be removed from the buffer.

Function 02h Return Keyboard Flags

Input: AH   = 02h

Output: AL   = Keyboard Flags
                Bit 7 INS key pressed (Insert mode on)
                Bit 6 CAPS LOCK key on
                Bit 5 NUM LOCK key on
                Bit 4 SCROLL LOCK key on
                Bit 3 ALT key pressed
                Bit 2 CTRL key pressed
                Bit 1 Left SHIFT key pressed
                Bit 0 Right SHIFT key pressed

Description:

Function 02h returns the Keyboard Flags Byte (40:17h and 40:18h in
the BIOS Data Area). The Keyboard Flags Byte describes the state of
certain keys.

Function 03h Set Typematic Rate Parameters

Input: AH = 03h
AL = 05h
BH = Typematic delay
        00h 250 ms
        01h 500 ms
        02h 750 ms
        03h 1000 ms
BL = Typematic rate

BL	Rate	BL	Rate
00h	30.0 characters per second	10h	7.5 characters per second
01h	26.7 characters per second	11h	6.7 characters per second
02h	24.0 characters per second	12h	6.0 characters per second
03h	21.8 characters per second	13h	5.5 characters per second
04h	20.0 characters per second	14h	5.0 characters per second
05h	18.5 characters per second	15h	4.6 characters per second
06h	17.1 characters per second	16h	4.3 characters per second
07h	16.0 characters per second	17h	4.0 characters per second
08h	15.0 characters per second	18h	3.7 characters per second
09h	13.3 characters per second	19h	3.3 characters per second
0Ah	12.0 characters per second	1Ah	3.0 characters per second
0Bh	10.9 characters per second	1Bh	2.7 characters per second
0Ch	10.0 characters per second	1Ch	2.5 characters per second
0Dh	9.2 characters per second	1Dh	2.3 characters per second
0Eh	8.6 characters per second	1Eh	2.1 characters per second
0Fh	8.0 characters per second	1Fh	2.0 characters per second

Output: None

Description:

Function 03h sets the keyboard typematic rate parameters. The typematic rate delay is the length of the delay between the first key character printed on the screen and first repeated character. The typematic rate is the number of characters to be repeated per second.

cont'd

Function 05h Push Character and Scan Code to Buffer

Input: AH = 05h
        CH = Scan Code to be pushed.
        CL = Character to be pushed.

Output: AL = 00h No error
            = 01h Keyboard buffer is full.
        CF = 0 No error
            = 1 Keyboard buffer is full.

Description: Function 05h places the specified character and scan
             code in the keyboard buffer.

Function 10h Enhanced Keyboard Read Character

Input: AH = 10h

Output: AH = 00h Scan code or character ID if special character
        AL = ASCII code

Description: Function 10h reads a character from the keyboard buffer
             and returns its ASCII code and scan code. Function 10h
             should be used with enhanced keyboards only.

Function 11h Enhanced Keyboard Return Status

Input: AH = 11h

Output: AH = Scan Code or character ID if special character
        AL = ASCII code of character
        ZF = 0 Character waiting
            = 1 No character waiting

Description: Determines if a character is waiting for input. If so, it
             returns the character and its scan code. It does not
             remove the character from the keyboard buffer. The
             character must be read via Function 10h to be removed
             from the buffer. Use only with enhanced keyboards.

Function 12h Return Enhanced Keyboard Flags

Input: AH   =   12h

Output: AX   =   Keyboard Flags
                     00h   Right SHIFT key pressed
                     01h   Left SHIFT key pressed
                     02h   CTRL key pressed
                     03h   ALT key pressed
                     04h   SCROLL LOCK is on
                     05h   NUM LOCK is on
                     06h   CAPS LOCK is on
                     07h   INS key pressed (Insert mode is on
                     08h   Left CTRL key is pressed
                     09h   Left ALT key is pressed
                     0Ah   Right CTRL key is pressed
                     0Bh   Right ALT key is pressed
                     0Ch   SCROLL LOCK key is pressed
                     0Dh   NUM LOCK key is pressed
                     0Eh   CAPS LOCK key is pressed
                     0Fh   SYSREQ key is pressed

Description:

Function 12h returns the Keyboard Flags at 40:17h and 40:18h and the Extended Keyboard Flags at 40:96h and 40:97h. These flags describe the state of certain keys on the keyboard. This function should be used only with enhanced keyboards.

cont'd

Function E0h Flash EPROM Programming

There are several types of Flash EPROM devices. The American Megatrends Flash programming utility (AMIFlash) must be generalized to be able to work with all types of Flash ROM hardware.

INT 16h Function E0h provides 14 system BIOS subfunctions that facilitate the use of the AMIFlash Flash EPROM programming utility so that AMIFlash can be used successfully with all types of Flash ROM hardware.

Function E0h Subfunction 00h Get Version Number of BIOS/Flash ROM Interface

Input: AH = E0h
        AL = 00h

Output: AL = 0FAh Successful
        BX = Version number in BCD format
        CF = 0 Successful
            = 1 Error

Description:

This subfunction returns the version number of BIOS/Flash interface implementation in BCD format in BX. For example, version number 2.00 is returned in BX as 0200h.

This subfunction can be used to determine whether the BIOS/Flash interface is implemented in the system BIOS. After returning from the subfunction, AX should be checked for 0FAH even CF is 0 (successful operation).

All registers except the returned registers are saved. The contents of AL and BX are destroyed if this subfunction is successful (CF = 0). The contents of AL should be unchanged if unsuccessful.

INT 16h Keyboard Service, Continued

Function E0h Subfunction 01h Save and Restore Status Requirement

Input: AH = E0h
           AL = 01h

Output: AL = 0FAh Successful
           BX = Number of bytes needed to save chipset environment
           CF = 0 Successful
              = 1 Error

Description:

This subfunction returns the data area space needed to save the current chipset status. The contents of AL and BX are destroyed if this subfunction is successful (CF = 0). The contents of AL should be unchanged if unsuccessful.

Function E0h Subfunction 02h Save Chipset Status and Prepare Chipset

Input: AH   = E0h
        AL   = 02h
        ES:DI = Pointer to start of buffer where chipset status will be saved

Output: AL   = 0FAh Successful
         CF   = 0 Successful
              = 1 Error

Description:

This function saves the current chipset status in the specified data area and then prepares the chipset to make the Flash EPROM accessible. The current cache memory status, power management status, shadow status, and other status is saved.

This subfunction should be invoked before programming the Flash EPROM so the system can be restored if a non-fatal error Flash utility error occurs. This function:

- saves chipset features, and
- disables Shadow RAM, cache memory, power management features, and other chipset features.

Disabling cache memory may be necessary to make the target ROM address space non-cacheable.

If the target ROM address space is cacheable only when shadowing is enabled (for instance, only shadow RAM is cacheable, but ROM is not cacheable), disabling shadow RAM also makes the target ROM address space non-cacheable and cache memory does not have to be disabled. But if the ROM is cacheable, then cache memory must be disabled.

The contents of AL are destroyed if successful. The contents of AL should be unchanged if unsuccessful.

Function E0h Subfunction 03h Restore Chipset Status

Input: AH   = E0h
             AL   = 03h
        ES:DI   = Pointer to start of buffer where chipset environment
                   will be restored.

Output: AL   = 0FAh Successful
             CF   = 0 Successful
                   = 1 Error

Description:

This function restores the chipset status from the specified data area
where the chipset status was saved by INT 16h Function E0h
subfunction 02h Chipset Status and Prepare Chipset.

The contents of AL are destroyed if successful. The contents of AL
should be unchanged if unsuccessful.

Function E0h Subfunction 04h Lower Programming Voltage Vpp

Input: AH = E0h
AL = 04h

Output: AL = 0FAh Successful
CF = 0 Successful
= 1 Error

Description:

This subfunction lowers programming voltage Vpp to the normal level.

The contents of AL are destroyed if this function is successful. The contents of AL should be unchanged if unsuccessful.

Lowering the Vpp programming voltage and write-protecting the Flash EPROM can be done in one operation in some Flash EPROMs. If the hardware supports this combination of functions, the calling program must only invoke INT 16h Function E0h Subfunction 04h and not Subfunction 06h.

Function E0h Subfunction 05h Raise Programming Voltage Vpp

Input: AH   = E0h
           AL   = 05h

Output: AL   = 0FAh Successful
           CF   = 0 Successful
                 = 1 Error

Description:

This subfunction raises the programming voltage to 12.0 Volt. This subfunction must wait until the voltage level is stabilized.

The contents of AL are destroyed if this function is successful. The contents of AL should be unchanged if unsuccessful.

Raising the Vpp programming voltage and write-protecting the Flash EPROM can be done in one operation in some Flash EPROMs. If the hardware supports this combination of functions, the calling program must only invoke INT 16h Function E0h Subfunction 05h and not Subfunction 06h.

Function E0h Subfunction 06h Flash Write Protect

Input: AH   = E0h
           AL   = 06h

Output: AL   = 0FAh Successful
           CF   = 0 Successful
                 = 1 Error

Description:

This subfunction write protects the Flash EPROM. The contents of AL are destroyed if this subfunction is successful. The contents of AL should be unchanged if unsuccessful.

Function E0h Subfunction 07h Flash Write Enable

Input: AH   = E0h
         AL   = 07h

Output: AL   = 0FAh Successful
         CF   = 0 Successful
              = 1 Error

Description:

This subfunction enables Flash EPROM programming. The contents of AL are destroyed if this subfunction is successful. The contents of AL should be unchanged if unsuccessful.

Function E0h Subfunction 08h Flash Select

Input: AH   = E0h
         AL   = 08h

Output: AL   = 0FAh Successful
         CF   = 0 Successful
              = 1 Error

Description:

This subfunction selects the Flash EPROM. In normal operation, a call to this subfunction is not necessary.

This function should be issued if both a standard EPROM and Flash EPROM reside on the motherboard. If this subfunction call was unnecessary, it returns with CF = 0.

The contents of AL are destroyed if this subfunction is successful. The contents of AL should be unchanged if unsuccessful.

INT 16h Keyboard Service, Continued

Function E0h Subfunction 09h Flash Deselect

Input: AH   = E0h
               AL   = 09h

Output: AL   = 0FAh Successful
               CF   = 0 Successful
                     = 1 Error

Description:

This subfunction deselects the Flash EPROM. In normal operation, a call to this subfunction is not necessary.

This function should be issued if both a standard EPROM and Flash EPROM reside on the motherboard. If this subfunction call was unnecessary, it returns with CF = 0.

The contents of AL are destroyed if this subfunction is successful. The contents of AL should be unchanged if unsuccessful.

Function E0h Subfunction 0Ah Verify Allocated Memory

Input: AH   = E0h
           AL   = 0Ah
           BX   = Offset of specified memory address
           ES   = Segment of specified memory address

Output: AL   = 0FAh Successful
           CF   = 0 Successful
                = 1 Error

Description:

This subfunction indicates if the address specified in ES:BX can be used. A call to this subfunction is not necessary in normal operation. If BX contains 0, this function returns with CF set.

If a certain memory region cannot be accessed (for example, 80000h – 9FFFFh may become inaccessible when shadowing is disabled) invoke this subfunction to verify the memory that the Flash EPROM programming utility will use.

If this subfunction call was unnecessary, it returns with CF = 0.

The contents of AL are destroyed if this subfunction is successful. The contents of AL should be unchanged if unsuccessful.

Function E0h Subfunction 0Bh Save Internal Cache Status

Input: AH = E0h
AL = 0Bh
ES:DI = Pointer to the beginning of a 4 KB buffer where the internal cache memory status is saved.

Output: AL = 0FAh Successful
CF = 0 Successful
= 1 Error

Description:

This subfunction saves the current status of the internal cache to the buffer pointed to be ES:DI. This subfunction returns with CF set if the requisite cache memory hardware is not available or this subfunction was called from protected mode.

The calling program must make sure that the buffer pointed to by ES:DI is at least 4 KB long.

The contents of AL are destroyed if this subfunction is successful. The contents of AL should be unchanged if unsuccessful.

Function E0h Subfunction 0Ch Restore Internal Cache Status

Input: AH   = E0h
            AL   = 0Ch
          ES:DI = Pointer to the beginning of a 4 KB buffer where the
                   internal cache memory status is restored.

Output: AL   = 0FAh Successful
            CF   = 0 Successful
                 = 1 Error

Description:

This subfunction restores the current status of the internal cache to the
buffer pointed to be ES:DI. This subfunction returns with CF set if the
requisite cache memory hardware is not available or this subfunction
was called from protected mode.

The calling program must make sure that the buffer pointed to by
ES:DI is at least 4 KB long.

The contents of AL are destroyed if this subfunction is successful. The
contents of AL should be unchanged if unsuccessful.

Function E0h Subfunction FFh Generate CPU Reset

Input: AH = E0h
AL = FFh

Output: None

Description:

This subfunction generates the CPU reset. A CPU reset is necessary to reboot the system after the Flash EPROM has been programmed successfully.

This subfunction does not return control to the calling program. The contents of all registers are destroyed by this subfunction call, since the system is rebooted when this subfunction is invoked.

Function F0h Set CPU Speed

Input: AH = F0h
AL = 00h or 01h Low Speed
02h High Speed

Output: None

Description:

Function F0h sets the CPU speed to Low or High. This function returns no values and does not destroy the contents of any registers. This function is only available if the BIOS date is after June 1992.

Function F1h Read CPU Speed

Input: AH = F1h

Output: AL = 00h or 01h Low Speed
= 02h High speed

Description:

Function F1h reads the current CPU speed. This function destroys the contents of AL, but no other registers. This function is only available if the BIOS date is after June 1992.

Function F4h Subfunction 00h Read Cache Controller Status

Input: AH = F4h
           AL   = 00h

Output: AH = None if cache controller cannot be enabled.
               = E2h Successful
           AL   = Cache Controller Status
                   00h   Cache controller not present
               = 01h   Cache memory enabled
               = 02h   Cache memory disabled
           CX   = Cache Memory Size
                   Bit 15   0 Cache size information is valid
                                 1 Cache size information is invalid
                   Bits 14–0   Cache memory size in KB
           DH = Cache Write Technology
                   Bit 7   0 Cache write information is valid
                                 1 Cache write information is not valid
                   Bits 6–1   Reserved, set to zero.
                   Bit 0   0 Write-through caching algorithm used
                                 1 Write-back caching algorithm used
           DL = Cache Type
                   Bit 7   0 Cache type information is valid
                                 1 Cache type information is not valid
                   Bits 6–1   Reserved, set to zero.
                   Bit 0   0 Cache type is direct-mapped
                               1 Cache type is two-way set-associative

Description:

Function F4h Subfunction AL = 00h returns cache controller status information. If unsuccessful, no register values are changed. The values in AX, CX, and DX are destroyed if successful. This function is only available if the BIOS date is after June 1992.

cont'd

Function F4h Subfunction 01h Enable Cache Controller

Input: AH = F0h
        AL = 01h

Output: AH = None if cache controller cannot be enabled.
            = E2h If cache controller can be enabled.

Description:

Function F4h Subfunction AL = 01h enables the cache controller. The contents of the registers are not changed if the cache controller cannot be enabled. The contents of AH are destroyed if successful. This function is only available if the BIOS date is after June 1992.

Function F4h Subfunction 02h Disable Cache Controller

Input: AH = F1h
        AL = 02h

Output: AL = None if cache controller cannot be disabled
            = E2h If successful

Description:

Function F4h Subfunction AL = 02h disables the cache controller. The contents of the registers are not changed if the cache controller cannot be enabled. The contents of AH are destroyed if successful. This function is only available if the BIOS date is after June 1992.

INT 17h Parallel Port Service

INT 17h controls the parallel ports. The BIOS uses three parallel ports, initialized to the following beginning I/O port addresses: 03BCh, 0378h, and 0278h, if present. Often, parallel ports 1 or 3 (LPT1 or LPT3) are attached to IRQ7 and parallel port 2 (LPT2) is attached to IRQ5, but this arrangement can easily be customized. The default values for the beginning parallel port I/O ports in the Hi-Flex AMIBIOS can be modified via AMIBCP.

INT 17h Functions

The INT 17h parallel printer functions are:

Function	Description
00h	Write Character
01h	Initialize Parallel Port
02h	Return Parallel Port Status

Function 00h Write Character

Input: AH = 00h
AL = Character
DX = Parallel Port Number. Index to parallel port lead address table at 40:08h.
00h LPT 1   01h LPT 2   02h   LPT 3

Output: AH = Port Status
Bit 7   Printer not busy if set to 1.
Bit 6   Printer acknowledge if set to 1.
Bit 5   Out of paper if set to 1.
Bit 4   Printer selected if set to 1.
Bit 3   I/O error if set to 1.
Bits 2–1 Reserved
Bit 0   Printer timed-out is set to 1.

Description:

Function 00h writes a character to the specified parallel port. The function status is returned in AH.

cont'd

Function 01h Initialize Parallel Port

Input: AH = 01h
         DX = Parallel Port Number. Index to parallel port address
               table at 40:08h.
               00h   LPT 1
               01h   LPT 2
               02h   LPT 3

Output: AH = Parallel Port Status
               Bit 7   Printer not busy if set to 1.
               Bit 6   Printer acknowledge if set to 1.
               Bit 5   Out of paper if set to 1.
               Bit 4   Printer selected if set to 1.
               Bit 3   I/O error if set to 1.
               Bits 2–1 Reserved
               Bit 0   Printer timed out if set to 1.

Description: Function 01h initializes the specified parallel port. The
              Parallel Port Status is returned in AH.

Function 02h Read Parallel Port Status

Input: AH = 02h
         DX = Parallel Port Number. Index to parallel port lead
               address table at 40:08h.
               00h   LPT1   01h   LPT2   02h   LPT 3

Output: AH = Port Status
               Bit 7   Printer not busy if set to 1.
               Bit 6   Printer acknowledge if set to 1.
               Bit 5   Out of paper if set to 1.
               Bit 4   Printer selected if set to 1.
               Bit 3   I/O error if set to 1.
               Bits 2–1 Reserved
               Bit 0   Printer timed out if set to 1.

Description: Function 02h returns the parallel port status in AH.

INT 18h ROM BASIC

Input: None

Output: None

Description: On the original IBM PC, INT 18h transferred control to ROM BASIC. ROM BASIC is not supported by IBM anymore. If INT 18h is invoked, the BIOS halts the system and displays:

```
NO BOOT DEVICE AVAILABLE
```

The only way to regain control is to reboot.

Other Uses of INT 18h

Some network cards contain boot ROMs so that a system attached to a network can boot without using a hard disk or floppy disk. These ROMs trap INT 18h to gain access to the system.

INT 19h Bootstrap Loader

Input: None

Output: None

Description:

INT 19h transfers control to the operating system. The BIOS reads the boot sector (sector 1, track 0) from the primary boot device (drive A: or C:) and writes that data to 0000:7C00h. The BIOS gives control to the data at that address, which in turn loads (boots) the operating system.

If the BIOS does not find a boot sector on the primary boot device, it looks for a boot sector on the secondary boot device. The primary and secondary boot devices are floppy drive A:, then hard disk drive C:.

If no boot sector is found on either drive A: or C:, INT 18h is invoked (see above).

cont'd

System Boot Up Sequence Option

The *System Boot Up Sequence* option in AMIBIOS Advanced CMOS
Setup permits you to set the boot sequence to either *C:, A:* or *A:, C:,* as
described in the following table.

If...	and...	then...
Advanced CMOS Setup *System Boot Up Sequence* is set to A:, C:,	a bootable floppy disk is in drive A:,	INT 19h reads the boot sector on the floppy disk and places its contents at 7C00h.
Advanced CMOS Setup *System Boot Up Sequence* is set to A:, C:,	Drive A: has no bootable disk:, or the floppy disk in drive A: is not bootable,	INT 19h invokes INT 18h. INT 18h displays: NO BOOT DEVICE AVAILABLE
Advanced CMOS Setup *System Boot Up Sequence* is set to C:, A:,	the boot sector is found on drive C:,	INT 19h reads the boot sector on the floppy disk and places its contents at 7C00h.
Advanced CMOS Setup *System Boot Up Sequence* is set to C:, A:,	Hard Disk Drive C: has no boot sector (the hard disk drive type is probably not properly configured),	INT 19h invokes INT 18h. INT 18h displays: NO BOOT DEVICE AVAILABLE

INT 1Ah Service

INT 1Ah functions set or read the system Real Time Clock and performs PCI and PCMCIA Socket Service functions. The Real Time Clock ISR is INT 70h. See the INT 08h discussion on page 186 for a discussion of timers used in ISA and EISA systems. The following graphic illustrates how the real time clock is used with the BIOS.

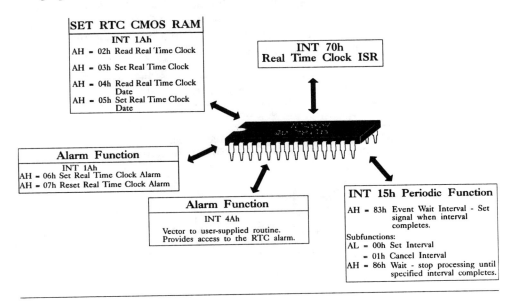

SET RTC CMOS RAM
INT 1Ah
AH = 02h Read Real Time Clock
AH = 03h Set Real Time Clock
AH = 04h Read Real Time Clock Date
AH = 05h Set Real Time Clock Date

INT 70h
Real Time Clock ISR

Alarm Function
INT 1Ah
AH = 06h Set Real Time Clock Alarm
AH = 07h Reset Real Time Clock Alarm

Alarm Function
INT 4Ah
Vector to user-supplied routine.
Provides access to the RTC alarm.

INT 15h Periodic Function
AH = 83h Event Wait Interval - Set signal when interval completes.
Subfunctions:
AL = 00h Set Interval
   = 01h Cancel Interval
AH = 86h Wait - stop processing until specified interval completes.

Socket Services

INT 1Ah Socket Services

Socket Services is an extension to system BIOS software interrupt 1Ah
Real Time Clock Service. All Socket Services are function calls to INT
1Ah. Socket Services provides the software interface to the hardware
that controls PCMCIA-compatible cards (memory and I/O) in sockets.
Socket Services provides the lowest level access to PCMCIA cards but
does not interpret the content of the cards. The following diagram
illustrates the AMIBIOS Socket Services work flow:

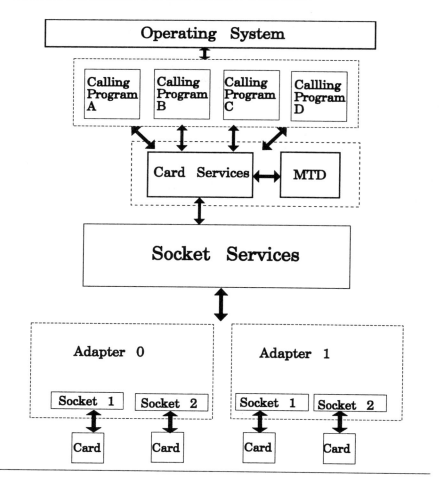

Adapters

Adapters are the hardware that connects the bus on the computer to the PC Card sockets. There can be several adapters in a computer. Socket Services can be used to report the number of adapters, windows, and EDC (Error Detection Code) generators provided for each adapter. Adapter power consumption and status change reporting can be controlled separately for each adapter. An adapter can have one or more sockets, as shown in the illustration on the previous page.

Sockets

Socket Services provides a universal interface to the hardware hat controls sockets for PC Cards. A socket is the physical 68-pin connector that a PC Card is inserted into. Socket Services can:

- report the characteristics of each socket,
- manage socket resources, and
- report the current socket settings.

PC Cards

Socket Services report the current PC Card status and read from or write to PC Cards that are not mapped to system memory or I/O space.

Mapping

PC Cards are often mapped to system memory or I/O space to provide better performance. XIP (Execute-In-Place — a specification that permits code to be directly executed from a PC Card) requires that PC Card memory arrays be mapped to system memory. Mapping occurs through a memory window.

Memory Windows

A window is an area in the host computer memory or I/O space through which a PC Card can be addressed. A memory window is composed of one or more contiguous 16 KB pages. Memory windows can address common or attribute memory. Memory windows can overlap only if one window at a time is mapped to system memory at the overlapping addresses while other windows that use the same address are disabled.

I/O Windows

I/O windows respond to I/O bus requests within their I/O port range by asserting Card Enable for the socket. The PC Card must then decode the address lines to decide how to respond to the request. I/O windows are not paged but can overlap and share I/O space if the socket supports the
-INPACK signal from the PC Card. But only one PC Card can respond to an I/O request.

Card Services

Card Services arbitrates the assignment of Socket Services resources. Card Services processes requests from multiple processes.

Card Services allocates and manages the resources of the system to the cards such as interrupt levels, DMA channels and memory windows. These activities can occur only after Socket Services has determined that there is a PC Card in one of the system sockets. Card Services also releases system resources for use by other system software if Socket Services determines that a particular PC Card has been removed from one of the system sockets. Card Services is the system software level interface used by the operating systems for PC Card and Socket Services.

Using Socket Services

Initializing Socket Services

AMIBIOS automatically initializes Socket Services, if present. Calling programs should check the version of Socket Services available to determine the service level.

Configuring Socket Services

Before using Socket Services, the calling program should determine:

- that Socket Services is installed by invoking INT 1Ah with AH = 80h Get Adapter Count,

- that the proper version of Socket Services is installed by invoking INT 1Ah with AH = 83h Get SS Info,

- verify the implementation version number by invoking INT 1Ah with AH = 9Dh Get Vendor Info,

- get the number of sockets and windows supported by each adapter, and other features (such as power management) available for each adapter by invoking INT 1Ah with AH = 84h Inquire Adapter, and

- get information about each individual socket by invoking INT 1Ah with AH = 8Ch Inquire Socket.

Table of Socket Services Configuration Information

For ease of access to adapters, sockets, and PC Cards, the calling program can build a table that contains the configuration information for all sockets and adapters including resource assignment.

Other PC Card-Related Software

Socket Services is virtualized by Card Services. Device drivers for different types of PC Cards reside above Card Services. These device drivers may map PC Cards to system I/O or system memory. Multiple drivers may share PC Cards, sockets, or windows. Card Services arbitrates request for Socket Services resources. Card Services also preserves and disseminates state information about PC Card resources.

When Status Changes

A calling program using Socket Services may need to be notified when:

• a PC Card is inserted or removed,

• a battery is low or dead, or

• a resource is busy or ready.

Status Change Handling

Socket Services provides asynchronous notification when the status of a socket changes. Each adapter can provide a hardware interrupt when there is a status change. While only one interrupt per handler is anticipated, the Socket Services interface allows status changes to be masked per each socket. Masking must be done in hardware because the hardware interrupt is managed by the Status Change Interrupt Handler.

If status change interrupts are supported, every program that calls Socket Services must specify the interrupt it uses for status changes. The interrupt must be one that is reported by INT 1Ah AH = 84h Inquire Adapter. A calling program can enable or disable this capability or can send the interrupt to a supported host interrupt level.

Using Socket Services, Continued

Status Change Interrupt Handler

The calling program must install a status change interrupt handler on the host interrupt level to monitor status change interrupts from Socket Services. The calling program can also poll for changes in socket and PC Card status.

When an adapter that is configured for status change interrupts recognizes a status change, it generates an interrupt that invokes the status callback handler supplied by the calling program.

This handler uses the Socket Services INT 1Ah AH = 9Eh Acknowledge Interrupt function to find which socket experienced the status change.

The handler records the information and completes the hardware interrupt processing. The calling program recognizes which socket requires attention and invokes INT 1Ah AH = 8Fh Get Status for PC Card and socket status.

Windows Supported

Socket Services uses a bitmap to return information on which windows can be mapped to a specific socket. The calling program should invoke INT 1Ah AH = 87h Inquire Windows to receive this information.

If a hardware implementation provides a single window per socket, Function INT 1Ah AH = 87h indicates the same value as the number of sockets supported by the adapter.

If a hardware implementation permits any adapter window to be mapped to any socket, the number of available windows will be returned. A window can be assigned to more than one socket but it is assumed that a window is mapped to only one socket at a time. A window can be shared between two sockets if it is remapped between accesses by the calling program.

Evaluate Windows Descriptions

Calling programs should evaluate the windows descriptions returned by Socket Services. Socket Services will fail invalid requests such as trying to map a window to an unsupported socket.

The calling program is responsible for preserving windows state information.

EDC Generators

Error Detection Code generators are optional. They are numbered from 0 to one less than the number on the adapter as returned by the INT 1Ah AH = 84h Inquire Adapter.

Using XIP (Execute-In-Place)

XIP applications require sockets that support memory-mapped windows. XIP applications also require exclusive full-time access to these memory-mapped windows. High-level software that uses Socket Services resources must make sure that resources used by XIP are dedicated to the XIP application.

Bus Expanders

It is possible to expand the number of PC Cards in a socket by plugging an expansion device that has room for two or more PC Cards into a single socket. Socket Services does not handle multiple PC Cards plugged into such a device.

There are several methods for permitting these type of devices to be used. You could address these sockets as if they existed on a different adapter. Software on the host computer could intercept Socket Services calls and filter the INT 1Ah AH = 80h Get Number of Adapter function calls and all function calls to the new adapter and its associated sockets.

Using Socket Services, Continued

Power Management

Socket Services provides two power conservation modes:

- all state information is maintained, and

- no state information is maintained.

The levels of power conservation are established by invoking INT 1Ah
AH = 86h Set Adapter.

Socket Services also manages power to PC Card sockets. Independent
controls and levels are provided for Vcc, Vpp1, and Vpp2. Because
available power levels are generally limited, Socket Services provides a
list of supported levels and then permits power adjustments by
manipulating an index to this list of power levels. The calling program
can invoke INT 1Ah AH = 84h Inquire Adapter to determine the level
of power management control available for adapters.

Socket Services does not deal with power management features on
individual PC Cards. This type of feature must be handled by card-
aware device drivers through a software service at a higher level.

PCMCIA PC Cards

PC Card Size

A PC Card is a small form factor electronic device a little thicker than a credit card. PC Cards provide functions such as added memory for data interchange between computers. Additionally, these cards are used to expand the I/O capabilities of a computer by adding such functions as serial or parallel ports, SCSI ports, Network Ports and Fax/Modems. The PC Card dimensions are shown below.

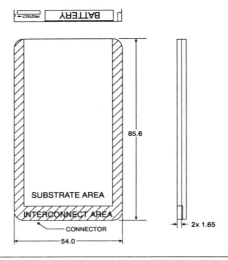

Card Types

The PCMCIA standards describes the physical, electrical and software specifications for the Cards. These specifications define four types of cards. All types use the same 68-pin edge connector for interfacing to the computer, but differ significantly in their width. The thickness of these types of cards is:

Type I   3.3 mm
Type II   5 mm
Type III 10.5 mm

The differences in the PC Card types are shown below.

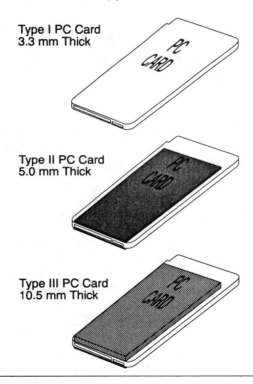

Type I PC Card
3.3 mm Thick

Type II PC Card
5.0 mm Thick

Type III PC Card
10.5 mm Thick

cont'd

Type I Cards

Type I Cards are used primarily for various types of memory upgrades such as RAM, FLASH, One Time Programmable (OTP), or electrically erasable/programmable read only memory (EEPROM).

Type II Cards

Type II cards can be used for memory enhancements as described as in Type I above or for I/O functions such as FAX/Modems, LAN connections, or other host communications.

Type III Cards

Type III PC Cards are twice the thickness of Type II cards and can be used for memory enhancements and/or I/O functions requiring additional head room on the card such as rotating media devices and radio communication devices.

Type IV Cards

The type IV specification has not been finalized as this book goes to press. Type IV PCMCIA PC Cards will probably be thicker than Type II Cards and will be able to contain storage devices with larger capacities.

Form Follows Function

Since all three card types adhere to the same electrical interface the type of card chosen by the card designer depends totally on the function being implemented. The functionality of the card depends on the components located inside the card and the software residing inside the computer.

PCMCIA PC Cards, Continued

Where Can PC Cards be Used?

PC Cards can be used in Laptop Computers, Palmtop Computers, Pen Computers, Desktop Computers, or any other type of computing device that adheres to the specifications. PC Cards make communication between portable computers and desktop computers or peripherals easy and affordable.

PCMCIA Hardware Standards

The following illustration is approximately the size of a PCMCIA PC Card:

cont'd

INT 1Ah Real Time Clock Service

Summary of INT 1Ah Real Time Clock Functions

INT 1Ah also provides functions for Socket Services, described on pages 340 through 394.

Function	Description
00h	Return Clock Tick Count
01h	Set Clock Tick Count
02h	Return Current Time
03h	Set Current Time
04h	Return Current Date
05h	Return Current Date
06h	Set Alarm
07h	Reset Alarm
80h - 9Ch	Socket Services functions (See page 340)
9Dh	Card Services functions
B1h	PCI BIOS functions (see page 396)

Function 00h Return Clock Tick Count

Input:　AH　=　00h

Output: AL　=　00h Midnight has not passed since last call.
　　　　　CX:DX　=　Clock Tick Count (CX is the MSB)

Description:

Function 00h returns the value of the timer tick counter from 40:6Ch through 40:6Fh. The value is the number of ticks counted since midnight. Approximately 18.2 timer ticks occur every second.

The contents of 40:70h Timer Overflow are returned in AL. This value is zero if the timer has not overflowed past 24 hours since the last call.

INT 1Ah Real Time Clock Service, Continued

Function 01h Set Clock Tick Count

Input: AH = 01h
CX:DX = Clock Tick Count (CX is MSB)

Output: None

Description:

Function 01h sets the clock tick counter in 40:6Ch – 6Fh to the value specified in CX and DX. Approximately 18.2 ticks occur a second. The Timer Overflow flag at 40:70h is reset to 0 by this function.

Function 02h Return Current Time

Input: AH = 02h

Output: CF = 0 Successful
= 1 Clock has stopped running.
CH = Number of Hours in binary coded decimal (BCD)
CL = Number of Minutes (in BCD)
DH = Number of Seconds (in BCD)
DL = 00h Standard time
= 01h Daylight savings time

Description:

Function 02h reads the current time from Real Time Clock CMOS RAM.

cont'd

INT 1Ah Real Time Clock Service, Continued

Function 03h Set Current Time

Input: AH = 03h
           CH = Number of Hours (in BCD)
           CL   = Number of Minutes (in BCD)
           DH = Number of Seconds (in BCD)
           DL   = 00h Standard time
                = 01h Daylight savings time

Output: AL   = Value written to CMOS RAM Register B

Description:

Function 03h writes a specified time to Real Time Clock CMOS RAM.

Function 04h Return Current Date

Input: AH = 04h

Output: CF   = 0 Successful
                = 1 Clock has stopped running.
           CH = Century (in BCD)
           CL   = Year (in BCD)
           DH = Month (in BCD)
           DL   = Day (in BCD)

Description:

Function 04h reads the current date from Real Time Clock CMOS RAM.

Function 05h Set Current Date

Input: AH   =   05h
          CH   =   Century (in BCD)
          CL   =   Year (in BCD)
          DH   =   Month (in BCD)
          DL   =   Day (in BCD)

Output: AL   =   Value written to Register B of RTC CMOS RAM

Description: This function writes the specified date to CMOS RAM.

Function 06h Set Alarm

Input: AH   =   06h
          CH   =   Hours (in BCD)
          CL   =   Minutes (in BCD)
          DH   =   Seconds (in BCD)

Output: CF   =   0 No error
              =   1 The alarm is already set.

Description: This function sets an alarm for the time specified in CMOS RAM and enables the clock interrupt request line (IRQ8). Trap the INT 4Ah vector (0:128h) and replace it with the address of your own alarm service routine.

Function 07h Reset Alarm

Input: AH   =   07h

Output: AL   =   Value written to Register B in RTC CMOS RAM

Description: This function resets all alarms in Real Time Clock CMOS RAM. It does not disable the clock interrupt request line (IRQ8).

cont'd

Socket Services Function Summary

Function	Name	Turn to
80h	Get Adapter Count	Page 341
83h	Get SS Info	Page 342
84h	Inquire Adapter	Page 343
85h	Get Adapter	Page 346
86h	Set Adapter	Page 347
87h	Inquire Window	Page 349
88h	Get Window	Page 356
89h	Set Window	Page 358
8Ah	Get Page	Page 360
8Bh	Set Page	Page 362
8Ch	Inquire Socket	Page 364
8Dh	Get Socket	Page 367
8Eh	Set Socket	Page 370
8Fh	Get Status	Page 373
90h	Reset Card	Page 376
95h	Inquire EDC (Error Detection Code)	Page 377
96h	Get EDC	Page 379
97h	Set EDC	Page 380
98h	Start EDC	Page 381
99h	Pause EDC	Page 382
9Ah	Resume EDC	Page 382
9Bh	Stop EDC	Page 383
9Ch	Read EDC	Page 383
9Dh	Get Vendor Info	Page 384
9Eh	Acknowledge Interrupt	Page 385
9Fh	Get and Set Prior Handler	Page 386
A0h	Get SS Addr	Page 388
A1h	Get and Set Access Offsets	Page 391
AEh	Vendor-Specific	Page 393

Socket Services Calling Conventions

Socket Services functions are invoked through software interrupt 1Ah. The general convention for invoking the socket services functions is:

Input: AH = Function number
          AL   = Adapter number
          BH = Window number
          BL   = Socket number or Page number

Other input parameters may be added, depending on the specific function.

Output: CF = 0 Successful
               = 1 Error
          AH = Error code

Function 80h Get Adapter Count

This function returns the number of adapters supported by Socket Services and can be used to determine the presence of the Socket Services handler.

Input: AH = 80h

Output: AL = Number of adapters (one-based)
           CF = 0 Successful. Socket Services handler present.
               = 1 Error. Socket Services handler not present.
           CX = the string *SS*

Even if the Socket Services handler is present, there may not be any adapter installed. In this case, this function should return with CF set, *SS* in CX, and 00h in AL. The caller of this function must handle this situation properly.

Function 83h Get SS Info

This function returns the version of both Implementor and PCMCIA Socket Services compliance levels. Version numbers are returned as binary coded decimals (BCD) values.

Input:	AH	=	83h
	AL	=	Adapter number (zero-based)
Output:	AH	=	Error code
		=	00h Successful
		=	01h Bad adapter
	AL	=	PCMCIA Socket Services Version Number
			00h Insures compatibility with Release 1.01.
	BX	=	Socket Services Interface Specification Compliance Level (0201h for PCMCIA V2.01)
	CF	=	0 Successful
		=	1 Error
	CH	=	Number of adapters supported by this handler.
	CL	=	First adapter supported by this handler.

If more than one type of adapter is present in the system, there may be more than one Socket Services handler present. This function determines the support level of Socket Services for the specified adapter.

Function 84h Inquire Adapter

This function returns information about the specified adapter.

Input: AH = 84h
AL = Adapter number (zero-based)
ES:EDI = Pointer to a buffer supplied by the calling program that will be filled with information about the adapter by Socket Services.

Output: AH = Error code
= 00h Successful
= 01h Bad adapter
BH = Number of windows (one-based)
BL = Number of sockets (one-based)
CF = 0 Successful
= 1 Error
CX = Number of EDCs (Error Detection Code) (can be 0 – the total number of sockets)
ES:EDI = Pointer to buffer containing adapter characteristics and power management tables.

The buffer pointed to by the contents of ES:EDI is supplied by the calling program and must have the following format:

```
typedef struct tagAISTRUCT {
    WORD wBufferLength;
    WORD wDataLength;
    ACHARTBL CharTable
    WORD wNumPwrEntries = NUM_ENTRIES;
    PWRENTRY PwrEntry[NUM_ENTRIES];
} AISTRUCT;
```

The CharTbl structure is defined below. wBufferLength must be set by the calling program to the size of AISTRUCT minus four bytes. wDataLength is set by Socket Services to the size of the information block returned. If the wDataLength value is greater than the wBufferLength value, the information is truncated.

PWRENTRY

PWRENTRY is a two-member structure. The first member is a binary value representing a DC voltage level in tenths of a volt with a maximum of 25.5 VDC. The second member specifies the power signals that may be set to the specified voltage level (either Vcc, Vpp1, or Vpp2). All sockets on an adapter should use the same power levels. Make one PWRENTRY for each supported voltage. PWRENTRY only indicates that it is possible to set power pins to a certain power level. It is up to the calling program to determine if the specified combination of power levels is valid for the PC Card in the socket. The PWRENTRY structure is shown below:

```
typedef struct tagPWRENTRY {
    BYTE PowerLevel;
    BYTE ValidSignals;
} PWRENTRY
```

where:

PowerLevel   the DC voltage level in tenths of a volt. Power levels from 0 (N/C) through 25.5 VDC are valid.

ValidSignals   flags that indicate if voltage is valid for specific signals. A combination of the following can be used:

Vcc   Voltage level valid for the Vcc signal
Vpp1   Voltage level valid for the Vpp1 signal
Vpp2   Voltage level valid for the Vpp2 signal

Sample AISTRUCT

```
AISTRUCT AdapterInfo = {
    24,              //Size of calling program-supplied buffer is 24 //bytes
    24,              //Size of data returned is 24 bytes
    {0,              //Indicators, power, and data bus width are controlled
                     //at the socket
    0xDEB8           //Status changes may be routed to IRQ levels
                     //3, 4, 5, 7, 9, 10, 11, 12, 14, and 15
                     //as an active high signal
    0},              //Status changes are not available on
                     //any level as an active low signal
    3,               //Number of PWRENTRY elements
    ((VCC | VPP1 | VPP2) << 8) | 0
                     //Vcc, Vpp1, and Vpp2 - No Connect
    ((VCC | VPP1 | VPP2) << 8) | 50
                     //Vcc, Vpp1, and Vpp2 - 5.0 VDC
    ((VPP | VPP2 | << 8) | 120
                     //Vpp1 and Vpp2 - 12.0 VDC
```

Function 84h Inquire Adapter, Continued

ACHATBL Structure

```
typedef struct tagACHATBL {    //Same format as Socket
                               //characteristics except
   WORD AdpCaps;               //CHARTBL has different values
   DWORD ActiveHigh;
   DWORD ActiveLow;
} ACHATBL;
```

AdpCaps

AdpCaps (Adapter capabilities) is structured as follows:

Indicators

0   There are individual indicators for each socket.
1   Indicators for write protect, card lock, battery status, busy status, and XIP status are shared by all sockets on the adapter.

Power Level

0   Power levels can be individually set for each socket.
1   The adapter requires all sockets to be set to the same power level controls.

Data bus width

0   Data bus width set individually for each window.
1   All windows on the adapter must use the same data bus width.

ActiveHigh

A doubleword bitmap of the status change interrupt levels that can be routed active high.

ActiveLow

A doubleword bitmap of the status change interrupt levels that can be routed active low.

Function 85h Get Adapter

This function returns the current configuration of the specified adapter.

Input: AH   = 85h

Output: AH   = Error code
             CF   = 0 Successful
                  = 1 Error
             DH   = Adapter attributes
                      Bit 1   Preserve state information in power-down
                               1 True
                      Bit 0   Reduce power consumption
                               1 True
             DI   = Status change interrupt routing
                      Bit 7   IRQ enabled
                               1 Status change is enabled.
                      Bit 6   IRQ high
                               1 Status change interrupt is active high.
                      Bits 4-0 IRQ level

Bit 0 of DH (Reduce power consumption) indicates if the adapter
hardware is attempting to conserve power. Before using the adapter,
full power must be restored via INT 1Ah AH = 86h Set Adapter.

If Bit 1 of DH (Preserve State Information) is set to 1, all adapter and
socket status are retained in reduced-power mode. If this bit is set to 0,
the software that placed the adapter in reduced-power mode must
save all adapter and socket status.

The ability to reduce power consumption is not available in all
adapters. Reduced power settings may not result in any power
savings. The Inquire Adapter function (AH = 84h) indicates if it is
possible to share the status change interrupt. This function returns the
form of interrupt sharing (if any) currently being performed.

Function 86h Set Adapter

This function sets the configuration of the specified adapter. The card status change interrupt is enabled or disabled through this function.

Input: AH = 86h

           AL = Adapter number (zero-based)

           DH = Adapter attributes

                    Bit 1   State information in power down

                                   1   Preserve status information

                    Bit 0   Power consumption

                                   1   Reduce

           DI   = Status change interrupt routing

                    Bit 7   IRQ enabled

                                   1   Status change is enabled.

                    Bit 6   IRQ high

                                   1   Status change interrupt is active high. If the adapter status change level is not programmable, this setting must match the actual hardware signal level.

                    Bits 4-0   IRQ level

Output: AH = Error code

                  = 00h Successful

                  = 01h Bad adapter

                  = 06h Bad IRQ

           CF = 0 Successful

                  = 1 Error

Function 86h Set Adapter, Continued

Bit 0 of DH (Reduce power consumption) indicates the adapter hardware is attempting to conserve power. Reduced power settings may not actually reduce power consumption because power management features are vendor-specific.

Before using the adapter, full power must be restored using this function.

If Bit 1 of DH (Preserve state information) is set to 1, all adapter and socket status are retained in reduced-power mode.

If this bit is set to 0, the software that placed the adapter in reduced-power mode must save all adapter and socket status.

Function 87h Inquire Window

This function returns information about the specified window on the specified adapter.

Input: AH = 87h
AL = Adapter number (zero-based)
BH = Window number (zero-based)
ES:EDI = Pointer to a buffer provided by the calling program that holds window information.

Output: AH = Error code
= 00h Successful
= 01h Bad adapter
= 11h Bad window

BL = Capabilities
Bit 7   Use PC Card -WAIT signal
1   Windows use the -WAIT signal from a PC Card to generate additional wait states.

Bits 6-3   Reserved (set to 0)
Bit 2   I/O space
1   The window can be used to map I/O ports on a PC Card to the host system I/O space.

Bit 1   Attribute memory
1   The window can be used to map PC Card attribute memory to the host computer system memory.

Bit 0   Common memory
1   The window can be used to map PC Card common memory to host computer system memory.

CF = 0 Successful
= 1 Error
CX = Bitmap of assignable sockets
ES:EDI = Pointer to either the memory window characteristics table (see pages 350 through 353) or the I/O window characteristics table (see pages 353 through 355.

Memory Window Characteristics Table

```
typedef struct tagMEMWINTBL {
    WORD   MemWndCaps;
    WORD   FirstByte;
    WORD   LastByte;
    WORD   MinSize;
    WORD   MaxSize;
    WORD   ReqGran;
    WORD   ReqBase;
    WORD   ReqOffset;
    BYTE   Slowest;
    BYTE   Fastest;
} MEMWINTBL;
```

where:

MemWndCaps is a set of memory window characteristic flags, as
    follows:

Memory Windows Characteristics Table Flags

Base   If set, the base address of the window is programmable
           within the range specified by FirstByte and LastByte. If set to
           0, the window base address is fixed in system memory at the
           location specified in FirstByte and LastByte is undefined.

Size   If set, the window size is programmable within the range
           specified by MinSize and MaxSize.

Enable   If set, the window can be disabled without reprogramming
           its characteristics. If 0, the calling program must preserve
           window state information before disabling the window.

8bit   If set, the window can be programmed for an 8-bit data bus
           width.

16bit   If set, the window can be programmed for a 16-bit data bus
           width.

Memory Window Characteristics Table Flags, cont'd

Balign   If set, the window base address must be a multiple of the window size. If 0, the base address can be any valid address.

Pow2   If set, a fixed-length window must be equal to a power of two of the ReqGran value. If 0, window size could be any value on a 4 KB boundary between 4 KB and 64 KB.

Calgn   If set, PC Card offsets must be in increments equal to the size of the window.

Pavail   If set, the window can be divided into multiple pages via hardware. If 0, the window can only be addressed as a single page. If 0, the calling program must preserve page state information before disabling the page.

Pshare   If set, the window paging hardware is sharable with another window. A request to use the paging hardware may fail if another window is using it. This value is only valid if Pavail is set.

*The calling program should check **Pshare** when using window paging. If set, the calling program must make sure that a subsequent INT 1Ah AH = 89h Set Window request is successful before using the window. To determine if the page is available, assign it to a window by invoking INT 1Ah AH = 89h Set Window and make sure AH = 00h upon return from Socket Services.*

Penbl   If set, the page can be disabled without reprogramming its characteristics.

Wp   If set, the PC Card memory window mapped to the host computer system can be write-protected.

cont'd

Memory Window Characteristics Table, resumed

FirstByte The first byte this window can use in the host memory
system. If the window base address is not programmable,
this is the same as the window base address.

LastByte The last byte this window can use in the host memory
system. The last byte of the window cannot exceed this
value. This value is not used if the window base address is
not programmable.

MinSize The minimum window size. The window must meet all
granularity and base requirements and must be within the
MinSize and *MaxSize* values.

MaxSize The maximum window size. The window must meet all
granularity and base requirements and must be within the
MinSize and *MaxSize* values. If *MaxSize* is 0, the window size
is the largest value that may be represented by the SIZE data
type plus one.

ReqGran The units required for defining the windows size because of
hardware constraints. If the window is a fixed size, this value
is the same as Min Size and MaxSize.

ReqBase If Balign is 0, this value specifies the boundary alignment for
setting the window base address via INT 1Ah AH = 89h Set
Window.

ReqOfst If *Calign* is 0, this value specifies the boundary alignment for
setting the window base address via INT 1Ah AH = 8Bh Set
Page. This field is undefined if *Calign* is set.

Slowest This value is the slowest access speed supported by this
window.

Fastest This value is the fastest access speed supported by this
window.

Memory Window Characteristics Table, resumed

Slowest and *Fastest* are in the format specified by the PCMCIA Device
Speed Code and Extended Device Speed Codes.

Bit 7 of *Slowest* and *Fastest* is reserved and is always set to 0.

I/O Window Characteristics Table

```
typedef struct tagIOWINTBL {
    WORD   IOWndCaps;
    WORD   FirstByte;
    WORD   LastByte;
    WORD   MinSize;
    WORD   MaxSize;
    WORD   ReqGran;
    BYTE   AddrLines;
    BYTE   EISASlot;
} IOWINTBL;
```

where:

IOWndCaps   is a set of I/O window characteristic flags, as follows:

I/O Window Characteristics Table Flags

Base   If set, the base address of the window is programmable
          within the range specified by FirstByte and LastByte. If set to
          0, the window base address is fixed in system I/O space at
          the location specified in FirstByte and LastByte is undefined.

Size   If set, the window size is programmable within the range
          specified by MinSize and MaxSize.

Wenable   If set, the window can be disabled without reprogramming
          its characteristics. If 0, the calling program must preserve
          window state information before disabling the window.

cont'd

I/O Window Characteristics Table Flags, cont'd

8bit   If set, the window can be programmed for an 8-bit data bus width.

16bit   If set, the window can be programmed for a 16-bit data bus width.

Balign   If set, the window base address must be a multiple of the windows size. If 0, the base address can be any valid address.

Pow2   If set, a fixed-length window must be equal to a power of two of the Reqgran value. If 0, window size could be any value between the *MinSize* and *MaxSize* values.

Inpck   If set, the window supports the -INPACK signal from a PC Card. -INPACK allows windows to overlap in I/O space.

EISA   If set, the window supports EISA-type I/O mapping as would an EISA system. EISASlot specifies the slot-specific address decodes for this window.

Cenable   If set, EISA-like common addresses can be ignored. If 0 and the window is programmed for EISA-like I/O mapping, the PC Card receives a Card Enable signal when an access is made to an EISA common address. This value is only valid if *EISA* is set.

I/O Window Characteristics Table, resumed

FirstByte   The first byte this window can use in the host I/O space. If the window base address is not programmable, this is the same as the window base address.

I/O Window Characteristics Table, cont'd

LastByte   The last byte this window can use in the host I/O space.
            The last byte of the window cannot exceed this value.
            This value is not used if the window base address is not
            programmable.

MinSize   The minimum window size. The window must meet all
            granularity and base requirements and must be within the
            MinSize and *MaxSize* values.

MaxSize   The maximum window size. The window must meet all
            granularity and base requirements and must be within the
            MinSize and *MaxSize* values. If *MaxSize* is 0, the window
            size is the largest value that may be represented by the
            SIZE data type plus one.

ReqGran   The units required for defining the window size because
            of hardware constraints. If the window is a fixed size, this
            value is the same as Min Size and MaxSize.

AddrLins   The number of address lines decoded by the window.
            Usually either 10 or 16. If a window only decodes 10
            address lines, accesses to address above 1 KB will drive
            Card Accesses to a PC Card when the ten least significant
            address lines fall within the range defined by the base
            address and the window size.

EISASlot   The upper byte for window-specific EISA I/O decoding.
            This value specifies the upper four address lines used for
            EISA slot-specific address that drive Card Enables. This
            filed is not used if *EISA* is 0.

Function 88h Get Window

This function returns the current configuration of the specified window on the specified adapter.

Input: AH = 88h
AL = Adapter number (zero-based)
BH = Window number (zero-based)

Output: AH = Error code
= 00h Successful
= 01h Bad adapter
= 11h Bad window
BL = Socket number (zero-based)
CF = 0 Successful
= 1 Error
CX = Size of window (In bytes for I/O windows. In 4 KB units for memory windows). If 0, the window is the maximum size that can be represented.
DH = Window state (bit-mapped)

The meaning of Bits 3 and 4 varies, depending on whether this function is reporting about an I/O window or a memory window.

Bit 4   EISA common I/O. This bit is only valid for I/O windows that have bit 3 set.
0   Access to I/O ports in EISA common I/O areas is ignored.
1   Access to I/O ports in EISA common I/O areas is enabled.

Bit 3   (If I/O window)
0   ISA I/O mapping
1   EISA I/O mapping

Bit 3   Memory page (if memory window)
0   Single page window
1   Window is divided into multiple 16 KB pages with PC Card offset addresses that can be set individually via Function AH = 8Bh Set Page.

Output: cont'd

DH = Window state (bit-mapped), cont'd

Bit 2   16/8-bit data path

0   The window can use an 8-bit data bus width.

1   The window can use a 16-bit data bus width.

Bit 1   Window enabling

0   The window is disabled.

1   The window is enabled and can map a PC Card to the host system memory or I/O space.

Bit 0   I/O Mapping

0   Common or attribute memory is mapped to the host memory space.

1   PC Card registers are mapped to the host I/O space.

DL = Access speed. Select only one. Not used for I/O windows. See the PCMCIA PC Card Standards 2.01 specification for the speed codes.

DI = Windows base address (In bytes if an I/O window. In 4 KB units if a memory window).

Function 89h Set Window

This function sets the configuration of the specified window on the specified adapter. The area of the PC Card memory array mapped to the host memory is managed by the INT 1Ah AH = 8Ah Get Page and INT A1h AH = 8Bh Set Page functions for memory-mapped windows.

Input: AH = 89h
AL = Adapter number (zero-based)
BH = Window number (zero-based)
BL = Socket number (zero-based)
CX = Window size (in 4 KB units for memory windows and in bytes for I/O windows)
DH = Window state (bit-mapped)

The meaning of Bits 3 and 4 varies, depending on whether this function is reporting about an I/O window or a memory window.

Bit 4   EISA common I/O. This bit is only valid for I/O windows that have bit 3 set.
0   Access to I/O ports in EISA common I/O areas is ignored.
1   Access to I/O ports in EISA common I/O areas is enabled.

Bit 3   (If I/O window)
0   ISA I/O mapping
1   EISA I/O mapping

Bit 3   Memory page (if memory window)
0   Single page window
1   Window is divided into multiple 16 KB pages with PC Card offset addresses that can be set individually via Function AH = 8Bh Set Page.

Function 88h Set Window, Continued

Output: cont'd

DH = Window state (bit-mapped), cont'd

    Bit 2   16/8-bit data path

        0 The window can use an 8-bit data bus width.

        1 The window can use a 16-bit data bus width.

    Bit 1   Window enabling

        0 The window is disabled.

        1 The window is enabled and can map a PC Card to the host system memory or I/O space.

    Bit 0   I/O Mapping

        0 Common or attribute memory is mapped to the host memory space.

        1 PC Card registers are mapped to the host I/O space.

DL = Access speed. Select only one. Not used for I/O windows. See the PCMCIA PC Card Standards 2.01 specification for the speed codes.

DI = Windows base address (In bytes if an I/O window. In 4 KB units if a memory window).

Output: AH = Error code

     = 00h Successful

     = 01h Bad adapter

     = 02h Bad attribute

     = 03h Bad base

     = 0Ah Bad size

     = 0Bh Bad socket

     = 17h Bad speed

     = 0Ch Bad type

     = 11h Bad window

   CF = 0 Successful

     = 1 Error

Function 8Ah Get Page

This function returns the current configuration for the specified page in the specified window on the specified adapter.

Input: AH = 8Ah
AL = Adapter number (zero-based)
BH = Window number (zero-based)
BL = Page number (zero-based)

Output: AH = Error code
= 00h Successful
= 01h Bad adapter
= 08h Bad page number
= 11h Bad window
CF = 0 Successful
= 1 Error
DI = Memory card offset (in 4 KB units)
DL = Page attributes
Bits 7-3   Reserved (set to 0)
Bit 2   Write-protection
1   Page is write-protected by page mapping hardware in the socket.
Bit 1   Page enable
1   PC Card attribute memory is mapped to system memory or I/O space (if page is also enabled).
Bit 0   Type of mapping
0   PC Card common memory is mapped to system memory (if page is also enabled).
1   PC Card attribute memory is mapped to system memory (if page is also enabled).

This function is valid for memory windows, not valid for I/O windows.

Function 8Ah Get Page, Continued

The maximum page number is the window size in bytes divided by 16 KB - 1. The associated socket number is implied by the prior INT 1Ah AH = 89h Set Window function call.

Page attributes indicate if the page is currently enabled.

Bit 1 of DL returned by Function 8Ah Get Page and Bit 1 of DH as returned by Function 88h Get Window must be set before you can map PC Card memory into system memory.

For windows with Bit 3 of DH set to 0 as returned by Function 88h Get Window, Bit 1 of DL as returned by Function 8Ah Get Page is ignored. The window is enabled and disabled by Bit 1 of DH as returned by Function 89h Set Window. Function 8Ah for windows with Bit 3 of DH set to 0 as returned by Function 88h Get Window supply the same value for Bit 1 of DH and Bit 1 of DL.

For windows with Bit 3 of DH set, Bit 1 of DH as returned by Function 88 Get Window globally enables or disables all pages in the window. After Bit 1 of DH has been set via Function 89h Set Windows, individual pages can be enabled and disabled via Function 8Bh Set Page and setting bit 1 of DL.

If the Wenable bit (see page 353) in the I/O window characteristics table is set as reported by Function 87h Inquire Window, Socket Services preserves the current state of DL bit 1 for every page in the window when Bit 1 of DH is changed by Function 89h Set Window. If Bit 1 of DH is 0 as returned by Function 87h Inquire Window, the calling program must:

- invoke Function 89h Set Window and set Bit 1 of DH, and then must

- invoke Function 8Bh Set Page to set Bit 1 of DL for each page in the window.

The memory card offset is the absolute memory card address (in 4 KB units) mapped to host system memory space for that page.

Function 8Bh Set Page

This function sets the configuration for the specified page in the specified window on the specified adapter.

Input: AH = 8Bh
AL = Adapter number (zero-based)
BH = Window number (zero-based)
BL = Page number (zero-based)
DI = Memory card offset (4 KB unit)
DL = Page attributes
  Bits 7-3 Reserved (set to 0)
  Bit 2   Write-protection
      1   Page is write-protected by page mapping hardware in the socket.
  Bit 1   I/O mapping enable
      1   PC Card attribute memory is mapped to system memory or I/O space (if page is also enabled).
  Bit 0   Memory mapping enable
      0   PC Card common memory is mapped to system memory (if page is also enabled).
      1   PC Card attribute memory is mapped to system memory (if page is also enabled).

Output: AH = Error code
= 00h Successful
= 01h Bad adapter
= 02h Bad attribute
= 07h Bad offset
= 08h Bad page
= 11h Bad window
CF = 0 Successful
= 1 Error

Function 8Bh Set Page, Continued

This function is valid for memory windows but is not valid for I/O windows. The maximum page number is equal to the window size in bytes divided by 16 KB - 1. The associated socket number is implied by the prior Set Window function call.

If the hardware does not allow individual pages to be disabled or enabled (the entire window can be disabled or enabled), this function should return an error on an attempt to disable a page.

The memory card offset is the absolute memory card address (in 4 KB units) mapped to host system memory space for that page.

Bit 1 of DL returned by Function 8Ah Get Page and Bit 1 of DH as returned by Function 88h Get Window must be set before you can map PC Card memory into system memory.

For windows with Bit 3 of DH set to 0 as returned by Function 88h Get Window, Bit 1 of DL as returned by Function 8Ah Get Page is ignored. The windows is enabled and disabled by Bit 1 of DH as returned by Function 89h Set Window. Function 8Ah for windows with Bit 3 of DH set to 0 as returned by Function 88h Get Window supply the same value for Bit 1 of DH and Bit 1 of DL.

For windows with Bit 3 of DH set, Bit 1 of DH as returned by Function 88 Get Window globally enables or disables all pages in the window. After Bit 1 of DH has been set via Function 89h Set Windows, individual pages can be enabled and disabled via Function 8Bh Set Page and setting bit 1 of DL.

If the Wenable bit (see page 353) in the I/O window characteristics table is set as reported by Function 87h Inquire Window, Socket Services preserves the current state of DL bit 1 for every page in the window when Bit 1 of DH is changed by Function 89h Set Window. If Bit 1 of DH is 0 as returned by Function 87h Inquire Window, the calling program must:

- invoke Function 89h Set Window and set Bit 1 of DH, and then must

- invoke Function 8Bh Set Page to set Bit 1 of DL for each page in the window.

Function 8Ch Inquire Socket

This function returns information about the specified socket on the specified adapter.

Input: AH = 8Ch
AL = Adapter number (zero-based)
BL = Socket number (zero-based)
ES:EDI = Pointer to buffer supplied by the calling program to hold the information about the socket.

Output: AH = Error code
= 00h Successful
= 01h Bad adapter
= 0Bh Bad socket
BH = Status change interrupt flags. Before an event can trigger a status change interrupt on a socket, the corresponding value in the Status Change Interrupt Mask parameter in INT 1Ah AH = 8Dh Set Socket must be set and status change interrupts must be enabled.
Bit 7 PC Card Card Detect signal
1 Enabled
Bit 6 PC Card RDY/BSY signal
1 Enabled
Bit 5 PC Card BVD2 (battery weak) signal
1 Enabled
Bit 4 PC Card BVD1 (dead battery) signal
1 Enabled
Bit 3 Externally-generated signal to insert a PC Card in the socket
1 Enabled
Bit 2 Externally-generated signal to eject a PC Card from the socket
1 Enabled
Bit 1 Externally-generated signal from a mechanical or electric card lock
1 Enabled
Bit 0 PC Card Write-Protect signal
1 Enabled

Output: cont'd

  CF = 0 Successful

    = 1 Error

  DH = Status change events that the socket can report on. If an event is not reportable by INT 1Ah AH = 8Fh Get Status, it is set to 0. The bit settings are exactly the same as for BH on the previous page.

  DL = Hardware indicators

    Bit 7 XIP status

      1 Enabled

    Bit 6 Card busy status

      1 Enabled

    Bit 5 Battery status

      1 Enabled

    Bit 4 Card lock status

      1 Enabled

    Bit 3 Externally-generated signal to insert a PC Card in the socket

      1 Enabled

    Bit 2 Externally-generated signal to eject a PC Card from the socket

      1 Enabled

    Bit 1 Externally-generated signal from a mechanical or electric card lock

      1 Enabled

    Bit 0 PC Card Write-Protect signal

      1 Enabled

  ES:EDI = Pointer to buffer supplied by the calling program to hold the information about the socket. The required table structure is shown below.

Socket Information Table Structure

```
typedef SISTRUCT {
   WORD  WBufferLength  //Size of buffer provided by //calling
                         program
   WORD  wDataLength    //Size of data returned is 10 bytes
   SCHARTBL CharTable;
} SISSTRUCT
```

cont'd

Socket Information Table Structure Example

```
SISTRUCT SocketInfo = {
    10,              //Size of buffer provided by calling //program is
                     10 bytes
    10,              //Size of data returned is 10 bytes
IF_MEMORY\IF_IO      //Socket support memory-only and
                     //I/O and memory interfaces
    0xDEB8,          //PC Card IRQ signal can be routed to IRQs
                     // 3, 4, 5, 7, 9, 10, 11, 12, 14, and 15
                     //as an active high signal.
    0},              //PC Card IREQ routing not available on //any
                     level as an active low signal.
};
```

Socket Characteristics Structure

```
typedef struct tagSCHARTBL {  //same as adapter
    WORD SktCaps;             //except for this member
    DWORD ActiveHigh;
    DWORD ActiveLow;
} SCHARTBL;
```

where:

SktCaps are flags that specify socket characteristics.

> IF_MEMRY The socket supports memory-only interfaces as per Release 2.01.

> IF_IO   The socket supports I/O port and memory interfaces as per Release 2.01.

ActvHgh   A bitmap of the IRQ levels available for routing an inverted PC Card IREQ signal when an unmasked event occurs.

ActvLw   A bitmap of the IRQ levels available for routing the normal PC Card IREQ signal when an unmasked event occurs. Normal PC Card IREQ signals can be shared in a host system.

Function 8Dh Get Socket

This function returns the current configuration of the specified socket on the specified adapter.

Input: AH = 8Dh
AL = Adapter number (zero-based)
BL = Socket number (zero-based)

Output: AH = Error code
= 00h Successful
= 01 Bad adapter
= 0Bh Bad socket
BH = Status change interrupt enable mask
Bit 7   Card detect change
1   Enabled
Bit 6   Ready change
1   Enabled
Bit 5   Battery warning change
1   Enabled
Bit 4   Battery dead change
1   Enabled
Bit 3   Insertion request
1   Enabled
Bit 2   Ejection request
1   Enabled
Bit 1   Card lock
1   Enabled
Bit 0   Write protect
1   Enabled
CF = 0 Successful
= 1 Error
CH = Bits 3-0 Vcc level
CL = Bits 7-4 Vpp1 level
Bits 3-0 Vpp2 level

cont'd

Function 8Dh Get Socket, Continued

Output: cont'd

DH = Bitmapped socket state

Bit 7	Card detect change	
	1 Enabled	
Bit 6	Ready change	
	1 Enabled	
Bit 5	Battery warning change	
	1 Enabled	
Bit 4	Battery dead change	
	1 Enabled	
Bit 3	Insertion request	
	1 Enabled	
Bit 2	Ejection request	
	1 Enabled	
Bit 1	Card lock	
	1 Enabled	
Bit 0	Write protect	
	1 Enabled	

DL = Indicators

Bit 7 XIP status
1 Enabled

Bit 6 Card busy status
1 Enabled

Bit 5 Battery status
1 Enabled

Bit 4 Card lock status
1 Enabled

Bit 3 Externally-generated signal to insert a PC Card in the socket
1 Enabled

Bit 2 Externally-generated signal to eject a PC Card from the socket
1 Enabled

Bit 1 Externally-generated signal from a mechanical or electric card lock
1 Enabled

Bit 0 PC Card Write-Protect signal
1 Enabled

Function 8Dh Get Socket, Continued

Output: cont'd

    DI   = IRQ level steering (valid I/O cards only)

Bit 9	I/O and memory interface	
	1 Enabled	
Bit 8	Memory interface	
	1 Enabled	
Bit 7	IRQ enabled	
	1 Enabled	
Bit 6	IRQ high	
	1 Enabled	
Bits 4-0	IRQ level	
	00h-0Fh	IRQ 00h-0Fh
	10h	NMI
	11h	I/O check
	12h	Bus error
	13h	Vendor-unique

The voltage levels Vcc, Vpp1, Vpp2 are the indexes into power management table.

Function 8Eh Set Socket

This function sets the current configuration of the specified socket on the specified adapter.

Input:

AH	=	8Eh		
AL	=	Adapter number (zero-based)		
BL	=	Socket number (zero-based)		
BH	=	Status change interrupt enable mask		
			Bit 7	Card detect change
				1 Enabled
			Bit 6	Ready change
				1 Enabled
			Bit 5	Battery warning change
				1 Enabled
			Bit 4	Battery dead change
				1 Enabled
			Bit 3	Insertion request
				1 Enabled
			Bit 2	Ejection request
				1 Enabled
			Bit 1	Card lock
				1 Enabled
			Bit 0	Write protect
				1 Enabled
CH	=	Bits 3-0	Vcc level	
CL	=	Bits 7-4	Vpp1 level	
		Bits 3-0	Vpp2 level	

Function 8Eh Set Socket, Continued

Input: cont'd
    DH = Bitmapped socket attributes
             Bit 7 Card detect change
                  1 Enabled
             Bit 6 Ready change
                  1 Enabled
             Bit 5 Battery warning change
                  1 Enabled
             Bit 4 Battery dead change
                  1 Enabled
             Bit 3 Insertion request
                  1 Enabled
             Bit 2 Ejection request
                  1 Enabled
             Bit 1 Card lock
                  1 Enabled
             Bit 0 Write protect
                  1 Enabled
    DL   = Indicators
             Bit 7 XIP status
                  1 Enabled
             Bit 6 Card busy status
                  1 Enabled
             Bit 5 Battery status
                  1 Enabled
             Bit 4 Card lock status
                  1 Enabled
             Bit 3 Externally-generated signal to insert a PC Card in the socket
                  1 Enabled
             Bit 2 Externally-generated signal to eject a PC Card from the socket
                  1 Enabled
             Bit 1 Externally-generated signal from a mechanical or electric card lock
                  1 Enabled
             Bit 0 PC Card Write-Protect signal
                  1 Enabled

cont'd

Input: *Continued*

DI = IRQ level steering (valid for I/O cards only)

Bit 9	I/O and memory interface	
	1 Enabled	
Bit 8	Memory interface	
	1 Enabled	
Bit 7	IRQ enabled	
	1 Enabled	
Bit 5	IRQ high	
	1 Enabled	
Bits 4-0	IRQ level	
	00h-0Fh	IRQ 00h-0Fh
	10h	NMI
	11h	I/O check
	12h	Bus error
	13h	Vendor-unique

Output: AH = Error code
= 00h Successful
= 01h Bad adapter
= 02h Bad attribute
= 0Bh Bad socket

CF = 0 Successful
= 1 Error

This function waits until the requested Vpp power level becomes valid.

Function 8Fh Get Status

This function returns the status of a PC Card in the specified socket on the specified adapter. This function must not be invoked during hardware interrupt processing. It should not be invoked by the calling program's status change hardware interrupt handler.

Input: AH = 8Fh
            AL = Adapter number (zero-based)
            BL = Socket number (zero-based)

Output: AH = Error code
               = 00h Successful
               = 01h Bad adapter
               = 0Bh Bad socket
            BH = Card state
                    Bit 7 Card changed
                          1 Enabled
                    Bit 6 Card Busy status
                          1 Enabled
                    Bit 5 Card insertion complete
                          1 Enabled
                    Bit 4 Card ejection complete
                          1 Enabled
                    Bit 3 Card insertion request pending
                          1 Enabled
                    Bit 2 Card ejection request pending
                          1 Enabled
                    Bit 1 Card lock
                          1 Enabled
                    Bit 0 Write protect
                          1 Enabled
            CF = 0 Successful
               = 1 Error

cont'd

Function 8Fh Get Status, Continued

Output: cont'd

    DH   = Socket state

        Bit 7 Card changed
              1 Enabled

        Bit 6 Card Busy status
              1 Enabled

        Bit 5 Card insertion complete
              1 Enabled

        Bit 4 Card ejection complete
              1 Enabled

        Bit 3 Card insertion request pending
              1 Enabled

        Bit 2 Card ejection request pending
              1 Enabled

        Bit 1 Card lock
              1 Enabled

        Bit 0 Write protect
              1 Enabled

    DL   = Card attributes (bitmapped)

        Bit 7 XIP status
              1 Enabled

        Bit 6 Card busy status
              1 Enabled

        Bit 5 Battery status
              1 Enabled

        Bit 4 Card lock status
              1 Enabled

        Bit 3 Externally-generated signal to insert a PC Card in the socket
              1 Enabled

        Bit 2 Externally-generated signal to eject a PC Card from the socket
              1 Enabled

        Bit 1 Externally-generated signal from a mechanical or electric card lock
              1 Enabled

        Bit 0 PC Card Write-Protect signal
              1 Enabled

Function 8Fh Get Status, Continued

Output: cont'd
DI = IRQ level steering (valid I/O cards only)
Bit 9   I/O and memory interface
           1 Enabled
Bit 8   Memory interface
           1 Enabled
Bit 7   IRQ enabled
           1 Enabled
Bit 5   IRQ high
           1 Enabled
Bits 4-0 IRQ level

00h-0Fh	IRQ 00h-0Fh
10h	NMI
11h	I/O check
12h	Bus error
13h	Vendor-unique

Function 90h Reset Socket

This function resets the specified socket on the specified adapter and returns the socket hardware to the power-on default state: Vcc, Vpp1, and Vpp2 are set to 5VDC, IRQ routing is disabled, memory-type mapping is set, and all windows, pages, and EDC generators are disabled. The calling program must make sure that a PC Card is not accessed before ready after this function returns.

Input:	AH	=	90h
	AL	=	Adapter number (zero-based)
	BL	=	Socket number (zero-based)
Output:	AH	=	Error code
		=	00h Successful
		=	01h Bad adapter
		=	0Bh Bad socket
		=	14h No PC Card in socket
	CF	=	0 Successful
		=	1 Error

This function sets the RESET pin on the card to the reset state and then resets the RESET pin to non-reset state, ensuring that the minimum reset pulse width is met. The caller must ensure that the card is not accessed before it is ready after returning.

Function 95h Inquire EDC

This function returns the capabilities of the specified EDC (Error Detection Code) generator.

Socket Services supports two types of EDC generation: 8-bit checksums and 16-bit CRC SDLC.

EDC generation can be produced by read or write accesses. Code that uses many sequential reads and writes must use EDC generation carefully. Bidirectional EDC generation may not work with flash EPROM programming routines because these routines typically require many reads and writes.

EDC generation may not be available with memory-mapped implementations. EDC generators must be configured via INT 1Ah AH = 97h Set EDC.

Input:	AH	=	95h
	AL	=	Adapter number (zero-based)
	BH	=	EDC generator number (zero-based)

Output:	AH	=	Error code
		=	00h Successful
		=	01h Bad adapter
		=	04h Bad EDC
	CF	=	0 Successful
		=	1 Error
	CX	=	Assignable sockets (Bit 0 is socket 0, bit 1 is socket 1, etc)

cont'd

Function 95h Inquire EDC, Continued

Output: cont'd

DH = EDC capabilities (Bit-mapped)

    Bits 7-5   Reserved (set to 0)

    Bit 4   Pausable EDC
             1 EDC generation can be paused.

    Bit 3   Memory-mapped support
             1 EDC generation is supported during window access.

    Bit 2   Register-based support
             1 EDC generation is supported through register-based access.

    Bit 1   Bidirectional code generation
             1 The EDC generator supports bidirectional code generation.

    Bit 0   Unidirectional code generation
             1 The EDC generator supports unidirectional code generation.

DL = Supported EDC types

    Bits 7-2   Reserved (set to 0)

    Bit 1   16-Bit CRC-SDLC
             1 The EDC generator supports 8-bit checksum code generation.

    Bit 0   8-Bit checksum
             1 The EDC generator supports 8-bit checksum code generation.

Not every hardware implementation provides EDC code generation.

The output of this function describes the EDC functions of the specified EDC generator.

EDC generators can be shared between sockets.

Card Services or higher-level software arbitrates the use of EDC generators.

Function 96h Get EDC

This function returns the current configuration of the specified EDC generator. A generator is not assigned if the socket number returned is zero.

Input: AH = 96h
AL = Adapter number (zero-based)
BH = EDC generator number (zero-based)

Output: AH = Error code
= 00h Successful
= 01h Bad adapter
= 04h Bad EDC
BL = Socket number of the physical socket that the EDC generator is assigned to (zero-based).
CF = 0 Successful
= 1 Error
DH = EDC attributes (Bit-mapped)
Bits 7-2 Reserved (set to 0)
Bit 1 If unidirectional only (Bit 0) is 1
0 EDC computing only on read accesses.
1 EDC computing only on write accesses.
Bit 0 Unidirectional only
0 EDC computing on both read and write accesses.
1 EDC computing in only one direction.
DL = EDC type (mutually exclusive bitmap)
Bits 7-2 Reserved (set to 0)
Bit 1 16-Bit CRC-SDLC EDC checksum generated by EDC.
Bit 0 8-Bit checksum generated by EDC.

Function 97h Set EDC

This function sets the error detection and correction configuration of the specified EDC generator.

Input: AH   = 97h
          AL   = Adapter number (zero-based)
          BH   = EDC generator number (zero-based)
          BL   = Socket number (zero-based)
          DH   = EDC attributes (Bit-mapped)
                  Bits 7-2 Reserved (set to 0)
                  Bit 1   EDC computes on reads or writes
                            0 Reads
                            1 Writes
                  Bit 0   Unidirectional
                            1 EDC generator compute in only one
                               direction.
          DL   = EDC type (mutually exclusive bitmap)
                  Bits 7-2 Reserved (set to 0)
                  Bit 1   16-Bit CRC-SDLC
                            1 16-bit EDC checksum generated.
                  Bit 0   8-Bit CRC-SDLC
                            1 8-bit EDC checksum generated.

Output: AH   = Error code
               = 00h Successful
               = 01h Bad adapter
               = 02h Bad attribute
               = 04h Bad EDC
               = 0Bh Bad socket
          CF   = 0 Successful
               = 1 Error

Function 98h Start EDC

This function starts the specified previously configured EDC generator.
This function load initialization values into the EDC generator.

Input:	AH	=	98h
	AL	=	Adapter number (zero-based)
	BH	=	EDC generator number (zero-based)

Output:	AH	=	Error code
		=	00h Successful
		=	01h Bad adapter
		=	04h Bad EDC
	CF	=	0 Successful
		=	1 Error

Function 99h Pause EDC

This function pauses EDC generation on the specified configured and computing EDC generator. This function is only supported if Bit 4 of DH is set when INT 1Ah AH= 95h Inquire EDC is invoked.

Input: AH   =   99h
         AL   =   Adapter number (zero-based)
         BH   =   EDC generator number (zero-based)

Output: AH   =   Error code
              =   00h Successful
              =   01h Bad adapter
              =   04h Bad EDC
         CF   =   0 Successful
              =   1 Error

Function 9Ah Resume EDC

This function resumes the EDC generation on the specified configured and paused EDC generator. This function can only be used if bit 4 of DH as returned by the INT 1Ah AH = 95h Inquire EDC function is set.

Input: AH   =   9Ah
         AL   =   Adapter number (zero-based)
         BH   =   EDC generator number (zero-based)

Output: AH   =   Error code
              =   00h Successful
              =   01h Bad adapter
              =   04h Bad EDC
         CF   =   0 Successful
              =   1 Error

Function 9Bh Stop EDC

This function stops the EDC generation on the specified configured and computing EDC generator.

Input: AH = 9Bh
           AL = Adapter number (zero-based)
           BH = EDC generator number (zero-based)

Output: AH = Error code
               = 00h Successful
               = 01h Bad adapter
               = 04h Bad EDC
           CF = 0 Successful
               = 1 Error

Function 9Ch Read EDC

This function reads the calculated EDC value computed by the specified EDC generator. The computed value may be incorrect if the EDC generator has been used incorrectly.

Input: AH = 9Ch
           AL = Adapter number (zero-based)
           BH = EDC generator number (zero-based)

Output: AH = Error code
               = 00h Successful
               = 01h Bad adapter
               = 04h Bad EDC
           CF = 0 Successful
               = 1 Error
           DX = Computed checksum or CRC. This can be an 8-bit or 16-bit value depending on the value of Bits 0 and 1 in DL as returned by INT 1Ah AH = 95h Inquire EDC.

Function 9Dh Get Vendor Info

This function returns information about the vendor implementing Socket Services for the specified adapter.

Input: AH = 9Dh
AL = Adapter number (zero-based)
BH = EDC generator number (zero-based)
ES:EDI = Address of buffer where vendor information is stored

Output: AH = Error code
= 00h Successful
= 01h Bad adapter
= 15h Bad function
CF = 0 Successful
= 1 Error
ES:EDI = Address of buffer where vendor information is stored
DX = Vendor release number in BCD

The buffer pointed to by the value in ES:EDI must have the following format:

```
typedef struct tagVISTRUCT {
   WORD wBufferlength = (BUF_SIZE - 4);
   WORD wDataLength;    Set by Socket Services
   char szImplementor[BUF_SIZE - 4];
} VISTRUCT;
```

If the wData Length value is greater than the wBufferLength value, the information is truncated.

Function 9Eh Acknowledge Interrupt

This function returns status change information for sockets on the specified adapter. Socket Services does not enable interrupts while this function is being performed.

The calling program should enable status change interrupts from adapter hardware via INT 1Ah AH = 86h Set Adapter.

The calling program must install an interrupt handler on the appropriate vector.

Specific events can be masked or unmasked for each socket via INT 1Ah AH = 8Eh Set Socket.

When a status change occurs, the calling program's status change handler receives control and invokes INT 1Ah AH = 9Eh Acknowledge Interrupt. This function permits Socket Services to prepare the adapter hardware to generate another interrupt if another status change occurs.

Socket Services preserves status change information if it is not preserved by the adapter hardware.

If this function is called and no status change has occurred on the specified adapter, Socket Services returns with AH and CX = 00h.

Input:	AH	=	9Eh
	AL	=	Adapter number (zero-based)
Output:	AH	=	Error code
		=	00h Successful
		=	01h Bad adapter
	CF	=	0 Successful
		=	1 Error
	CX	=	A bitmap that represents the sockets that have changed status.

Function 9Fh Get and Set Prior Handler

This function replaces or acquires the entry point of a prior handler for the specified adapter.

If this Socket Services handler is the first installed in the INT 1Ah chain, the values returned when this function is issued with BL = 0 should be the entry point to the Time of Day handler.

This function might fail if the Socket Services it addresses are in the system BIOS ROM as the first extension to the Time of Day handler. To circumvent this problem, register the value returned by this function to this Socket Services with a replacement Socket Services implementation.

Warning

This function should only be used with the first adapter serviced by a Socket Services handler as returned by Function 83h Get SS Info. If a handler services more than one adapter, subsequent requests to the handler for adapters other than the first adapter will return the same information and set the same internal variables.

Warning

A calling program should not add Socket Services that increase the number of adapters or sockets supported.

To provide support for additional adapters and sockets, new Socket Services handlers should be added to the end of the handler chain. Adjusting internal prior handlers should be used only to replace an old Socket Services implementation with an updated version.

Function 9Fh Get and Set Prior Handler, Continued

Input: AH   = 9Fh
               AL   = Adapter number (zero-based)
               BL   = Mode
                     00h   Get prior handler
                     01h   Set prior handler
          CX:DX   = If BL = 1, contains a pointer to a new prior handler. It now returns the entry point of the old prior handler.

Output: AH   = Error code
                     00h   Successful
                     01h   Bad adapter
                     15h   Bad function
            CF   = 0 Successful
                 = 1 Error
         CX:DX   = Contains a pointer to a new prior handler and returns the entry point of the old prior handler.

Function A0h Get and Set SS Addr

> **Warning**
>
> This function should only be used with the first adapter serviced by a Socket Services handler as returned by Function 80h Get SS Info. If a handler services more than one adapter, subsequent requests to the handler for adapters other than the first adapter will return the same information and set the same internal variables.

This function returns code and data area descriptions and provides a method for passing address mode-specific data area descriptors to a Socket Services handler.

If Socket Services must access other memory regions, the value in CX is the number of unique memory regions that Socket Services must address as well as the main data segment.

Card Services uses the entry point returned by this function to establish the appropriate address mode-specific pointers to the code and main data areas before calling the entry point.

The entry points returned by this function must receive control from a CALL instruction. The real mode, 16:16, and 16:32 entry points require a FAR CALL. The 00:32 entry point requires a NEAR CALL. When using an entry point that has been returned by this function in all address modes except real mode, the calling program must establish a pointer to the main data area in DS:ESI.

Input:
AH = A0h
AL = Adapter number (zero-based)
BH = Mode
    00h   Real mode
    01h   16:16 Protected mode
    02h   16:32 Protected mode
    03h   00:32 Protected mode

Function A0h Get and Set SS Addr, Continued

Input: cont'd

    BL = Subfunction

        BL = 00h Socket Services returns the number of additional data areas in this parameter.

        BL = 01h Socket Services returns a description of any additional data areas in the buffer supplied by the calling program at ES:EDI.

        BL = 02h Socket Services accepts the number of mode-specific pointers to additional data areas in the buffer pointed to in ES:EDI specified in CX.

  ES:EDI = Contains a pointer to a buffer supplied by the calling program. The buffer must be the appropriate length.

Output: AH = Error code

        00h   Successful

        01h   Bad adapter

        02h   Bad attribute

        15h   Bad function

        16h   Bad mode

    CF = 0 Successful

        = 1 Error

    CX = Number of additional data areas.

        If BL = 00h Socket Services returns the number of additional data areas in this parameter.

        If BL = 01h Socket Services returns a description of any additional data areas in the buffer supplied by the calling program at ES:EDI.

        If BL = 02h Socket Services accepts the number of mode-specific pointers to additional data areas in the buffer pointed to in ES:EDI specified in CX.

  ES:EDI = Contains a pointer to a buffer supplied by the calling program. The buffer must be the appropriate length.

> **Warning**
> Any CS selector should be readable and executable so Socket Services can reference constant data that may reside in ROM. The calling program must also make sure that Socket Services has the appropriate privileges to permit access to I/O ports.

cont'd

Function A0h Get and Set SS Addr, Continued

Buffer Table Entry if BL = 00h

Offset	Description
00h	32-bit linear base address of the code segment in system memory.
04h	Limit of the code segment. This value must be less than 64 KB in real mode and 16:16 in protected mode.
08h	Entry point offset. This value must be less than 64 KB in real mode and 16:16 in protected mode.
0Ch	32-bit linear base address of the main data segment in system memory. This field is ignored if 00:32 (flat) protected mode addressing is used.
10h	The limit of the data segment. This value must be less than 64 KB in real mode and 16:16 in protected mode.
14h	The data area offset. This field is only used if 32-bit protected mode addressing is used.

Buffer Table Entry if BL = 01h

Offset	Description
00h	32-bit linear base address of the additional data segment in system memory. This field is ignored if 00:32 (flat) protected mode addressing is used.
04h	Limit of the code segment. This value must be less than 64 KB in real mode and 16:16 in protected mode.
08h	Data area offset. This field is only used if 00:32 (flat) protected mode addressing is used.

Buffer Table Entry if BL = 02h

Offset	Description
00h	32-bit offset. This field is ignored if 16:16 protected mode addressing is used. 16:16 protected mode addressing assumes 0 in this field.
04h	Selector. This field is only used if 00:32 (flat) protected mode addressing is used.
08h	Reserved

Function A1h Get Access Offsets

This function fills the buffer pointed to by ES:EDI with an array of offsets for low-level, adapter-specific, optimized PC Card access routines for adapters that use registers or I/O ports to access PC Card memory. Adapters that access PC Card memory through windows mapped to host system memory do not support this function.

It is assumed that all requested offsets are in the Socket Service code segment. All sockets on an adapter must use the same entry point for a certain address mode. These offsets can be different for different address modes. A calling program can use the values returned by this function to create an internal table, permitting the routines at these offsets to be called in a manner appropriate to the address mode they will be used in.

16-bit offsets are returned in all modes. The offset must be combined with information returned by Function A0h Get and Set SS Addr that describes the location of the code segment. Offsets returned by this function are relative to the code segment.

For real, 16:16, and 16:32 address modes, the routines at these offsets use FAR RET instructions to return to the calling program, so this function must be invoked with a FAR CALL instruction. In 00:32 (flat) protected address mode, the routines at the returned offsets use NEAR RET instructions and must be invoked with a NEAR CALL instruction.

Input:	AH	=	A1h
	AL	=	Adapter number (zero-based)
	BH	=	Mode
			00h Real mode
			01h 16:16 Protected mode
			02h 16:32 Protected mode
			03h 00:32 Protected mode
	CX	=	Number of access offsets
	ES:EDI	=	Pointer to a buffer supplied by the calling program for the array of access offsets. The value in CX specifies the number of entries in the buffer.

cont'd

Function A1h Get Access Offsets, Continued

Output: AH   = Error code
           = 00h   Successful
           = 01h   Bad adapter
           = 15h   Bad function
           = 16h   Bad Mode

      CF   = 0 Successful
          = 1 Error

      DX   = Number of access offsets supported by this Socket Services handler for the specified adapter.

   ES:EDI = Pointer to a buffer supplied by the calling program for the array of access offsets. The value in CX specifies the number of entries in the buffer.

Offset Order

Offsets are returned in the following order:

1 Set Address,
2 Set Auto Increment,
3 Read Byte,
4 Read Word,
5 Read Byte with Auto Increment,
6 Read Word with Auto Increment,
7 Read Words,
8 Read Words with Auto Increment,
9 Write Byte,
10 Write Word,
11 Write Byte with Auto Increment,
12 Write Word with Auto Increment,
13 Write Words,
14 Write Words with Auto Increment,
15 Compare Byte,
16 Compare Byte with Auto Increment,
17 Compare Words, and
18 Compare Word with Auto Increment.

Function AEh Vendor-Specific

This function handles vendor-specific information. The vendor can add proprietary extensions to Socket Services via this interface.

See the vendor technical documentation for additional information about INT 1Ah AH = AEh.

Input: AH   = AEh
             AL   = Adapter number (zero-based)
                         all other registers are vendor-specific

Output: AH   = Error code
             CF   = 0 Successful
                   = 1 Error

Socket Services Error Codes

Code	Explanation
00h	Successful
01h	Invalid adapter
02h	Invalid attribute
03h	Invalid base system memory address
04h	Invalid EDC generator
06h	Invalid IRQ level
07h	Invalid card offset
08h	Invalid Page
09h	Incomplete read request
0Ah	Invalid window size
0Bh	Invalid socket
0Dh	Invalid window type
0Eh	Invalid Vcc level
0Fh	Invalid Vpp1 and Vpp2 level
11h	Invalid window
12h	Incomplete write request
14h	No card present
15h	Function not supported
16h	Invalid mode
17h	Invalid speed
18h	Busy

INT 1Ah Function 9Dh Intel ExCA Card Service Functions

INT 1Ah Function 9Dh supports the following Card Service functions, as specified in the Intel ExCA specifications.

Type	AL Value	Function
Client Services	00h	Get Number of Sockets
	02h	Register Client
	03h	Deregister Client
	05h	Register SCB
	06h	Deregister SCB
	0Ah	Get Status
	0Bh	Reset Card
	1Ch	Modify Window
	1Eh	Map Mem Page
Resource Management	19h	Request I/O
	1Ah	Release I/O
	1Bh	Request Memory
	1Dh	Release Memory
	22h	Request IRQ
	23h	Release IRQ
Bulk Memory Services	14h	Open Region
	15h	Read Memory
	16h	Write Memory
	17h	Copy Memory
	18h	Erase Memory
	24h	Close Region
Client Utilities	0Ch	Get First Tuple
	0Dh	Get Next Tuple
	0Eh	Determine First Region
	0Fh	Determine Next Region
	10h	Get First Region
	11h	Get Next Region
	12h	Get First Partition
	13h	Get Next Partition
Advanced Client Services	1Fh	Return SS Entry
	20h	Map Log To Phy
	21h	Map Log Phy To Log
	01h	Initialize
	04h	Enumerate Clients
	07h	Register MTD
	08h	Deregister MTD
	09h	Enumerate MTDs

Peripheral Component Interconnect (PCI) BIOS Calls

PCI is a way to physically interconnect highly integrated peripheral components and processor/memory systems. PCI BIOS functions provide a software interface to the PCI hardware.

PCI is an Intel specification for a 486 CPU Local Bus standard. The PCI specification includes electrical specifications for peripheral chip makers and the logic requirements for a PCI Controller. PCI ia a local bus standard that permits a variety of I/O components to be directly connected to the CPU bus using no glue logic. PCI includes a CPU-to-local bus bridge with FIFO buffers. PCI signals are multiplexed. Unlike other local bus specifications, PCI has a standalone controller to manage data transfer between PCI peripherals, memory, and the CPU.

PCI Features

Up to ten PCI peripherals can be used in the same system on the PCI bus, including the PCI Controller and an optional expansion bus controller for the EISA, ISA, or MCA buses. PCI uncouples the CPU from the expansion bus while still maintaining a 33 MHz 32-bit path to peripheral devices. The PCI bus works at 33 MHz and can use either a 32-bit or 64-bit data path to the CPU.

Queued Reads and Writes

The PCI Controller queues reads and writes between the memory/CPU and PCI peripheral devices.

Concurrent Operation of CPU and Bus Masters

The CPU in a PCI system runs concurrently with PCI bus mastering peripherals. Although bus mastering peripheral devices are specified, impressive data transfer rates can be achieved without splitting resource utilization between the CPU and a bus mastering device. PCI peripheral devices can operate at 33 MBs in an ISA environment.

PCI Bus Mastering

Up to ten bus mastering devices can operate simultaneously on the PCI bus. PCI devices can be bus masters, slaves, or a combination of bus master and slave. PCI supports full burst mode for both reads and writes. The 486 CPU only permits burst mode on reads.

Multiplexing

PCI is a multiplexed version of the Intel 80486 bus. Multiplexing allows more than one signal to be sent on the same electrical path. The control mechanisms are extended to optimize I/O support.

PCI Device Drivers

The system BIOS in a PCI system provides information about where the PCI device is in memory or I/O space and which interrupt vector the PCI device will generate. This information comes directly from the configuration registers of the peripheral component, not from CMOS RAM or an internal BIOS table. PCI BIOS functions can access these configuration registers and provide this information.

Expansion ROM Code

All expansion ROM in a PCI system is fully relocatable. PCI expansion ROM can call a PCI system BIOS function to see where its device is placed in memory or I/O space.

cont'd

PCI BIOS Calls, Continued

PCI BIOS Interface

All software in a system that uses the PCI bus should use system BIOS functions to access PCI features. The system BIOS in a PCI system supports multiple operating and addressing modes. Some of the functions of the system BIOS in a PCI system are:

- allows the calling program to find a PCI Controller,
- provides access to special PCI functions,
- allows the calling program to determine the interrupt level, and
- allows the calling program to access configuration space (either memory or I/O ports).

Address Modes and PCI BIOS Calls

PCI-specific BIOS function calls can be used in real mode, 16-bit protected mode, or 32-bit protected mode. Real mode function calls are made via INT 1Ah AH = B1h. Protected mode access is provided by calling the BIOS through a protected mode entry point, specified by calling INT 1Ah Function B1h AL = 01h/81h PCI BIOS Present.

INT 1Ah Function B1h Calling Conventions

Every PCI function can be invoked with two codes: one for 32-bit mode and the other for all other modes.

The EAX, EBX, ECX, and EDX registers and all flags may be modified by every function call. All other registers will be preserved. CF indicates the completion status of the function call.

Protected Mode PCI BIOS Function Calls

Access the protected mode interface by calling through a protected mode entry point provided by the INT 1Ah Function B1h AL = 01h/81h PCI BIOS Present function. The code segment descriptor must specify protection level 0. All INT 1Ah Function B1h PCI BIOS functions must be invoked with CPL = 0. The code segment descriptor must permit access to the 64 KB of code that starts at the 16-byte boundary immediately below the protected mode entry point.

Function B1h Subfunction AL = 01/81 PCI BIOS Present

This subfunction indicates if the PCI BIOS interface is present. The current PCI BIOS interface version level is also returned. Information about hardware mechanisms for accessing PCI configuration space and PCI Special Cycles support is also provided.

Input: AH   =   B1h

AL   =   01h real mode operation

=   81h protected mode operation

BH   =   EDC generator number (zero-based)

Output: AH   =   00h PCI BIOS interface present

=   Any other value is an error code

AL   =   Hardware mechanism

Bit 5   1 Special cycle supported via Config mechanism 1

Bit 4   1 Special cycle supported via Config mechanism 2

Bit 1   1 Config Mechanism #2 supported

Bit 0   1 Config Mechanism #1 supported

BH   =   Interface Level Major Version (in BCD)

BL   =   Interface Level Minor Version (in BCD)

CF   =   0 PCI BIOS interface present

=   1 No PCI BIOS interface present

CL   =   Number of PCI buses in system (zero-based)

EDI   =   Physical address of entry point to PCI BIOS functions for protected mode access

EDX   =   "PCI"

Function B1h Subfunction AL = 02/82 Find PCI Device

This subfunction returns the location of PCI devices. Specify the Device ID in CX, Vendor ID in DX, and a Device Index in SI. This function returns the PCI bus number in BL and the Device Number of the specified *(nth)* device in BH.

You can find all PCI devices with the same Vendor ID and Device ID by making consecutive calls to this function and incrementing the Device Index by one each time until code 86h is returned in AH.

Input:	AH	=	B1h
	AL	=	02h real mode operation
		=	81h protected mode operation
	CX	=	Device ID (0 through 65535)
	DX	=	Vendor ID (1 through 65534)
	SI	=	Device Index (0 through *n*)
Output:	AH	=	00h Successful
		=	82h Incorrect Device ID
		=	83h Incorrect Vendor ID
		=	86h Device not found
	BH	=	Device Information
		=	Bits 7-3 Device Number
	BL	=	Bus Number (0 through 255)
	CF	=	0 No error
		=	1 Error

Function B1h Subfunction AL = 03/83 Find PCI Class Code

This subfunction returns the location of PCI devices with the specified Class Code. Specify the Class Code in ECX and a Device Index in SI. The function returns the Bus Number in BL, the Device Number in BH, and the Function Number of the *nth* device in the bottom three bits of BH.

You can find all PCI devices with the same Class Code by making consecutive calls to this function and incrementing the Device Index by one each time until code 86h is returned in AH.

Input:	AH	=	B1h
	AL	=	03h real mode operation
		=	83h protected mode operation
	ECX	=	Class Code in low three bytes
	SI	=	Device Index (0 through *n*)
Output:	AH	=	00h Successful
		=	86h Device not found
	BH	=	Bits 7-3 Device Number
			Bits 1-0 Function Number
	BL	=	Bus number (0 through 255)
	CF	=	0 No error
		=	1 Error

Function B1h Subfunction AL = 06/86 Generate Special Cycle

This subfunction generates PCI Special Cycles that are broadcast on a specific PCI bus.

Input: AH   = B1h
           AL   = 06h real mode operation
                = 86h protected mode operation
           EDX = Special Cycle Data

Output: AH   = 00h Successful
                = 81h Function not supported
           CF   = 0 No error
                = 1 Error

Function B1h Subfunction AL = 08/88 Read Configuration Byte

This subfunction reads individual bytes from the configuration space of the specified PCI device.

Input: AH   = B1h
           AL   = 08h real mode operation
                = 88h protected mode operation
           BH   = Bits 7-3   Device Number
                   Bits 2-0   Function Number
           BL   = Bus Number (0 through 255)
           DI   = Register Number (0 through 255)

Output: AH   = 00h Successful
                = 84h Incorrect Bus Number
           CF   = 0 No error
                = 1 Error
           CL   = Byte read

Function B1h Subfunction AL = 09/89 Read Configuration Word

This subfunction reads individual words from the configuration space of the specified PCI device. The Register Number must be a multiple of 2.

Input: AH = B1h
        AL = 09h real mode operation
            = 89h protected mode operation
        BH = Bits 7-3   Device Number
               Bits 2-0   Function Number
        BL = Bus Number (0 through 255)
        DI = Register Number (0 through 255)

Output: AH = 00h Successful
            = 84h Incorrect Bus Number
            = 87h Incorrect Register Number
        CF = 0 No error
            = 1 Error
        CX = Word read

Function B1h Subfunction AL = 0A/8A Read Configuration Dword

This subfunction reads individual doublewords from the configuration space of the specified PCI device. The Register Number must be a multiple of 4.

Input: AH = B1h
           AL = 0Ah real mode operation
               = 8Ah protected mode operation
           BH = Bits 7-3 Device Number
                 Bits 2-0 Function Number
           BL = Bus Number (0 through 255)
           DI = Register Number (0 through 255)

Output: AH = 00h Successful
               = 84h Incorrect Bus Number
               = 87h Incorrect Register Number
           CF = 0 No error
               = 1 Error
           ECX = Doubleword read

Function B1h Subfunction AL = 0B/8B Write Configuration Byte

This subfunction writes individual bytes to the configuration space of the specified PCI device.

Input:

	AH	=	B1h
	AL	=	0Bh real mode operation
		=	8Bh protected mode operation
	BH	=	Bits 7-3 Device Number
			Bits 2-0 Function Number
	BL	=	Bus Number (0 through 255)
	CL	=	Byte value to write
	DI	=	Register Number (0 through 255)

Output:

	AH	=	00h Successful
		=	84h Incorrect Bus Number
	CF	=	0 No error
		=	1 Error

Function B1h Subfunction AL = 0C/8C Write Configuration Word

This subfunction writes individual words to the configuration space of the specified PCI device. The Register Number must be a multiple of 2.

Input: AH   =   B1h
         AL   =   0Ch real mode operation
              =   8Ch protected mode operation
         BH   =   Bits 7-3   Device Number
                  Bits 2-0   Function Number
         BL   =   Bus Number (0 through 255)
         CX   =   Word value to write
         DI   =   Register Number (0 through 255)

Output: AH   =   00h Successful
              =   84h Incorrect Bus Number
              =   87h Incorrect Register Number
         CF   =   0 No error
              =   1 Error

Function B1h Subfunction AL = 0D/8D Write Configuration Dword

This subfunction writes individual doublewords to the configuration space of the specified PCI device. The Register Number must be a multiple of 4.

Input: AH = B1h
           AL   = 0Dh real mode operation
               = 8Dh protected mode operation
           BH = Bits 7-3   Device Number
                    Bits 2-0   Function Number
           BL   = Bus Number (0 through 255)
           ECX = Doubleword value to write
           DI   = Register Number (0 through 255)

Output: AH = 00h Successful
                  = 84h Incorrect Bus Number
                  = 87h Incorrect Register Number
           CF   = 0 No error
                  = 1 Error

INT 1Ah Function B1h Error Codes

The following error codes may appear in AH after any INT 1Ah Function B1h function call.

AH Value	Description
00h	Successful
81h	Function Not Supported
82h	Incorrect Device ID
83h	Incorrect Vendor ID
84h	Incorrect Bus Number
86h	Device Not Found
87h	Incorrect Register Number
EEh	Internal Error

INT 1Bh Ctrl Break

Input: None

Output: None

Description:

INT 1Bh is called by the operating system to terminate the current application when you press CTRL BREAK. The BIOS sets this routine to an IRET instruction. The next time the operating system boots, it resets the routine to point to its own interrupt service routine.

INT 1Ch Periodic Timer Interrupt

Input: None

Output: None

Description:

The system timer calls INT 08h 18.2 times per second. After each call to INT 08h, INT 1Ch is called to permit any applications program to access the system timer.

The BIOS sets this routine to an IRET instruction. The next time the operating system boots, it resets the routine to point to its own interrupt service routine.

INT 1Dh Video Parameter Table

Input: None

Output: None

Description:

The vector for INT 1Dh points to a table of video parameters.

INT 1Eh Floppy Disk Parameter Table

Input: None

Output: None

Description:

The vector for INT 1Eh points to a table of floppy disk parameters.

INT 1Fh Video Graphics Characters

Input: None

Output: None

Description:

The vector for INT 1Fh points to a table of video graphics characters.

INT 4Ah User Alarm Interrupt

Input: None

Output: None

Description:

The Real Time Clock generates an interrupt request at the hour, minute, and second specified by INT 1Ah Function 06h when the Real Time Clock alarm is activated. INT 4Ah is invoked when the alarm occurs. The calling program must redirect the INT 4Ah vector to a routine that processes the alarm.

INTs 70h through 77h

An ISA system has two interrupt controllers. The second controller uses INTs 70h to 77h. Only INTs 70h, 74h, 75h, 76h, and 77h are described. You cannot revector INTs 70h – 77h to your own routine.

INT 70h Real Time Clock Interrupt (IRQ8)

Input: None

Output: None

Description:

The BIOS services INT 70h by determining the reason the interrupt was called and correcting the situation that caused INT 70h. INT 70h ticks approximately 1,024 times per seconds.

INT 71h IRQ9

Input: None

Output: None

Description:

When IRQ9 occurs, the interrupt is routed through the IRQ2 transfer vector (INT 0Ah) by the BIOS and the slave interrupt controller's interrupt is cleared so the interrupt appears to be an IRQ2.

INT 74h PS/2 Mouse Interrupt (IRQ12)

Input: None

Output: None

Description:

INT 74h is the interrupt service routine for BIOS PS/2-type mouse support. The PS/2-type mouse sends data to the keyboard controller. The keyboard controller generates IRQ12. Mouse data is transmitted in packets. The BIOS INT 74h collects these packets and stores them in the extended BIOS data area. INT 74h also sets the appropriate flags.

INT 75h Math Coprocessor Interrupt (IRQ13)

Input: None

Output: None

Description:

INT 75h is called when the math coprocessor attached to the system generates an exception and the exception interrupt has been enabled. This interrupt is passed on to the BIOS INT 02h NMI processing routine.

INT 76h Hard Disk Drive Interrupt (IRQ14)

Input: None

Output: None

Description:

The hard disk drive controller calls INT 76h when a hard disk drive access has been completed.

INT 77h Power Down Interrupt (IRQ15)

Input: None

Output: None

Description:

Some Power Management AMIBIOS interpret an INT 77h from applications software programs as a signal that the system should suspend activity and go to a power down state.

Chapter 13

Power Management AMIBIOS

Power management is the coordination and manipulation of power-consuming computer system component devices to minimize the system power consumption and maximize battery life. Power management techniques include turning power off to a specific device and slowing or stopping the device's clock.

Power management features are useful in small portable computers, such as laptops, notebook, and handheld models. Since many of these computers run on battery power, a primary design goal is to conserve power use so the system can run as long as possible without being recharged.

System BIOS is a Logical Place to Start

Because it directly controls system hardware, the system BIOS is the logical place to implement power management.

The AMIPMBIOS (American Megatrends Power Management BIOS) does just that, and AMIPMBIOS adheres to the APM specification.

APM

The Advanced Power Management (APM) specifications were
developed jointly by Intel and Microsoft. APM is a layered approach
to power management. APM specifies a cooperative approach: the
BIOS, operating system, and applications programs work together to
reduce power consumption and conserve battery power.

APM uses a system-wide view of power management where the BIOS,
operating system, and software applications programs all play a role.
The operating system can provide precise power management
information to the BIOS, permitting the BIOS to intelligently conserve
power use. The APM BIOS functions are listed on pages 240 through
260.

APM Features

- APM can be implemented in any operating system. Microsoft
  offers APM support in MS-DOS 5.0 and above and Microsoft
  Windows 3.1 and above. APM is compatible with applications
  that are not aware of APM.

- APM is an open platform-independent specification that can be
  implemented on any Intel x86-based microprocessor.
  Additional APM support is provided in the Intel 386SL and
  486SL CPUs. Intel and Microsoft made APM an open
  specification for all AMIPMBIOS.

- APM is simple for PC users. Microsoft has shipped APM
  drivers for MS-DOS 5.0 and Windows 3.1. Once configured,
  the end user does not have to configure or adjust any
  parameters.

APM Power States

The APM specification defines four power states:

Power State	affects...
Ready	applies to both individual system components and to the system as a whole.
Standby	applies to both individual system components and to the system as a whole.
Suspend	a low power condition that applies to the system as a whole but not to individual components.
Off	applies to both individual system components and to the system as a whole.

Ready State

In Ready, the system or device is fully powered up and ready for use. The system can be active or idle.

Standby State

This is an intermediate system-dependent state that tries to conserve power. The Standby state is entered when the CPU is idle and no device activity occurs for a prespecified length of time. The system does not return to the Ready State until:

- a device raises a hardware interrupt, or

- any controlled device is accessed.

All data and operational parameters are preserved when the system is in Standby.

cont'd

Suspend State

The Suspend state is the lowest level of power consumption available that still preserves operational data and parameters. This state can be initiated either by AMIPMBIOS or software one layer above the BIOS.

AMIPMBIOS can place the system in Suspended state with no notification if it detects a situation that requires an immediate response, for example, when the battery power becomes critically low.

When the system is in Suspend state, no computation is performed until normal activity is resumed and the system leaves this state. Activity cannot resume unless signaled by an external event, such as a key press, Real Time Clock alarm, and so on.

Off State

The system is powered down and inactive in Off state. Data and operational parameters may or may not be preserved in this state.

State Changes

The system and devices in the system can change from one power state to another by explicit command or automatically, based on APM parameter settings and system activity.

Power capabilities differ from device to device. Some devices may not be able to enter all states. Some devices may have built-in automatic power management features invisible to the system. These devices are outside the scope of this manual.

BIOS Power Management

Power Management

Power management features control the power consumption of many system components. Almost every facet of power consumption is monitored. When the system is idle for an end user-specified period of time, the system automatically enters Power Down Mode. The end user can also power down the system by pressing an externally-mounted *Power Down* switch.

IDLE Mode

In IDLE Mode, the CPU receives a very low clock frequency and all other clocks except the DRAM refresh are stopped. The clock can also be stopped for a static CPU. Pressing the externally-mounted *IDLE* switch brings the system out of IDLE Mode.

Power Management Interrupt

INT 77h is the Software Power Management Interrupt (SPMI) in the AMIPMBIOS. The request to change the state of the machine to Power Down Mode comes to the BIOS via OEM-specified sequence microcode.

Microsoft Windows Support

AMIPMBIOS automatically supports True Suspend/Resume power management features under Windows 3.0 and 3.1 in Real and Protected Mode.

OS/2, Unix, and Xenix Support

All AMIPMBIOS power management features work under OS/2, Unix, Xenix, DOS, and any other operating environment.

cont'd

BIOS Power Management, Continued

Modes

The power management scheme is implemented in different levels. Each level saves more power than the previous level and each level can be accessed directly, or incrementally. These levels are:

Full On Mode This is full power mode. A system built on a power management chipset initially powers on in this mode. The LCD and hard disk drive are powered off in inactive for a set length of time. The timeout values are set via AMIBIOS Setup and AMIBCP. When AMIPMBIOS determines that the system does not need maximum power, it enters IDLE Mode.

IDLE Mode is entered when the CPU has been idle for a specified length of time. AMIPMBIOS automatically enters this mode. AMIPMBIOS returns to FULL ON Mode when additional power is required.

SLEEP Mode AMIPMBIOS determines if the system performance has dropped to a level such that the system can function efficiently in SLEEP mode. SLEEP Mode can only be entered from IDLE Mode. The length of time that the BIOS waits before entering SLEEP mode is set in AMIBIOS Setup and AMIBCP.

SUSPEND Mode uses the least amount of power necessary for the system to function. SUSPEND mode is entered from SLEEP Mode. The system can go from IDLE mode directly to SUSPEND Mode via timers configured by AMIBIOS Setup and AMIBCP. If an external switch is pressed, the system can go to SUSPEND Mode from any other mode. Pressing the switch again returns the system to FULL ON Mode.

Chapter 14

EISA Overview

EISA is an acronym for Extended Industry Standard Architecture. EISA is a superset of the Industry Standard Architecture (ISA), based on the original IBM AT specifications. The EISA specifications allow 32-bit memory addressing to be used by the microprocessor, DMA devices, and bus mastering devices. EISA devices can also perform either 16-bit or 32-bit data transfers.

EISA Features

The EISA specification has the following features:

- bus mastering, with an arbitration scheme to prioritize bus access and use,
- 32-bit burst mode DMA and three additional DMA transfer modes,
- sixteen additional data lines, allowing 32-bit data transfers,
- eight additional address lines, allowing up to 4 GB of address space,
- complete compatibility with XT and ISA standards, and
- both level-triggered and edge-triggered interrupts.

EISA and ISA Differences

One of the most important differences between ISA and EISA is that EISA system configuration is done through software, rather than the hardware switches used by an ISA system.

I/O ports, ROM addresses, IRQ lines, and DMA lines for EISA motherboards and EISA adapter cards are configured via an EISA Configuration Utility (ECU), where an ISA adapter card uses DIP switches and jumpers.

EISA Bus Specifications

32-Bit Expansion Slots

EISA computers have 32-bit expansion slots that are fully compatible
with 8-bit and 16-bit ISA expansion slots. EISA expansion slots have
188 pins. The upper 98 pins are exactly the same as the standard ISA
pinouts. The lower 90 pins are used for EISA bus signals.

Bus Transfer Rate

Data can flow on the EISA bus much faster than on the ISA Bus. Not
only does EISA provide a wider 32-bit bus, it also provides a
maximum 33 MBs bus transfer rate. An ISA bus can transfer data at a
maximum rate of only 8 MBs.

EISA systems can achieve higher throughput by using high-speed
burst transfers, which use only one clock cycle. Normal EISA (ISA-
compatible) transfers use two clock cycles.

EISA Bus and the ISA Bus

Specification	EISA Bus	ISA Bus
Data Lines	32	16
Address Lines	32	24
Bus Clock Rate	about 8 MHz	about 8 MHz
Bus Modes	8-, 16-, and 32-bit	8- and 16-bit
Burst Transfer Rate	33 MBs	8 MBs at 0 wait states
DMA	8, 16, and 32-bit DMA	8- and 16-bit DMA
Normal DMA Transfer Rate	5.3 Mbs	1.2 – 1.6 Mbs
Maximum DMA Transfer Rate	33 Mbs	4 Mbs
DMA Cycle Time	0.12 – 1.0 μseconds	1.25 – 1.67 μseconds
Adapter Card Pin Count	188 pins	98 pins
Bus Master	Multiple intelligent 8-, 16-, and 32-bit bus masters	Limited bus mastering
Configuring Adapter Cards	ECU Autoconfiguration. DIP switch and Jumper setting.	DIP switch and jumper setting.

32-bit Memory Addressing

Thirty-two memory address lines are available in EISA systems. EISA systems use 80386 or 80486 processors that allow 32-bit memory addressing. Up to 4 GB of physical RAM can be configured in an EISA system.

An ISA adapter card used in an EISA system can address only up to 16 MB of memory because it uses 24-bit ISA memory addressing. EISA devices can use all available system memory.

EISA Bus Masters

A bus master is a device that takes control of the bus during the data transfers supervised by the bus master. The EISA specification permits up to fifteen intelligent bus mastering devices. Although it is possible to add bus mastering to an ISA system, it can only be done on a limited scale and the bus master cannot be intelligent. With an EISA bus master, the microprocessor does not have to monitor all data transfers. An intelligent EISA bus mastering device uses a dedicated I/O processor and local memory to facilitate and manage data transfers on the EISA bus.

Bus Master Arbitration

The memory refresh circuitry, DMA, and each EISA expansion slot in an EISA system has a preassigned bus master priority level. Each priority level has its own line to the central arbitration point.

EISA bus arbitration determines the latency of each device on the bus. The EISA bus master then knows how much system response time to allocate for all devices on the bus. Several I/O processors can run concurrently on an EISA bus.

Arbitration Priority

Memory refresh and DMA have the highest priority. The assignment of arbitration levels 1 – 15 to bus master expansion slots is defined by the EISA motherboard manufacturer.

cont'd

The following diagram illustrates the relationship between the components involved in arbitration. Up to 15 bus masters are shown, but current EISA chipsets support only up to 8 bus masters.

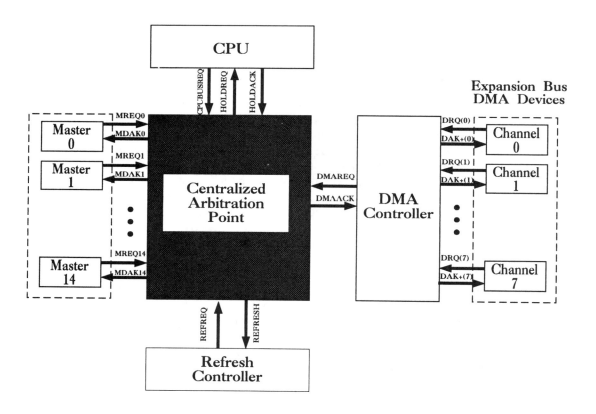

Bus Masters, Continued

Common Clock Signal

EISA devices can synchronize data transfers to a common clock signal generated and optimized by the EISA motherboard.

Type of Data Transfer	Rate
Standard transfers	two clock cycles
EISA burst transfers	one clock cycle
Bus masters slave devices	1.5 clock cycles

Bus Master Components

An EISA bus master includes a dedicated I/O processor and local memory. The I/O processor drives the address, data, and control signals for intelligent peripherals, which become slave devices during a bus cycle. Bus masters improve system performance by doing simple tasks that would otherwise be the responsibility of the host processor.

EISA DMA

EISA DMA devices have seven channels, just like ISA, but DMA transfer is much faster and supports 8-, 16-, and 32-bit data transfers.

cont'd

DMA Modes

DMA Mode	Description
ISA-compatible	DMA request and acknowledge cycles are performed during each DMA transfer cycle.
Block Transfer	1. The peripheral device that requires service makes a DMA request. 2. The DMA controller performs a DMA acknowledge cycle and executes DMA transfer cycles continuously until the DMA request is removed or the terminal count is reached. Devices that use ISA-compatible timing should not use this mode.
Demand Transfer	1. The peripheral device that requires service makes a DMA request. 2. The DMA controller performs a DMA acknowledge cycle. 3. Bus transfers continue until the terminal count register value is reached. Devices that use ISA-compatible timing should not use this mode.
Cascade	1. A bus mastering device that wants bus ownership asserts a DMA request on the channel. 2. The DMA controller performs a DMA acknowledge cycle. 3. Bus ownership is transferred to the bus-mastering requester. DMA channel 4 uses this mode to cascade DMA channels 0 – 3 Controller Block to the DMA Channels 4 – 7 Controller Block. A DMA channel can be programmed in cascade mode for use with external 16-bit bus masters.

EISA Data Transfer Cycles

Four cycle control sequences for transferring data between the DMA device and memory are available. These cycles are:

EISA Cycle Type	Execution Rate
ISA-compatible	Executes one transfer in eight bus cycles. Two additional bus cycles are added for each wait state. ISA DMA devices can use this cycle to transfer data to or from 8-, 16-, or 32-bit memory.
Type A	Executes one transfer cycle in six bus cycles (longer if the transferred data requires data size translation). Supports 8-, 16-, and 32-bit DMA devices. Data size translation is performed automatically for transfers to mismatched memory.
Type B	Executes one transfer in four bus cycles (longer if the transferred data requires data size translation). Supports 8-, 16-, and 32-bit DMA devices and performs automatic data-size translation for transfers to mismatched memory. Transfer time can be cut in half in some ISA devices by using this type of transfer.
Type C (Burst DMA)	Executes one transfer cycle in one bus cycle. Adds one cycle for each simultaneous transfer and each additional wait state. Supports 8-, 16-, and 32-bit DMA devices and performs automatic data-size translation for transfers to mismatched memory.

Using Type A and B Faster than ISA-Compatible

Most ISA-compatible DMA devices can transfer data about 120% faster by programming the EISA DMA controller to use Type A and B transfers instead of ISA-compatible timing.

Benefits of Arbitration

Arbitration provides increased efficiency and performance. Arbitration manages the time between the DMA device request and the grant events. Arbitration does not decrease ISA compatibility. Existing hardware and software can take advantage of arbitration without modification.

cont'd

EISA DMA Cycle Type Characteristics

DMA Cycle Type	Size of Transfer	Maximum Transfer Rate (MBs)	Compatibility
ISA-Compatible	8-bit	1.0	All ISA
ISA-Compatible	16-bit	2.0	All ISA
Type A	8-bit	1.3	Mostly ISA
Type A	16-bit	2.6	Mostly ISA
Type A	32-bit	5.3	EISA Only
Type B	8-bit	2.0	Some ISA
Type B	16-bit	4.0	Some ISA
Type B	32-bit	8.0	EISA Only
Burst DMA (Type C)	8-bit	8.2	EISA only
Burst DMA (Type C)	16-bit	16.5	EISA Only
Burst DMA (Type C)	32-bit	33.0	EISA Only

Interrupt Handling Under EISA

The original PC and ISA buses use edge-triggered interrupts. Edge-triggered interrupts are easy to implement but are also susceptible to false triggering and cannot be shared with other interrupts. Edge-triggered interrupts are signalled by the rising edge of the interrupt signal wave form. Other than the line that the signal came from, there is no way for the EISA system to distinguish between edge-triggered interrupts. Therefore, edge-triggered interrupts cannot be shared.

EISA supports edge-triggered interrupts to maintain ISA compatibility, but also provides level-triggered interrupts. Level-triggered interrupts are less susceptible to noise and allow multiple peripherals to share the same interrupt level. Level-triggered interrupts are signaled by a continuous logic-level voltage, permitting interrupt sharing.

EISA System Configuration

EISA permits automatic configuration of system resources and adapter cards. EISA decreases the need for switches and jumpers. EISA specifies a product identification code for EISA motherboards and adapter cards. An EISA computer automatically compares the product identifier for all EISA adapter cards with the product ID in EISA Extended CMOS RAM, and configures the adapter card accordingly.

EISA Configuration Files

EISA adapter cards are shipped with a configuration file (CFG file). EISA motherboards are shipped with both a CFG file and an ECU. The ECU configures adapter cards with EISA .CFG files and stores the configuration information in EISA Extended CMOS RAM. The ECU minimizes conflicts or contention between EISA adapter cards by controlling the assignment of all necessary system resources.

Configuration Characteristics

EISA configuration consists of:

- an ECU for EISA motherboard and adapter card configuration,
- CFG files for the EISA motherboard and adapter cards,
- EISA Extended CMOS RAM to store configuration parameters,
- a way to save and restore the configuration parameters,
- BIOS routines to read from and write to CMOS RAM, and
- automatic detection and initialization of adapter cards by the BIOS during the Power-On Self Test (POST).

Adapter Cards and EISA Slot Numbers

Each ISA or EISA adapter card is installed in a motherboard expansion slot. The slots are numbered from 1 to 15. The EISA motherboard is always slot 0. Each EISA expansion slot has a unique I/O address space of 1,024 bytes (1 KB). The BIOS uses the registers and information written to EISA Extended CMOS RAM to initialize the adapter cards in BIOS POST. If an ISA adapter card is in an expansion slot, I/O space is limited to 00100h – 003FFh. The ECU can display the proper switch and jumper settings for the ISA adapter card or device if a CFG file is provided with the ISA adapter card or device.

EISA Configuration Utility

The ECU reads and writes the system configuration parameters so that
a conflict-free environment can be established.

CFG Files

The ECU reads the CFG files provided by the EISA adapter card
manufacturer. The CFG file has the product ID and the product's
system resource requirements and initialization information.

Configuration Data Stored in EISA Extended CMOS RAM

Initialization information is read by the ECU and stored in EISA
Extended CMOS RAM. A backup copy of EISA Extended CMOS RAM
configuration data is also stored on disk. The BIOS reads CMOS RAM
and executes the initialization instructions during POST.

EISA System Resources

EISA system resources include:

- DMA channels,
- memory,
- interrupt request lines (IRQs), and
- I/O ports.

The ECU verifies that the resources requested by the EISA adapter
card are not already assigned to another device and then allocates
them. The allocation information is stored in EISA Extended CMOS
RAM and is accessed by the BIOS during POST.

EISA Configuration Overlay Files

Manufacturers may not be able to perform all initializations in the
framework of a CFG file. Features and resources may be specific to the
adapter card and may not be configurable by the ECU. For these
situations, the EISA specification permits CFG file extensions (overlay
files).

EISA Product ID

I/O port addresses 0zC80 – 0zC83h (z = the slot number) store the
EISA four-byte compressed product ID number. The I/O port
information differs for motherboards and adapter cards.

For an EISA motherboard

I/O Port	Description	
0C80h	Bit 7	Reserved. Should be 0.
	Bits 6–2	First letter of the manufacturer code.
	Bits 1–0	First two bits of the second letter of the manufacturer code.
0C81h	Bits 7–5	Remaining bits of the second letter of the manufacturer code.
	Bits 4–0	Third letter of the manufacturer code.
0C82h	Bits 7–0	Manufacturer's product number.
0C83h	Bits 7–0	Product revision number.

For an EISA Adapter Card

I/O Port	Description	
zC80h	Bit 7	Reserved. Should be 0.
	Bits 6–2	First letter of the manufacturer code.
	Bits 1–0	First two bits of the second letter of the manufacturer code.
zC81h	Bits 7–5	Remaining bits of the second letter of the manufacturer code.
	Bits 4–0	Third letter of the manufacturer code.
zC82h	Bits 7–4	Second hex digit of the product number.
	Bits 3–0	First hex digit of the product number.
zC83h	Bits 7–4	Product revision level.
	Bits 3–0	Third hex digit of the product number.

CFG Filenames

CFG filenames must consist of an exclamation point, the product ID, and the DOS file extension *.CFG*, as shown in the following sample. !AMI87B1.CFG is a sample CFG file. The following table identifies the components of this CFG file name:

Code	Description
!	Identifies a CFG file.
AMI	Manufacturer ID.
87	Product Number.
B1	Product Revision Level.

Duplicate File Names

The ECU renames CFG files when it finds duplicate CFG filenames. The ECU changes the exclamation point in the filename to the number of the duplicate. For example, if the ECU finds multiple CFG files for AMI87B1, the first CFG file is named !AMI87B1.CFG, the next 1AMI87B1.CFG, the next 2AMI87B1.CFG, and so on.

EISA BIOS

The EISA BIOS works with the ECU to initialize the system. EISA BIOS POST routines use the information stored in EISA Extended CMOS RAM to initialize the system. EISA POST is described in more detail on page 166.

The BIOS also accesses EISA Extended CMOS RAM. The EISA BIOS provides software routines to read and write EISA configuration information to and from EISA Extended CMOS RAM. These routines can be called using a software INT instruction. There are two BIOS INT 15h Function D8h routines used by the ECU to manipulate the information in CMOS RAM. Detailed explanations of these routines begin on page 279.

Chapter 15

8042 Keyboard Controller BIOS

The 8042 Keyboard Controller BIOS provides ISA-compatible and
extended keyboard commands. It supports ISA (AT-compatible) and
PS/2-compatible keyboards, mouses, and pointing devices. The
keyboard controller in most ISA and EISA systems is an Intel 8042.
The 8042 is a single-chip microcomputer that supports an Intel 80286,
80386, or 80486 PC keyboard interface.

Programming the 8042

To program the 8042, you need an assembler. Avocet Systems, Inc.
makes an 8042/8742 Assembler. *You cannot reprogram the keyboard
controller already in your computer.*

Keyboard Controller BIOS Features

The Keyboard Controller AMIBIOS automatically detects the keyboard
type. It operates at 6 – 12 MHz and supports:

- PS/2-type mouse devices, if hardware support is present,
- 83 or 84-key keyboards,
- 101 or 102-key enhanced keyboards, and
- other enhanced and PS/2-type keyboards.

8042 and 8742

The 8042 is an EPROM and the 8742 is an EEPROM. In this book, 8042
refers to both the 8042 and the 8742, since the functionality of these
two devices is equivalent.

Keyboard Controller Functions

The following figure graphically illustrates the function of the keyboard controller in ISA and EISA systems:

Keyboard

Sends a
Keyboard Make/Break
Scan Code.

Keyboard Controller

Sends a
Make/Break
System Scan Code.

INT 09h

BIOS

Queries Shift/Toggle State Flags.

Handles internal Function Requests.

Converts System Scan Code
to 16-Bit Character Code.

Sends to INT 16h.

The following figure describes the functions performed by the keyboard controller:

Keyboard
Controller

Receives and Translates Serial Data

1. Receives serial data from keyboard.
2. Checks parity.
3. Translates the data to a system scan code, if necessary.
4. Places received and processed data in the data buffer.
5. Notifies the interrupt processor.

Executes System Commands

1. Executes commands via the controller command buffer.
2. Places the result in the data buffer.
3. Interrupts the system microprocessor.

Reports Errors

Transmits/Receives System Data

1. Places it in system buffer.
2. Interts a parity bit.
3. Sends it to the keyboard in serial format.

It also receives keyboard responses and reports to the system microprocessor.

cont'd

Keyboard Controller Receives Data from the Keyboard

The keyboard sends data in an 11-bit serial format to the keyboard controller.

Step	Performed by	Action
1	the keyboard	The data begins with a start bit (low level), followed by 8 data bits (least significant data bit first), an odd parity bit, and a stop bit (high level).
2	the keyboard	Data sent is synchronized with the keyboard clock.
3	the keyboard controller	On receiving a byte of data from the keyboard, the keyboard controller places the data in its one-byte receive-data buffer and disables the keyboard interface until that data is picked up by the system microprocessor. This avoids data overrun.
4	the microprocessor	Reads the data from the keyboard controller receive-data buffer.
5	the keyboard controller	**Error Processing** **Parity Error** The controller requests that the keyboard resend the data. If the error is repeated, the controller sets the parity error bit in its status register. **Timeout Error** The keyboard controller sets the timeout bit in the status register if all eleven bits are not received within two milliseconds from the start of the transmission. If either error occurs, FFh is placed in the input data buffer.

Keyboard Controller Functions, Continued

Possible Errors When Sending Data to the Keyboard

Data is sent to the keyboard in the same serial format as data received from the keyboard.

If...	then...
the time between request to send and start of transmission is greater than 15 milliseconds,	the transmit timeout error bit is set in the status register.
the duration of transmission is greater than 2 milliseconds,	the transmit timeout error bit is set in the status register.
the acknowledgement by the keyboard has a parity error (the keyboard must acknowledge every transmission from the controller),	the keyboard controller sets both the parity and transmit timeout error status bits.
the acknowledgement does not arrive within 25 milliseconds,	both the receive and transmit timeout error bits are set.

Other Error Results

- FEh is placed in the data buffer if any of these errors occur.

- There are no retries on errors that occur during transmissions to the keyboard.

Keyboard Inhibit

The keyboard can sometimes be inhibited by shorting a jumper. See the owner's manual for your system for more information.

All transmissions from the system to the keyboard still occur when the keyboard is inhibited. The keyboard controller tests all data received from the keyboard. If this data is a response to a command sent to the keyboard, it is placed in the data buffer. It is ignored otherwise.

Keyboard Controller and System Interface

The system communicates with the keyboard controller through an input buffer, an output buffer, and a status register.

System to Keyboard Communication Method	Reads	Writes
Keyboard status register	64h	Not Applicable
Keyboard output buffer	60h	Not Applicable
Keyboard input buffer	The keyboard controller interprets the data as a command when the input data is written through I/O port 64h. If the input data is written through I/O port 60h, the data is interpreted either as: ■ a parameter attached to a keyboard command to the controller, or ■ an item of data to be transmitted to the keyboard.	

I/O Port 64h Keyboard Controller Status Register

Bit	Description
7	Parity Error 0 No parity error. 1 The last byte received from the keyboard had a parity error. The keyboard sends data with odd parity.
6	Timeout Error 0 No timeout error. 1 A data transmission from the keyboard to the keyboard controller was not completed within the predefined time limit.
5	Auxiliary Output Buffer Full 0 Keyboard data. 1 Mouse data.
4	Inhibit Switch This bit reflects the state of the keyboard inhibit switch. It is updated when the controller writes to the output buffer. 0 Keyboard inhibited. 1 Keyboard not inhibited.
3	Command or Data Used by the keyboard controller to determine whether the input buffer contains the command or data. 0 The system writes to the input buffer through I/O port 60h. 1 The system writes to the input buffer through I/O port 64h.
2	System Flag The keyboard controller can set this bit to 0 or 1 depending on the command from the system. It is set to 0 after power on reset.
1	Input Buffer Full 0 The keyboard controller input buffer (60h or 64h) is empty. 1 The system has written to the input buffer. It is reset to 0 when the controller reads the input buffer.
0	Output Buffer Full 0 The keyboard controller output buffer has no data. 1 The keyboard controller has written to the output buffer. The keyboard controller returns to 0 when the system reads the output buffer (60h).

Keyboard Controller I/O Ports

The 8042 keyboard controller has two 8-bit I/O ports, 60h and 64h. One port is an input port and the other an output port. The following table lists the bit definitions for the I/O ports:

I/O Port 60h or 64h Keyboard Input Port Definitions

Bit	Description
7	Keyboard inhibit switch 0 Keyboard inhibited. 1 Keyboard not inhibited.
6	Display type switch 0 Primary display is CGA (Color Graphics Adapter). 1 Primary display is monochrome (MDA).
5	Manufacturing diagnostics. 0 The system BIOS performs diagnostics on the motherboard in an infinite loop. 1 Any other function.
4	RAM on the Motherboard 0 256 KB RAM on motherboard. 1 512 KB or greater RAM on motherboard.
3	Unused in ISA and PS/2 systems, but can be configured for clock switching.
2	Unused in ISA and PS/2 systems, but can be configured for clock switching.
1	Unused in ISA systems. Used for mouse data in PS/2 systems.
0	Unused in ISA systems. Used for keyboard data in PS/2 systems.

Keyboard Controller I/O Ports, Continued

I/O Port 64h Keyboard Output Port Definitions

Bit	Description
7	Keyboard data (output). The data is being transferred.
6	Keyboard clock (output). The clock signal is used for data transfer.
5	Output buffer full interrupt to the system from the mouse 0 IRQ12 is not generated. 1 IRQ12 is generated.
4	Output buffer full interrupt to the system from the keyboard 0 IRQ1 is generated. 1 IRQ1 is not generated.
3	Unused in ISA systems. Used for mouse clock output in PS/2 systems.
2	Unused in ISA systems. Used for mouse data output in PS/2 systems.
1	Gate address 20 of system processor 0 The system processor address 20 is inhibited on the system bus. Address 20 remains zero for any system processor bus cycle. 1 The system processor address 20 is allowed on the system bus.
0	Reset to the system processor 0 Reset the system microprocessor. 1 No reset. The software should set this bit to 1 and keep it set for the system microprocessor to work.

Commands to Keyboard Controller

System Commands to the 8042 Keyboard Controller are sent via I/O port address 60h or 64h.

Command	ISA/EISA	MCA (PS/2)
00h-1Fh	Read 8042 RAM to I/O port 60h. The address is specified in bits D5-D0 of the command. These commands to the controller are used exclusively with the AMIBIOS system BIOS.	Read 8042 RAM to I/O Port 60h. The address is specified in bits D5-D0 of the command. These commands to the controller are used exclusively with the AMIBIOS system BIOS.
20h	Read Controller Command Byte. The 8042 places the command byte in the output buffer, making it available in I/O port 60h.	Read Controller Command Byte. The 8042 places the command byte in the output buffer, making it available in I/O port 60h.
20h-3Fh	Read 8042 RAM to I/O port 60h. The address is specified in bits D5-D0 of the command.	Read 8042 RAM to I/O port 60h. The address is specified in bits D5-D0 of the command.
40h-5Fh	Write Controller RAM. The next byte from the system in I/O port 60h is stored in 8042 RAM locations 20h-3Fh. These commands simulate commands 60h-7Fh. These commands to the controller are used exclusively with the AMIBIOS system BIOS.	Write Controller RAM. The next byte from the system in I/O port 60h is stored in 8042 RAM locations 20h-3Fh. These commands simulate commands 60h-7Fh. These commands to the controller are used exclusively with the AMIBIOS system BIOS.
60h	Write Controller Command Byte. The next byte of data from the system in I/O port 60h is used as the Controller Command Byte (CCB).	Write Controller Command Byte. The next byte of data from the system in I/O port 60h is used as the Controller Command Byte (CCB).

Commands to Keyboard Controller, Continued

Command	ISA/EISA	MCA (PS/2)

60h	The Controller Command Byte format is:
	
	Bit 7 Reserved
	Bit 6 IBM PC compatibility mode
	        1 The controller converts the scan code received to the PC-compatible scan code. It also converts the two-byte break sequence from the AT-compatible keyboard to the one-byte PC break code format.
	Bit 5 Reserved in ISA Systems. Should be 0 for proper operation.
	        in PS/2 Systems: Disable Mouse
	        1 Disable the mouse interface by driving the clock line low. Data is not received.
	Bit 4 Disable keyboard
	        1 Disables the keyboard interface by driving the *clock* line low. Data is not received.
	Bit 3 Inhibit override
	        1 Disables the keyboard inhibit function through the keyboard lock.
	Bit 2 System Flag
	        The keyboard controller writes the value written in this bit to bit 2 of the status register.
	Bit 1 Not used in ISA systems. Should be zero.
	        In PS/2 systems:
	        1 The controller generates an interrupt to the system when it places mouse data in the output buffer.
	Bit 0 Used in both ISA and PS/2 systems.
	        1 The controller generates an interrupt to the system when it places keyboard data in the output buffer.	

60h-7Fh	Write Controller RAM. The next byte from the system in I/O port 60h is stored in 8042 RAM locations 20h-3Fh.	Write Controller RAM. The next byte from the system in I/O port 60h is stored in 8042 RAM locations 20h-3Fh.
A0h	Output Copyright Message. A string of standard ASCII characters that ends with a null (0) is placed in I/O port 60h.	Output Copyright Message. A string of standard ASCII characters that ends with a null (0) is placed in I/O port 60h.
A1h	Output Controller Version Number. A single byte of the controller version number in standard ASCII format is placed in I/O port 60h. This command to the controller is used exclusively with the AMIBIOS system BIOS.	Output Controller Version Number. A single byte of the controller version number in standard ASCII format is placed in I/O port 60h. This command to the controller is used exclusively with the AMIBIOS system BIOS.

Commands to Keyboard Controller, Continued

Command	ISA/EISA	MCA (PS/2)
A2h	Resets keyboard controller lines P22 and P23 low. These lines can be used for speed switching via the keyboard controller. This command to the controller is used exclusively with the AMIBIOS system BIOS. After executing this command, the keyboard controller sends one garbage byte to the system, indicating completion. The system must clear the garbage byte.	Not valid.
A3h	Sets keyboard controller lines P22 and P23 high. These lines can be used for speed switching via the keyboard controller. This command to the controller is used exclusively with the AMIBIOS system BIOS. After executing this command, the keyboard controller sends one garbage byte to the system, indicating completion. The system must clear the garbage byte.	Not valid.
A4h	Write Clock = Low. Resets an internal flag that indicates that the system clock is Low. 0 indicates that the clock is Low. This command to the controller is used exclusively with the AMIBIOS system BIOS.	Test password installed. Checks to see if a new password has been installed. The result is in I/O port 60h: FAh Password installed. F1h Password not installed.
A5h	Write Clock = High. Sets an internal flag to indicate that the clock is High. 1 indicates that the clock is High. This command to the controller is used exclusively with the AMIBIOS system BIOS.	Load Security. Initiates the password load procedure. The data stream following the command is the new password and is terminated by a null (0). The password is stored in scan code format.
A6h	Read Clock. Returns an internal flag to indicate that the clock is Low or High. 1 indicates that the clock is High. This command to the controller is used exclusively with the AMIBIOS system BIOS.	Enable security. Enables keyboard controller security features. Valid only when a new password is installed.

Command	ISA/EISA	MCA (PS/2)
A7h	Write Cache Bad. Resets an internal flag to indicate that the cache is bad. 0 indicates that the cache is bad. This command to the controller is used exclusively with the AMIBIOS system BIOS.	Disable Auxiliary Device. Disables the clock line of the auxiliary device and sets bit 5 of the CCB. All data transmissions to or from the auxiliary device are blocked by this command.
A8h	Write Cache Good. Sets an internal flag to indicate that the cache is good. 1 indicates that the cache is good. This command to the controller is used exclusively with the AMIBIOS system BIOS.	Enable Auxiliary Device. Enables the clock line to the auxiliary device and clears bit 5 of the CCB (see the Command 60h description).
A9h	Read Cache Bad or Good. Returns an internal flag to indicate that the cache is bad or good. 0 indicates that the cache is bad. This command to the controller is used exclusively with the AMIBIOS system BIOS.	Auxiliary device Interface Test. Checks the clock and data lines of the auxiliary device. The test result is placed in I/O port 60h: 00h Successful 01h Clock line stuck on Low. 02h Clock line stuck on High. 03h Data line stuck on Low. 04h Data line stuck on High.
AAh	Self Test. The keyboard controller runs an internal diagnostics test. 55h is placed in the output buffer if the test is successful. FCh appears in the output buffer if the test is not successful.	Self Test. The keyboard controller runs an internal diagnostics test. 55h is placed in the output buffer if the test is successful. FCh appears in the output buffer if the test is not successful.
ABh	Interface Test. Instructs the controller to test keyboard clock and data lines. The test result placed in the output buffer is: **Result** **Description** 00 No error detected. 01 Keyboard clock line stuck low. 02 Keyboard clock line stuck high. 03 Keyboard data line stuck low. 04 Keyboard data line stuck high.	
ADh	Disable Keyboard. Disables the keyboard clock line and sets Bit 4 in the CCB. Any keyboard command enables the keyboard.	Disable Keyboard. Disables the keyboard clock line and sets Bit 4 in the CCB. Any keyboard command enables the keyboard.
AEh	Enable Keyboard. Enables the keyboard clock line and clears Bit 4 in the CCB (see Command 60h).	Enable Keyboard. Enables the keyboard clock line and clears Bit 4 in the CCB (see Command 60h).

Commands to Keyboard Controller, Continued

Command	ISA/EISA	MCA (PS/2)
B0h	Resets the keyboard controller P10 line low. This command to the controller is used exclusively with the AMIBIOS system BIOS. After executing this command, the keyboard controller sends one garbage byte to the system, indicating completion. The system must clear the garbage byte.	Not valid.
B1h	Resets the keyboard controller P11 line low. This command to the controller is used exclusively with the AMIBIOS system BIOS. After executing this command, the keyboard controller sends one garbage byte to the system, indicating completion. The system must clear the garbage byte.	Not valid.
B2h	Resets the keyboard controller P12 line low. This command to the controller is used exclusively with the AMIBIOS system BIOS. After executing this command, the keyboard controller sends one garbage byte to the system, indicating completion. The system must clear the garbage byte.	Resets keyboard controller P12 line low. This command to the controller is used exclusively with the AMIBIOS system BIOS. After executing this command, the keyboard controller sends one garbage byte to the system, indicating completion. The system must clear the garbage byte.
B3h	Resets the keyboard controller P13 line low. This command to the controller is used exclusively with the AMIBIOS system BIOS. After executing this command, the keyboard controller sends one garbage byte to the system, indicating completion. The system must clear the garbage byte.	Resets the keyboard controller P13 line low. This command to the controller is used exclusively with the AMIBIOS system BIOS. After executing this command, the keyboard controller sends one garbage byte to the system, indicating completion. The system must clear the garbage byte.

Commands to Keyboard Controller, Continued

Command	ISA/EISA	MCA (PS/2)
B4h	Resets the keyboard controller P22 line low. This command to the controller is used exclusively with the AMIBIOS system BIOS. After executing this command, the keyboard controller sends one garbage byte to the system, indicating completion. The system must clear the garbage byte.	Not valid.
B5h	Resets the keyboard controller P23 line low. This command to the controller is used exclusively with the AMIBIOS system BIOS. After executing this command, the keyboard controller sends one garbage byte to the system, indicating completion. The system must clear the garbage byte.	Not valid.
B8h	Sets the keyboard controller P10 line high. This command to the controller is used exclusively with the AMIBIOS system BIOS. After executing this command, the keyboard controller sends one garbage byte to the system, indicating completion. The system must clear the garbage byte.	Not valid.
B9h	Sets the keyboard controller P11 line high. This command to the controller is used exclusively with the AMIBIOS system BIOS. After executing this command, the keyboard controller sends one garbage byte to the system, indicating completion. The system must clear the garbage byte.	Not valid.

Command	ISA/EISA	MCA (PS/2)
BAh	Sets the keyboard controller P12 line high. This command to the controller is used exclusively with the AMIBIOS system BIOS. After executing this command, the keyboard controller sends one garbage byte to the system, indicating completion. The system must clear the garbage byte.	Sets the keyboard controller P12 line high. This command to the controller is used exclusively with the AMIBIOS system BIOS. After executing this command, the keyboard controller sends one garbage byte to the system, indicating completion. The system must clear the garbage byte.
BBh	Sets the keyboard controller P13 line high. This command to the controller is used exclusively with the AMIBIOS system BIOS. After executing this command, the keyboard controller sends one garbage byte to the system, indicating completion. The system must clear the garbage byte.	Sets the keyboard controller P13 line high. This command to the controller is used exclusively with the AMIBIOS system BIOS. After executing this command, the keyboard controller sends one garbage byte to the system, indicating completion. The system must clear the garbage byte.
BCh	Sets the keyboard controller P22 line high. This command to the controller is used exclusively with the AMIBIOS system BIOS. After executing this command, the keyboard controller sends one garbage byte to the system, indicating completion. The system must clear the garbage byte.	Not valid.
BDh	Sets the keyboard controller P23 line high. This command to the controller is used exclusively with the AMIBIOS system BIOS. After executing this command, the keyboard controller sends one garbage byte to the system, indicating completion. The system must clear the garbage byte.	Not valid.
C0h	Read Input Port. The keyboard controller reads the input port and places the data in the output buffer.	Read Input Port. The keyboard controller reads the input port and places the data in the output buffer.
C2h	Not valid.	Poll Input Port High. Bits 7-4 of the Input Port are placed in Bits 7-4 of I/O Port 64h.
C3h	Not valid.	Poll Input Port Low. Bits 3-0 of the Input Port are placed in Bits 3-0 of I/O Port 64h.

Commands to Keyboard Controller, Continued

Command	ISA/EISA	MCA (PS/2)
C8h	Unblock keyboard controller lines P22 and P23. The system can make lines P22 and P23 active low or active high via D1h after this command executes. Issue this command before issuing D1h. This command to the controller is used exclusively with the AMIBIOS system BIOS.	Not valid
C9h	Block keyboard controller lines P22 and P23. The system *cannot* make lines P22 and P23 active low or active high via D1h after this command executes. Issue this command before issuing D1h. This command to the controller is used exclusively with the AMIBIOS system BIOS.	Not valid
CAh	Read Mode. This command outputs information about the keyboard controller mode (ISA or PS/2) to I/O Port 60h Bit 0. 0 ISA (AT) interface 1 PS/2 (MCA) interface This command to the controller is used exclusively with the AMIBIOS system BIOS.	Read Mode. This command outputs information about the keyboard controller mode (ISA or PS/2) to I/O Port 60h Bit 0. 0 ISA (AT) interface 1 PS/2 (MCA) interface This command to the controller is used exclusively with the AMIBIOS system BIOS.
CBh	Write Mode. Sets or resets the keyboard controller mode between AT (ISA) and PS/2. Before writing this mode, read the mode byte using command CAh. Then modify only bit 0, leaving the other bits unchanged, and write the mode byte back.	Write Mode. Sets or resets the keyboard controller mode between AT (ISA) and PS/2. Before writing this mode, read the mode byte using command CAh. Then modify only bit 0, leaving the other bits unchanged, and write the mode byte back.
D0h	Read Output Port. Outputs the status of the keyboard controller output port (P2) to I/O Port 60h. The keyboard controller reads the output port and places the data in the output buffer.	Read Output Port. Outputs the status of the keyboard controller output port (P2) to I/O Port 60h. The keyboard controller reads the output port and places the data in the output buffer.
D1h	Write Output Port. The data byte that follows this command is written to the keyboard controller output port (P2). Writes data via I/O port 60h to the output port. Make sure that output port bit 0 is not written as 0, because a 0 in bit 0 resets the system processor.	Write Output Port. The data byte that follows this command is written to the keyboard controller output port (P2). Writes data via I/O port 60h to the output port. Make sure that output port bit 0 is not written as 0, because a 0 in bit 0 resets the system processor.
D2h	Not valid.	Write Keyboard Output Buffer. This command sends the data byte that follows the command in I/O Port 60h straight to the system as it is initiated by the device.

Commands to Keyboard Controller, Continued

Command	ISA/EISA	MCA (PS/2)
D3h	Not valid.	Write Auxiliary Device Output Buffer. The next data byte in I/O Port 60h from the system is made available immediately to the system as if it is initiated by an auxiliary device.
D4h	Not valid.	Write Auxiliary Device. The next data byte to I/O Port 60h is transmitted to an auxiliary device.
E0h	Read Test Inputs. This command makes the status of the Test inputs T0 and T1 available to the system at I/O Port 60h. The T0 status is in Bit 0 (0 is enabled). The T1 status is in Bit 1 (0 is enabled).	Read Test Inputs. This command makes the status of the Test inputs T0 and T1 available to the system at I/O Port 60h. The T0 status is in Bit 0 (0 is enabled). The T1 status is in Bit 1 (0 is enabled).
F0h-FFh	Pulse Output Port. Bits 3-0 of the output port of the keyboard controller may be pulsed low for approximately 6 μseconds. Bits 3–0 of this command specify the output port bits to be pulsed. The corresponding bits in the command indicate the bits to be pulsed. 0 Bit should be pulsed. 1 Bit should not be modified. Note that bit 0 of the output port is connected to the reset of the system processor, so the processor can be reset by pulsing this bit.	Pulse Output Port. Bits 1-0 of the output port of the keyboard controller may be pulsed low for approximately 6 μseconds. Bits 1–0 of this command specify the output port bits to be pulsed. The corresponding bits in the command indicate the bits to be pulsed. 0 Bit should be pulsed. 1 Bit should not be modified. Note that bit 0 of the output port is connected to the reset of the system processor, so the processor can be reset by pulsing this bit.

Keyboard Controller/Keyboard Interface

The keyboard controller communicates with the keyboard over a clock line (bit 6 of output port 5) and a data line (bit 7 of the output port).

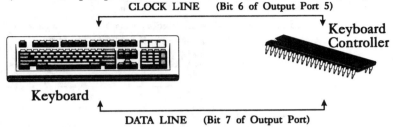

CLOCK LINE   (Bit 6 of Output Port 5)

Keyboard Controller

Keyboard

DATA LINE   (Bit 7 of Output Port)

The keyboard controller reads the data line through test input T1 and the clock line through test input T0. The keyboard supplies the clock for all data transmission to and from the keyboard.

Data is made available after the rising edge of the clock and is sampled on the falling edge as shown in the following pulse diagram:

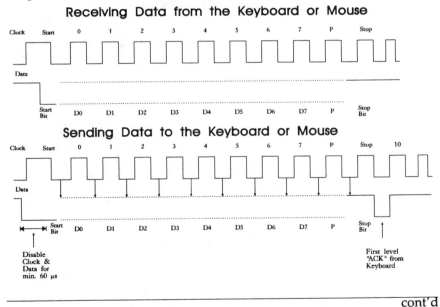

Receiving Data from the Keyboard or Mouse

Sending Data to the Keyboard or Mouse

cont'd

Keyboard/Keyboard Controller Communication Protocol

Step	Performed by	Action
1	the keyboard	The keyboard first checks the clock line for a high level when the keyboard wants to send data. *The keyboard controller can prevent the keyboard from sending data by driving the clock line low through bit 6 of the output port.*
2	the keyboard	Sends the data if the clock and data lines are high (enabled). Otherwise it stores data in its own buffer.
3	the keyboard	Checks the state of the clock line at an interval of 60 μseconds, to sense whether the keyboard controller intends to send data.
4	the keyboard controller	The keyboard controller forces the clock and data line low for more than 60 μseconds and then releases the clock line with the data line low when it wants to send data.
5	the keyboard	The low data line is accepted by the keyboard as a start bit (request to send) and the keyboard starts clocking the data in. After the tenth bit, the keyboard forces the data line low for one clock period (the stop bit) to inform the keyboard controller that the keyboard has received the data.

Appendix A

AMIBIOS Error Messages

Beep Codes

Beeps	Error message	Explanation
1	Refresh Failure	Bad memory refresh circuitry on the motherboard.
2	Parity Error	Parity error in the first 64 KB block of memory.
3	Base 64 KB Memory Failure	Memory failure in first 64 KB.
4	Timer Not Operational	Memory failure in the first 64 KB of memory or Timer 1 on the motherboard is not functioning.
5	Processor error	The CPU on the motherboard generated an error.
6	8042 – Gate A20 Failure	The BIOS cannot switch to protected mode.
7	Processor Exception Interrupt	The CPU generated an exception interrupt.
8	Display Memory Read/Write Error	The system video adapter is either missing or its memory is faulty. This is not a fatal error.
9	ROM Checksum Error	The ROM checksum value does not match the value encoded in the BIOS.
10	CMOS Shutdown Register Read/Write Error	The shutdown register for CMOS RAM failed.
11	Cache Error/ External Cache Bad	The external cache is faulty.

What to Do If the Computer Beeps

Beeps	Action
1, 2, or 3	Reseat the memory SIMMs or DIPs. If it still beeps, replace memory.
6	▪ Replace the keyboard fuse (if it has one), or ▪ Attach a different keyboard, or ▪ Reseat the keyboard controller chip. If it still beeps, replace the keyboard controller.
8	Replace the video adapter or the RAM on the video adapter.
9	Probably needs a new BIOS ROM chip.
11	Reseat the cache memory on the motherboard. If it still beeps, replace the cache memory.
4, 5, 7, or 10	Replace the motherboard.

AMIBIOS Displayed Error Messages

POST displayed error messages have the following format:

> ERROR *Message Line 1*
> ERROR *Message Line 2*
> Press <F1> to RESUME

Press <F1> to RESUME is not displayed if *Wait for <F1> If Any Error* in Advanced CMOS Setup has been Disabled.

> RUN SETUP

can appear. Press F1 to run AMIBIOS Setup.

Error Message	Explanation
8042 Gate – A20 Error	Gate A20 on the keyboard controller (8042) is not working.
Address Line Short!	Error in the address decoding circuitry on the motherboard.
C: Drive Error	Hard disk drive C: does not respond. Run the Hard Disk Utility. Also, check the C: hard disk type in Standard CMOS Setup.
C: Drive Failure	Hard disk drive C: does not respond. Replace the hard disk drive.
Cache Memory Bad, Do Not Enable Cache!	Cache memory is defective. Replace it.
CH-2 Timer Error	ISA systems have two timers. There is an error in timer 2.
CMOS Battery State Low	CMOS RAM is powered by a battery. The battery power is low. Replace the battery.
CMOS Checksum Failure	After CMOS RAM values are saved, a checksum value is generated for error checking. The previous value is different from the current value. Run AMIBIOS Setup.
CMOS System Options Not Set	The values stored in CMOS RAM are either corrupt or nonexistent. Run AMIBIOS Setup.
CMOS Display Type Mismatch	The video type in CMOS RAM does not match the type detected by the BIOS. Run AMIBIOS Setup.
CMOS Memory Size Mismatch	The amount of memory on the motherboard is different than the amount in CMOS RAM. Run AMIBIOS Setup.
CMOS Time and Date Not Set	Run Standard CMOS Setup to set the date and time.
D: Drive Error	Hard disk drive D: does not respond. Run the Hard Disk Utility. Also, check the D: hard disk type in Standard CMOS Setup.
D: drive failure	Hard disk drive D: does not respond. Replace the hard disk.
Diskette Boot Failure	The boot disk in floppy drive A: cannot be used to boot the system. Use another boot disk and follow the screen instructions.
Display Switch Not Proper	Some systems require a video switch to be set. Turn the system off, set the switch properly, then power on.
DMA Error	Error in the DMA controller.
DMA #1 Error	Error in the first DMA channel.
DMA #2 Error	Error in the second DMA channel.

AMIBIOS Displayed Error Messages, Continued

Error Message	Explanation
FDD Controller Failure	The BIOS cannot communicate with the floppy controller. Check all connections after the system is powered down.
HDD Controller Failure	The BIOS cannot communicate with the hard disk drive controller. Check all connections after the system is powered down.
INTR #1 Error	Interrupt channel 1 failed POST.
INTR #2 Error	Interrupt channel 2 failed POST.
Invalid Boot Diskette	The BIOS can read the disk in floppy drive A:, but it cannot boot the system with it. Use another boot disk.
Keyboard Locked...Unlock	The keyboard is locked.
Keyboard Error	Timing problem with the keyboard. Set the *Keyboard* option in Standard CMOS Setup to *Not Installed* to skip keyboard routines.
KB/Interface Error	Error in the keyboard connector.
No ROM BASIC	Cannot find a bootable sector on either A: or C:. The BIOS calls INT 18h which generates this message. Use a bootable disk.
Off Board Parity Error	Parity error in memory on an adapter card. The format is: OFF BOARD PARITY ERROR ADDR (HEX) = (XXXX) *XXXX* is the hex address where the error occurred. Run AMIDiag to find and correct memory problems.
On Board Parity Error	Parity error in motherboard memory. The message format is: ON BOARD PARITY ERROR ADDR (HEX) = (XXXX) *XXXX* is the hex address where the error occurred. Run AMIDiag to find and correct memory problems.
Parity Error ????	Parity error in system memory, but the address of the error is unknown. Run AMIDiag to find and correct memory problems.

EISA Error Messages

Message	Explanation
EISA CMOS Checksum Failure	The Checksum for EISA Extended CMOS RAM is incorrect. Replace the battery for EISA Extended CMOS RAM.
EISA CMOS Inoperational	Read/Write error in EISA CMOS RAM. Replace the battery.
Expansion Board not ready at Slot *X, Y, Z*	Cannot find the adapter card in Slot *X, Y,* or *Z*. Make sure the adapter card is in the correct slot and is properly seated.
Fail-Safe Timer NMI Inoperational	Devices that depend on the fail-safe NMI timer cannot operate correctly.
ID information mismatch for Slot *X, Y, Z*	The ID of the EISA adapter card in Slot *X, Y,* or *Z* does not match the ID in EISA Extended CMOS RAM. Run the ECU.
Invalid Configuration Information for Slot *X, Y, Z*	Configuration data for EISA adapter cards *X, Y,* or *Z* is not correct. The adapter card cannot be configured. Run the ECU.
Software Port NMI Inoperational	The software port NMI is not working. You can continue, but the system can fail if an NMI occurs.

ISA NMI Messages

ISA NMI Message	Explanation
Memory Parity Error at *xxxxx*	Memory failed. If the memory location can be determined, it is displayed as *xxxxx*. If not, the message is *Memory Parity Error ????*.
I/O Card Parity Error at *xxxxx*	An expansion card failed. If the address can be determined, it is displayed as *xxxxx*. If not, the message is *I/O Card Parity Error ????*.
DMA Bus Time-out	A device has driven the bus signal for more than 7.8 μseconds.

EISA NMI Error Messages

EISA NMI Message	Explanation
BUS Timeout NMI at Slot *n*	There was a Bus Timeout NMI at Slot *n*.
(E)nable (D)isable Expansion Board?	An adapter card generated an NMI. Type E to enable the adapter card or D to disable it.
Expansion Board Disabled at Slot *n*	The EISA adapter card in Slot *n* has been disabled.
Expansion Board NMI at Slot *n*	An adapter card NMI was generated from Slot *n*.
Fail-Safe Timer NMI	A fail-safe timer NMI has been generated.
Software Port NMI	A software port NMI has been generated.

Appendix B

Upgrading the BIOS

Although American Megatrends does not sell upgrade BIOS, some AMIBIOS distributors do. Call American Megatrends Sales at 404-263-8181 for information about an upgrade AMIBIOS.

Ordering an Upgrade System BIOS

Have the following information when ordering an upgrade BIOS:

- manufacturer and model number of your computer,
- number of BIOS ROMs,
- processor type and speed,
- chipset part numbers,
- date of BIOS,
- BIOS Identification string, and
- RAM configuration and speed.

Identifying BIOS ROMs

The BIOS ROM chips have the AMIBIOS label and a part number. There are either one, two, or four BIOS ROMs.

Finding the Processor Type and Speed

The AMIBIOS System Configuration screen displays the processor type. AMIDiag Version 4.0 or later also displays this information.

Finding the Chipset Part Numbers

Your computer probably uses an integrated chipset. This chipset consists of 3 to 6 square flat chips with pins on all four sides. They can be socketed but are probably mounted directly on the motherboard. The manufacturer's name (CHIPs, OPTi, Symphony, VLSI, Intel, TI, ETEQ, and so on) and logo are printed on the chip as well as the part number (such as 82C100, 62C200, 87C711).

cont'd

Finding the BIOS Date

AMIDiag Version 4.0 or later displays this information. But the quickest method is to read the AMIBIOS System Configuration Screen that appears at system boot. The BIOS date is 8 bytes located at F:FFF5h in memory.

Finding the BIOS Identification String

The BIOS Reference or Identification String is displayed at the bottom of the first AMIBIOS screen. If the system has a Hi-Flex AMIBIOS, press INS during system power-on to display the two additional reference strings.

See Appendix D, beginning on page 469, for additional information about BIOS Identification Strings.

Why You Should Update the System BIOS

A system BIOS upgrade can offer additional support that might be useful. See Appendix C for a list of AMIBIOS features for each release of the AMIBIOS since 1986. Some of the potential benefits include:

- configure new higher-density drives,
- eliminate controller or device driver translation for MFM, RLL, or ESDI hard disk drives with 1,024 or fewer cylinders via the user-definable hard disk drive types,
- user-defined hard drives types for IDE and other nonstandard drives,
- performance improvement,
- use a PS/2-type mouse or keyboard,
- use Advanced CMOS Setup and Advanced Chipset Setup options. The newer AMIBIOS provide many more Setup options, permitting more control over more system functions, and
- use the hard disk utilities that come with the AMIBIOS.

Upgrading the Keyboard BIOS

Only system BIOS upgrades are discussed in this book. Changing the Keyboard Controller BIOS is not recommended. About the only reason to replace the keyboard BIOS is if this chip or the BIOS on the chip is faulty. In a few rare cases, the keyboard controller BIOS must be replaced when a new system BIOS is installed.

Upgrading the BIOS, Continued

What If the BIOS in My System is not an AMIBIOS?

In most cases, it does not matter. You can usually upgrade from a
Phoenix, Award, or other brand to a new AMIBIOS.

Potential Problems of Upgrading the BIOS

Do not try to perform a BIOS upgrade without consulting a dealer or
distributor. If you choose the wrong BIOS, it may not work and may
corrupt CMOS RAM to the point that the system can be unusable.

This is not a complete disaster. If CMOS RAM is bad, remove the
battery and leave the system alone for about 30 minutes. Make sure
you know the hard disk drive type before you do this.

Then replace the battery and turn the system on. CMOS RAM should
be blank, since it has been without power. You are now free to
configure the system from scratch. Enter the date, time, disk
configuration information, monitor type and other basic system
configuration, store it in CMOS RAM, and reboot.

Installing System BIOS ROM

The ROM BIOS chips are installed in 28-pin DIP sockets. One to four
BIOS chips may be present. The following table identifies the BIOS
ROMs.

If you have ...	the ROM size is...	the chip type is...	and the number of BIOS chips is...
an EISA System	128 KB	27010 or	1 ROM chip or
		27512	2 ROM chips
		27256	4 ROM chips
an ISA (AT-compatible) System	64 KB	27512 or	1 ROM chip or
		27256 or	2 ROM chips or
		27128	4 ROM chips

cont'd

Installing System BIOS ROM, Continued

Removing the Old BIOS ROMs

Use an IC remover or a screwdriver to gently remove the old BIOS
ROM chips. Do not use excessive force to remove the chips. Applying
excessive force can damage the motherboard.

Unpacking the New BIOS ROM Chips

Unpack the BIOS ROM chips. See the following table to identify BIOS
chip labels. Inspect chips for bent pins. Using pliers, gently straighten
any bent pins so that all pins are parallel and straight.

Install each ROM chip so that pin 1 of a ROM is inserted in pin 1 of
the corresponding socket, and all other pins on the ROM chip fit in the
pin sockets by number. Press each ROM firmly but gently into the
socket.

Steps to Upgrade the System BIOS

Step	Action
1	Wear an antistatic wristband to properly ground yourself.
2	Turn the computer off and remove the cover.
3	Unpack the ROM BIOS chips on a grounded antistatic mat.
4	Check the size and number of the existing ROM BIOS chips. An ISA Hi-Flex AMIBIOS is available in the following sets: One 27512 ROM chip (64 KB) Two 27256 ROM chips (32 KB each) Four 27128 ROM chips (16 KB each) Read the system documentation to verify that the set of Hi-Flex AMIBIOS you received is the proper size and number for the motherboard.
5	Remove the old chips. Note which chips are ODD and EVEN (for a two-chipset) or which chips are numbered 0, 1, 2, and 3 (for a four-chipset). The new chips should directly replace the old chips (the EVEN chip from the new set should replace the old EVEN chip and the new ODD chip replaces the old ODD chip).
6	Install the chips. Each ROM chip is notched and there is a corresponding notch on the receiving ROM socket. Make sure that the chips are oriented such that the notch on the chip matches the notch on the socket.
7	Replace the cover.

Appendix C

AMIBIOS History

The major upgrades, features, and newly-supported devices are listed for each BIOS release in this Appendix.

American Megatrends, Inc. has been selling AT-compatible system BIOS since 1986. AMIBIOS has always included all standard IBM AT BIOS features and has always been noted for its performance. This appendix lists many of the additional features added by American Megatrends since 1986.

If the Motherboard has Cache Memory

In general, older AMIBIOS (AMI BIOS and AMI BIOS Plus) for non-American Megatrends motherboards with cache memory are customized. Contact the motherboard manufacturer if you want to upgrade the BIOS. An AMIBIOS on an American Megatrends motherboard usually has a BIOS ID that begins with DAMI, DAMX, or EDAMI.

AMI 286 and 386 BIOS — January 1987

- 1.44 MB 3½" floppy disk drive support
- Support for IDE hard disk drives
- User-defined hard disk drive type 47
- INT 15h Function 4Fh Keyboard Intercept Support
- INT 15h Function C0h PS/2 Mouse Support

AMI 286 and 386 BIOS — 6/17/1988

Reference Number

The BIOS reference number appears on the bottom line of the screen during startup, as follows:

```
Ref. TTTT-XXXX-042088-Kn
```

TTTT   BIOS type
XXXX   customer number
042088   the BIOS release date
K*n*   the keyboard BIOS version number. If *n* is 0, it is not an American Megatrends keyboard BIOS.

A new INT 13h function, AH = 19h Park Heads, has been added. DL must contain the drive number (80h or 81h).

INT 13h Function AH = 08h Return Parameter — This function returns the actual number of cylinders in the hard disk drive. Previously, the highest number returned was 1,024.

Using Default Values for C&T NEAT- and 386 CHIPSet-based systems — The C&T NEAT or C&T 386 chipset registers can be programmed incorrectly. When this happens, the system can be difficult to boot. By pressing INS at power-on or after a hard reset, the end users can program the chipset registers with default values stored in CMOS RAM, thereby booting the system. The end user then must run Setup to optimize configuration values.

Enhanced IRMA 3270 Emulation support.

Improved 1.44 MB 3½" drive compatibility.

Supports Toshiba ND-04DT-A 360 KB floppy.

AMI 286 and 386 BIOS — 9/25/1988

INT 10h — Video I/O functions execute approximately 25% faster.

Extended Setup for the BIOS for the NEAT 286 and C&T 386 Chipsets — EASY SETUP is now available for the BIOS for the C&T NEAT and 386 chipsets. It configures DRAM wait states, clock speed, and shadowing options.

Translates 80286 LOADALL — This feature is included only in the AMI 386 BIOS. OS/2, RAMDRIVE, and certain other programs use the 80286 LOADALL instruction, which does not exist in the 80386 instruction set. The BIOS translates LOADALL to an 80386 format, but needs an extra 100 bytes to do so. The BIOS can either use the BIOS Stack Area from 0:300h–0:400h, or use the top 1 KB of user memory (at 639K). Typing 1 specifies that the BIOS should use the BIOS Stack Area at 0:300h. Typing 2 specifies that the BIOS should use the top 1 KB of the DOS memory area.

OS/2 can be booted from a 1.44 MB 3½" floppy.

ESDI, SCSI and RLL hard disk drives - If one of these types of hard drives is in a system, the BIOS Date should be 092588 or later.

AMI 286 and 386 BIOS — 12/15/1988

Configure Workstations — The end user can configure file servers or diskless workstations by bypassing keyboard, video, and floppy error messages.

No <F1> after Error Message — The end user does not have to press <F1> after an error message.

Serial Ports — A maximum of four serial ports is supported. The COM1 starting I/O port is 3F8h, COM2 is 2F8h, COM3 is 3E8h, and COM4 is 2E8h. The BIOS only supports data transfer and programmability for COM1 and COM2.

cont'd

System Configuration — A new System Configuration Screen displays number and type of drives installed, total RAM, math coprocessor presence, amount of cache memory, and other system configuration data.

1,024 Cylinders — The BIOS recognizes a maximum of 1,024 cylinders on a hard disk drive. The BIOS has resolved DOS and SpeedStore problems when using a drive with more than 1,024 cylinders. Problems with a Western Digital WD1003V-MM2 hard drive controller and a Miniscribe hard disk drive have been resolved.

82C302C Support — The 82C302C uses a 4 KB page size instead of the 2 KB page size used by the 82C302. This BIOS automatically detects which chip is in the system and provides the appropriate support.

C&T 386 Soft Reset Bypass — In previous BIOS, BIOS default values or user-configured Extended CMOS Setup values were programmed into the chipset registers at cold boot and soft reset. Now they are set only at cold boot.

C&T 386 Memory — The BIOS will now accept 256 KB RAM chips in banks 0 and 1 and 1 MB RAM chips in banks 2 and 3. The BIOS automatically assigns physical banks 2 and 3 as logical banks 0 and 1 and uses all available memory.

C&T 386 and NEAT Clock Switching — Clock switching via a keyboard controller pin, programming the processor clock speed, or programming the processor clock and bus speed are now supported. A keyboard controller pin can also be used to switch the Turbo LED pin on and off.

Additional NEAT Feature — The BIOS for the NEAT chipset now supports the 80386SX processor and 80387SX math coprocessor.

82C212B Support for NEAT BIOS — The BIOS for the NEAT chipset automatically detects the 82C212 or 82C212B and programs the chipset registers accordingly. Extended CMOS Setup supports both chips.

AMI 286 and 386 BIOS — 2/25/1989

64 MB of System Memory — Support for up to 64 MB has been added (if the system hardware supports memory above 16 MB).

IDE — Support for Conner IDE interface drives has been added.

OS/2 — Support for OS/2 in the scratch RAM area has been added. You must use Type 47 for hard disk drives when using OS/2.

SCSI — Support for the Western Digital 8-Bit SCSI Controller has been added.

AMI 286 and 386 BIOS — 3/25/1989 and 3/30/1989

New CMOS Setup Utility Features:

- full-screen editing,
- user-defined drive types for drives C: and D:, and
- bypass keyboard, floppy and video error reporting.

Diagnostics for 1.44 MB Floppy Drives — The BIOS Diagnostics utility will now run on 1.44 MB floppy drives.

Diagnostics for User-Defined Hard Drives — The BIOS Diagnostics utility will now support any user-defined hard disk drive.

NEAT and C&T 386 Chipset BIOS — Previous BIOS products forced the system to 1 DRAM wait state if only 1 bank of memory was used. The BIOS now allows 0 wait states if selected by the end user in Extended CMOS Setup.

AMI 386 Mark II AT/XT BIOS — 4/25/1989

Automatic CMOS Memory Size Adjustment — In previous versions of this BIOS, the end user had to execute Setup twice when setting the *Shadow RAM* and *256KB Relocation* options.

No System Configuration Screen — The BIOS System Configuration screen is no longer displayed.

AMI 286 and 386 BIOS — 4/30/1989

User-defined Drive Type 47 implemented in CMOS Setup.

AMI 286 and 386 BIOS — 9/15/1989

INT 15h — Function 87h now returns error codes via I/O port 80h.

POST — The keyboard timeout period in POST has been enlarged to accommodate some keyboards with a slow response time.

Seek — The timeout values for hard disk Seek have been enlarged to accommodate some slow hard disk drives.

Floppy Test — Previous BIOS products did not test the floppy disk drives if no floppy drives were configured in CMOS RAM. If floppy drives are part of the system, they are now tested.

AMI 286 and 386 BIOS — 12/15/1989

Western Digital 8-bit SCSI Controller support was added. A problem with some Western Digital 8-bit hard drive controllers that conflicted with the BIOS when accessing the BIOS data area was corrected.

AMI BIOS — 4/9/1990

IDE hard drive support has been fixed. To use an IDE drive in your system, the BIOS Date should be 040990 or later.

PS/2-compatible mouse support has been added.

INT 19h Bootstrap Loader has been modified to support the IBM Token Ring Network Card.

Floppy controller reset was added during bootup to work with DR DOS.

Up to 4 GB of RAM is recognized with some chipsets.

AMI BIOS — 10/15/1990

Hard drive type 47 will now work under Novell.

The POST memory test performs faster.

INT 15h Block Memory Move now performs faster.

AMI BIOS for Headland HT12 Chipset — 11/15/1990

Shadowing — Older versions of the BIOS for the HT12 chipset may have had problems configuring shadowing under these conditions:

- the motherboard has 1 MB,
- the user selects remapping and no shadowing, and
- then disables remapping and enables shadowing.

This release fixes the above problem.

Error Message — This release also eliminates the CMOS Memory Size Mismatch error message when the end user toggles the shadowing and remapping options.

AMI BIOS for HT12 Chipset — 10/15/1990

Shadowing — The previous version of this BIOS had trouble with shadowing when SIMM Bank1 had 256 KB RAM and BANK2 had 1 MB RAM for a total of 2.4 MB of motherboard system RAM. ROM Diagnostics may not work with this configuration either. This is a hardware problem, but American Megatrends implemented a BIOS solution.

AMI BIOS — 2/2/1991

The AMI BIOS now runs OS/2 in CGA mode.

New BIOS Setup screens — Advanced CMOS Setup and Advanced CHIPSET Setup have been added to BIOS Setup.

INT 15h Function C2h PS/2 Mouse Support was added.

Hi-Flex AMIBIOS Release — 3/15/1991

Turbo Switch 8042 Pins — The following 8042 keyboard controller pins can be used for Turbo Switch Input Pins: 27, 28, 29, 30, 31, and 33. Pins 23 and 24 cannot be used as Turbo Switch Input Pins. Pins 23, 24, 27, 28, 29, and 30 can be used for clock switching.

Turbo Switch Option has been added to Advanced CHIPSET Setup. It can be Enabled or Disabled. If the Turbo Switch option is Present and Enabled and the Turbo Switch is Low at Power-On, the CPU speed is set low. Otherwise, the speed is set in Standard CMOS Setup.

Three BIOS ID Strings — The last two (of three) BIOS Identification Strings do not appear on the screen. Press INS during POST to display these strings.

Timer Channel 1 — The Timer Channel 1 test for refresh has been removed, which corrects a problem on some 33 MHz 486 systems.

The BIOS now recognizes up to 4 GB of RAM without customization.

AMIBIOS 4/4/1991, 5/5/1991, 7/7/1991, and 9/6/1991

No major features added.

AMIBIOS 12/12/1991

Peripheral Setup and Power Management Setup added.

BIOS Size — The run-time BIOS size is only 32 KB.

Serial Ports — Baud rates up to and including 19,200 bps are now supported.

Setup Option — The Daylight Saving option has been removed from Standard CMOS Setup.

INT 15h — Function AH = C1h Get Extended Data has been added.

Processor — The BIOS automatically detects the following processor types: Intel 80486DX, 80486DX2, 80486SX, 80386DX, and 80386SX.

8042 Pin — Pin 32 of the keyboard controller can be used to remove the password checking facility. If pin 32 of the keyboard controller is connected to GND, the password is set as uninstalled. Please note that a null password is not a valid password.

Password — The password option in Advanced CMOS Setup has only two settings: Setup or Always. Please note that Bit 7 of CMOS register 34h is available for use.

AMIBIOS 06/06/1992 and 11/11/1992

New Features

■ 2.88 MB 3½" floppy drive support has been added in the BIOS.

■ INT 16h has these new functions:
- Function F0h Set CPU Speed
- Function F1h Read CPU Speed
- Function F4h Subfunction 00h Read Cache Controller Status
- Function F4h Subfunction 01h Enable Cache Controller
- Function F4h Subfunction 02h Disable Cache Controller

■ *Boot Sector Write Protection* — This Advanced CMOS Setup option warns the end user any time a program attempts to format or write to the boot sector on the hard disk drive.

■ *Auto Detect Hard Disk Drive* — this AMIBIOS Setup main menu option detects hard drive parameters for IDE, SCSI, and other non-MFM drives.

■ AMIBIOS now automatically detects AMD386DXL, Cyrix Cx486SLC and Cx486DLC, IBM 486SLC,and Intel 80486DX, 80486DX2, 80486DX3, 80486SX, 80386DX, 80386SX, and Overdrive™ processors.

Appendix D

AMIBIOS Identification Strings

The BIOS Identification strings contain characters in a prearranged sequence that identify BIOS characteristics and features.

In a Hi-Flex AMIBIOS, there are up to three BIOS Identification strings that can be displayed.

Only Identification String 1 appears automatically at the bottom of the screen during boot-up. The end user must press INS while the BIOS boot screen is being displayed to force BIOS Identification Strings 2 and 3 appear.

The three BIOS Identification strings are described on the following pages.

Identification String Line 1

The BIOS identification string appears on the bottom of the screen during BIOS POST. The bytes of Identification String 1 are numbered as follows:

```
xx          -xxxx      -xxxxxxx   -xxxxxxxxx  -xxxxxx    -xxxxxxxx   -x
12          4-7        9-14       17-24       26-31      33-40       42
```

Byte	Description
1	Processor Type 0 8086 or 8088 2 80286 3 80386 4 80486
2	Size of BIOS 0 64 KB BIOS 1 128 KB BIOS
4–5	Major Version Number
6–7	Minor Version Number
9–15	Reference Number
17	Halt on Post Error. Set to 1 if On.
18	Initialize CMOS in every boot. Set to 1 if On.
19	Block pins 22 and 23 of the keyboard controller. Set to 1 if On.
20	Mouse support in BIOS and keyboard controller. Set to 1 if On.
21	Wait for F1 if error found. Set to 1 if On.
22	Display Floppy error during POST. Set to 1 if On.
23	Display Video error during POST. Set to 1 if On.
24	Display Keyboard error during POST. Set to 1 if On.
26–27	BIOS Date. Month (1-12).
28–29	BIOS Date. Date (1-31).
30–31	BIOS Date. Year (0-99).
33–40	Chipset Identification. BIOS Name.
42	Keyboard controller version number.

Identification String Line 2

```
xxx-x     -xxxx    -xx              -xx     -xxxx    -xx      -xx      -xxx
123 5     7-10     12-13            15-16   18-21    23-24    26-27    29-31
```

Byte	Description
1–2	Pin number for clock switching through keyboard controller.
3	Indicates High signal on pin switches clock to High(H) or Low (L).
5	Clock switching through chipset registers 0 No clock switching through chipset registers. 1 Clock switching through chipset registers.
7–10	Port address to switch clock high through special port.
12–13	Data value to switch clock high through special port.
15–16	Mask value to switch clock high through special port.
18–21	Port Address to switch clock low through special port.
23–24	Data value to switch clock low through special port.
26–27	Mask value to switch clock low through special port.
29–31	Turbo Switch Input Pin information (Pin number for Turbo Switch Input Pin).

Identification String Line 3:

```
xxx      -x      -xxxx    -xx     -xx     -xxxx    -xx     -xx-xx   -xx
1-3      5       7-10     12-13   15-16   18-21    23-24   26-27    29-30

-x       -x
31       33
```

Byte	Description
1–2	Keyboard Controller Pin number for cache control. Pin number for Cache Control.
3	Keyboard Controller Pin number for cache control. Indicates whether High signal on the pin enables (H) or disable (L) cache.
5	1 The High signal is used on the Keyboard Controller pin.
7–10	Cache Control through Chipset Registers: 0 Cache control off 1 Cache Control on
12–13	Port Address to enable cache through special port.
15–16	Data value to enable cache through special port.
18–21	Mask value to enable cache through special port.
23–24	Port Address to disable cache through special port.
26–27	Data value to disable cache through special port.
29–30	Mask value to disable cache through special port.
31	Reset memory controller Pin number for Resetting the 82335 Memory controller.
33	BIOS Modified Flag This byte is incremented each time the BIOS is modified. It is incremented from 1 to 9, then from A to Z, and then reset to 1. If this byte is a 0, then the BIOS has not yet been modified.

AMI BIOS and AMI BIOS Plus Identification Strings

AMI BIOS and AMI BIOS Plus were sold from 1986 through 1990. The general format of the BIOS Reference string in this type of AMI BIOS:

```
Ref. TTTT-XXXX-042088-Kn
```

TTTT	BIOS type
XXXX	customer number
042088	the BIOS release date
K*n*	the keyboard BIOS version number. If *n* is 0, it is not an American Megatrends Keyboard Controller BIOS.

Appendix E

Old AMI BIOS POST Checkpoint Codes

The following table lists the BIOS POST checkpoint codes for
American Megatrends BIOS with a BIOS date before 4/9/90.

Code	Description
01h	The NMI is Disabled. The 80286 register test is about to start.
02h	The 80286 register test is done.
03h	The ROM checksum is OK.
04h	8259 Programmable Interrupt Controller initialization completed successfully.
05h	The CMOS pending interrupt is disabled.
06h	The video has been disabled and the system timer counter test has completed.
07h	The test of channel 2 of the 8253 Programmable Interval Timer has completed.
08h	The delta count test of channel 2 of the 8253 Programmable Interval Timer is over.
09h	The delta count test of channel 1 of the 8253 Programmable Interval Timer is done.
0Ah	The delta count test of channel 0 of the 8253 Programmable Interval Timer is done.
0Bh	The parity status has been cleared.
0Ch	The memory refresh and system timer tests have completed.
0Dh	The memory refresh link toggling test has completed.
0Eh	The refresh period On/Off 50% test has completed.
10h	Confirmed refresh is On. About to start 64 KB base memory test.
11h	The address line test passed.
12h	The 64 KB base memory test completed successfully.
13h	The interrupt vectors have been initialized.
14h	The 8042 keyboard controller test passed.
15h	The CMOS RAM read and write tests passed.
16h	The CMOS RAM checksum and battery tests passed.
17h	Monochrome mode has been set.
18h	Color mode has been set.
19h	Searching for optional video ROM.
1Ah	The optional video ROM control test has passed.

Old BIOS Checkpoint Codes, Continued

Code	Description
1Bh	The display memory read/write test passed.
1Ch	The display memory read/write test for an alternate display passed.
1Dh	The video retrace test passed.
1Eh	The global equipment byte has been set for video.
1Fh	The mode set call for Monochrome and Color test passed.
20h	The video test passed.
21h	The video display test passed.
22h	The power-on message display test passed.
30h	The virtual mode memory test is about to begin.
31h	The virtual mode memory test has started.
32h	The processor is in virtual mode.
33h	The memory address line test is in progress.
34h	The memory address line test is in progress.
35h	POST has calculated the amount of memory below 1 MB.
36h	The memory size computation routine has completed.
37h	The memory test is in progress.
38h	All memory below 1 MB has been initialized.
39h	All memory above 1 MB has been initialized.
3Ah	The memory size has been displayed.
3Bh	The test on memory below 1 MB will be done next.
3Ch	The memory test on all memory below 1 MB completed successfully.
3Dh	The memory test on all memory above 1 MB completed successfully.
3Eh	Entering real mode next via the Shutdown byte.
3Fh	Shutdown was successful. Now in real mode.
40h	Disabling the Gate A20 address line next.
41h	The Gate A20 line has been successfully disabled.
42h	The DMA controller test will be done next.
4Eh	The address line test passed.
4Fh	The processor is in real mode after Shutdown.
50h	The DMA page register test completed successfully.
51h	The first DMA Controller base register test is about to start.
52h	The first DMA Controller channel test has completed. Beginning the channel test on the second DMA Controller.
53h	The second DMA Controller base register test is about to start.
54h	Beginning test of the F/F latch from the first DMA controller.
55h	The F/F latch test passed for both DMA controllers.
56h	The programming of both DMA controllers has completed.

Old BIOS Checkpoint Codes, Continued

Code	Description
57h	Initialization of the 8259 Programmable Interrupt Controller has completed.
58h	The 8259 Programmable Interrupt Controller mask register test completed successfully.
59h	The 8259 Programmable Interrupt Controller mask register test completed successfully. Now checking the slave interrupt controller mask register.
5Ah	Starting the timer and keyboard interrupt level tests.
5Bh	The timer interrupt test completed successfully.
5Ch	Testing the keyboard interrupt next.
5Dh	An error occurred — the timer/keyboard interrupt is not at the proper level.
5Eh	The 8259 Programmable Interrupt Controller had an error.
5Fh	The 8259 Programmable Interrupt Controller test completed successfully.
70h	The keyboard test is starting.
71h	The keyboard BAT test completed successfully.
72h	The keyboard test completed successfully.
73h	The keyboard global data initialization completed successfully.
74h	Configuring the floppy drives next.
75h	The floppy drive configuration completed successfully.
76h	Hard disk drive configuration is about to start.
77h	Hard disk drive configuration completed successfully.
79h	Initializing the timer data area next.
7Ah	Verifying CMOS RAM battery power next.
7Bh	The CMOS RAM battery power has been verified.
7Dh	Analyzing the diagnostic test results for memory next.
7Eh	The CMOS RAM memory size update test passed.
7Fh	Testing the optional ROM at C000:0h next.
80h	The keyboard has been sensed to enable BIOS Setup.
81h	The optional ROM at C000:0H test passed.
82h	The printer global data initialization has completed.
83h	The RS-232C global data initialization has completed.
84h	The 80287 math coprocessor test has completed successfully.
85h	Displaying the soft error message next.
86h	Passing control to the adaptor ROM at E00:0h next.
87h	The E000:0h adaptor ROM test passed.
00h	Control has been passed to the INT 19h Bootstrap Loader.

Acronyms and Abbreviations

ACK	Acknowledge (Keyboard command and serial communications signal)
ACR	Hard Disk Drive Adapter Controller Register
ALE	Address Latch Enable (x86 processor signal)
ANSI	American National Standards Institute
ARLL	Advanced Run Length Limited (method of encoding hard disk data)
ARB	Access Rights Byte (part of i286, i386, and i486 instruction)
ASCII	American Standard Code for Information Interchange
ASIC	Application-Specific Integrated Circuit
ASR	Hard Disk Adapter Status Register
AT	Advanced Technology
b	Binary
BAT	Basic Assurance Test (keyboard diagnostic)
BCD	Binary-coded decimal
BIOS	Basic Input Output System
bps	Bits per second
CAS	Column Address Strobe (RAM signal)
CCB	Command Control Block (disk drive data structure)
CGA	Color Graphics Adapter
CLK	Clock signal (line) on a microprocessor
CMOS	Complementary Metal Oxide Semiconductor
COM1	Serial Communications Port 1
COM2	Serial Communications Port 2
COM3	Serial Communications Port 3
COM4	Serial Communications Port 4
CRC	Cyclic Redundancy Check
CSB	Command Specify Block (disk drive data structure)
CTS	Clear To Send (serial communications signal)
DAC	Digital to analog converter
DCC	Display combination code
DIN	Deutsche Industrie Normal
DIP	Dual Inline Package
DMA	Direct Memory Access
DPL	Descriptor Privilege Level (part of x86 instructions)

cont'd

Acronyms and Abbreviations, Continued

DSR	Data Set Ready (serial communications signal)
DSR	Device Service Routine
DTR	Data Terminal Ready (serial communications signal)
EA	Effective Address
EBCDIC	Extended Binary-Coded Decimal Interchange
ECC	Error Checking and Correction
EGA	Enhanced Graphics Adapter
EIA	Electronic Industries Association
EISA	Extended Industry Standard Architecture
EOI	End of Interrupt
EPL	Extended Privilege Level
EEPROM	Electronically Erasable Programmable Read-Only Memory
EPROM	Erasable Programmable Read-Only Memory
ESDI	Enhanced Small Device Interface
ETB	End of Transmission Block
FCB	Format Control Block (data structure for disk information)
GB	Gigabytes
GDT	Global Descriptor Table
GDTR	Global Descriptor Table Register
h	Hexadecimal
ICW	Interrupt Control Word
IDE	Intelligent Device Electronics (method of accessing hard disk drives)
IDT	Interrupt Descriptor Table
INT	Software interrupt
I/O	Input/Output
IRQ	Interrupt Request Line
IRET	Return from an Interrupt
ISA	Industry Standard Architecture (AT-compatible)
ISR	Interrupt Service Return
ISR	Interrupt Status Register
KB	Kilobytes (1,024 bytes)
KBs	Kilobytes per second
Kb	Kilobits (1,024 bits)
Kbs	Kilobits per second
LDT	Local Descriptor Table
LDTR	Local Descriptor Table Register

LED	Light-Emitting Diode
LID	Logical ID
LPT1	Parallel Printer Port 1, DOS reserved word
LPT2	Parallel Printer Port 2, DOS reserved word
LPT3	Parallel Printer Port 3, DOS reserved word
LSB	Least Significant Bit (or Byte)
LSI	Large Scale Integration
LUN	Logical Unit Number (SCSI device identifier)
MB	Megabytes (1,048,576 or 2^{20} bytes)
MBs	Megabytes per second
Mb	Megabits (1,048,576 bits)
Mbs	Megabits per second
MCGA	Modified Color Graphics Adapter (video standard used only in low-end PS/2® models)
MDA	Monochrome Display Adapter
MFM	Modified Frequency Modulation (a method of encoding hard disk data)
MGA	An obsolete Graphics Adapter (IBM PCJr only)
MHz	Megahertz
MMU	Memory Management Unit
MSB	Most Significant Byte (or Bit)
MTBF	Mean Time Between Failure
MTTR	Mean Time To Repair
NCB	Network Control Block (data structure for networked disk drives)
NMI	Nonmaskable Interrupt
OCW	Operation Control Word (Programmable Interrupt Controller)
OEM	Original Equipment Manufacturer
OS/2	Operating System /2
PC	Personal Computer
PCB	Printed Circuit Board
PCLK	Peripheral Clock
PEL	Picture Element (pixel)
PGA	Professional Graphics Array
PIC	Programmable Interrupt Controller
PIO	Programmed Input/Output

cont'd

PIT	Programmable Interval Timer
POR	Power-On Reset
POST	Power-On Self Test
RAM	Random Access Memory
RAS	Row Address Strobe (RAM signal)
RGB	Red-Green-Blue
RI	Ring Indicator (serial communications signal)
RLL	Run Length Limited (method of encoding hard disk data)
ROM	Read-Only Memory
RS232C	Industry standard serial controller interface
RTC	Real Time Clock
RTS	Request To Send (serial communications signal)
SCSI	Small Computer Systems Interface
SDLC	Synchronous Data Link Communications
SIMM	Single Inline Memory Module
SIP	Single Inline Package
SMD	Surface Mount Device
SMT	Surface Mount Technology
SSB	Sense Summary Block (data structure for hard disks)
TB	Terabytes
TID	Target ID (SCSI device identifier)
TSS	Task State Segment (part of x86 instructions)
TTL	Transistor-To-Transistor Logic
UART	Universal Asynchronous Receiver/Transmitter
VGA	Video Graphics Array
VLSI	Very Large Scale Integration
XMS	Extended Memory Specification
XT	Extended Technology

Additional Reading

The following books and articles are recommended for additional information about BIOS and related subjects:

Boston, Michael and Narushoff, Paul. *System BIOS for IBM PC/XT/AT Computers and Compatibles*, Phoenix Technical Reference Series. Reading, MA: Addison-Wesley Publishing Company. 1989.

Brown, Ralf, and Kyle, Jim, *PC Interrupts*. Reading, MA: Addison-Wesley Publishing Company. 1991.

Cohen, Howard N. and John Hanel. "A Timing-Independent BIOS." *Byte IBM Special Edition*, Fall 1987, pp. 219–222.

Duncan, Ray. *Advanced MS-DOS Programming*. Redmond, WA: Microsoft Press, 1989.

Duncan, Ray. *IBM ROM BIOS*. Redmond, WA: Microsoft Press, 1988.

Extended Industry Standard Architecture Technical Reference. New York, NY: BCPR Services. 1989.

Glass, L. Brett. "Inside EISA." *Byte*, November 1989, pp 417–425.

Intel Corporation. *i486 Programmer's Reference Manual*. Santa Clara, CA: Intel Corporation. 1989.

Intel Corporation, Microsoft Corporation. *Advanced Power Management (APM) Interface Specification*. 1993

Intel Corporation. *ExCa Card Services Specification*. Hillsboro, OR: 1993

Intel Corporation. *PCI BIOS Specification*. Hillsboro, OR: 1993

Kliewer, Bradley Dyck. *EGA/VGA Programmer's Reference Guide*. New York, NY, McGraw-Hill Book Company, 1988.

Norton, Peter and Wilton, Richard. *The New Peter Norton Programmer's Guide to the IBM PC and PS/2*. Redmond WA: Microsoft Press, 1988.

PCMCIA. *PC Card Standard*. Personal Computer Memory Card International Association, 1992

PCMCIA. *Socket Services Interface Specification*. Personal Computer Memory Card International Association, 1992.

Schulman, Andrew, et al. *Undocumented DOS*. Reading, MA: Addison-Wesley Publishing Company, 1991.

SCSI Specification X3T9.2. ANSI Committee, 1991.

Shiell, Jon. "IBM PC Family BIOS Comparison." *Byte IBM Special Edition*, Fall 1987, pp. 173–180.

Small Computer System Interface (SCSI) Specification. ANSI X3.131-1991.

White, George. "A Bus Tour." *Byte*, September 1989, pp. 296–302.

Wilton, Richard. *Programmer's Guide to PC and PS/2 Video Systems*. Redmond, WA: Microsoft Press, 1987.

Index

Index, Continued